No Stone
Unturned

D1234987

Praise for *No Stone Unturned: A Remarkable Journey to Identity*

An inspirational and courageous debut memoir of a woman's years-long search for her birth mother. —*Kirkus Reviews*

If ever a cable series suggested its own sequel that promised to be just as or more captivating than the original, *The Handmaid's Tale*, this would be it. And writer Nadean Stone has provided a true-life look at how such a shocking dystopia can play out in the next generation. Stone, one of the more than 600,000 babies deemed "illegitimate" in Canadian census records from the period, tells a tale that's often raw with emotion, recounting a grim childhood and her winding, but determined journey to find her birth mother—and herself. —*The Parklander Magazine*

This is a must-read! I couldn't put it down. I felt like I was sitting in a room talking to Nadean the entire time I read this book. It makes you laugh and cry and giggle at times, but such a fabulous read. —*Love Reading, the UK's Leading Book Recommendation Website*

Nadean Stone's *No Stone Unturned* is a fast page-turning saga of personal hardships, triumphs, loss, and love. Her perseverance to find the truth about her family and what it really means validates the spirit of humanity. A must-read! —*Jane Ubell-Meyer, CEO and Founder of Bedside Reading*

Despite the current trend to openness in adoption records in Canada, Nadean Stone's story highlights the difficulties many adoptees continue to experience due to the treatment of unmarried mothers and their children during the postwar adoption mandate. Through challenges and hardships, grief and loss, Nadean's persistence and courage will keep you riveted. —*Valerie Andrews, Executive Director, Origins Canada*

This book is a MUST READ. Never judge a book by its cover. Don't let the beauty and softness of Nadean fool you. She is tough as stone. *No Stone Unturned* is a real-life story which contains all the elements for a great movie: Real-life drama, pain, suspense, romance, royalty, politics, and more. You will cry, laugh, and get angry. Thank you, Nadean, for being transparent and opening up your soul to share such personal details. —*Margie Diaz, Association of Legal Administrators*

Once started you cannot put this book down. An amazing story that will grip you and astound you with the sheer courage and perseverance of its author. Nadean's style of writing is uncomplicated and flowing, void of sentimentality, and this adds to the tremendous impact this book has on its reader. An outstanding tribute to the remarkable strength embodied in human nature. —*Elizabeth Taylor-Margalit, UK*

Just finished reading and this book is honestly one of the best l have ever read. I could not put it down and I felt as if I was right in the moment with her. I laughed at times and I literally had tears streaming down my face at times. All the makings of a great movie and I would be first in line to buy tickets. This book is not only a story of the quest of the author to find her birth mother with the odds stacked against her. It is the life story of a courageous woman who perseveres despite many hardships, and still has the ability to love unconditionally. All of us can learn a lesson from her by reading this! —*Andrea S*

Once the tears subsided—going back and forth from sad tears to happy tears—I took time to reflect on the total story. This is one of those true stories where you ask, "How did this person survive so many struggles life threw her way"? Told in chronological order of her life, Ms. Stone brings the reader inside to experience the emotional roller coaster that was her life. There was no whitewash and "no stone unturned" in the telling of each event. The fact that Ms. Stone kept a positive outlook throughout her life is an amazing story in itself! —*Claudia H*

If you're not sobbing by page 155, you are not human. This is an extraordinary beautiful story about a very, very brave woman, mother, accountant, journalist, friend, wife, lover. She is the kind of heroine women and men can be proud of. Persistence is omnipotent. And, Nadean, the real woman, and Nadean, the protagonist, are full of the brilliance and courage a hero needs to conquer her dramatic need and to cope with the tragedy imposed upon her. If you need some courage and inspiration, this is your book. I couldn't put it down. —*Happy Consumer*

I simply could not put this book down. Nadean Stone's story, from the day she is given away after the luck of a coin toss, to the day she finally finds her family, again, by pure luck, and everything in between, including a whole lot of bad luck, is mind-boggling. Written from the heart by one tough and determined lady—it is unbelievable what she lived through, and that she survived, and endured, and clearly remains a positive and loving woman is perhaps something of a miracle. I am in awe. Give this one to everyone you know who needs inspiration to keep on smiling, keep on loving, keep on doing the right thing and never, ever give up. —*Charryl Y*

This book is a life story that everyone should read! Men & woman alike! I read it in two days, I bawled, I chuckled and it moved my soul. To love and be courageous in times when you can barely crawl. To have faith, never say never!! I'm so inspired! Go get this book! —*Jenny B*

No Stone Unturned by Nadean Stone IS TRULY (caps on purpose) a remarkable journey to identity and so much more. This non-fiction catches your attention from the minute you open the book and read the first page. It's a fascinating journey of Nadean Stone's fearlessness and determination to never quit even when all odds seem to be against her. I was moved and inspired as I lived through all the personal challenges and pain she experienced. Nadean gives us a peek into her soul and her deep love of family. Her story allows you to experience a mother's unstoppable love. Her story illustrates compassion, wisdom, forgiveness and fairness for everyone during times of despair and tragedy. I deeply connected to the story. I lived every page as if it were my own. If you have ever felt like giving up on life or anything, this book will give you faith, hope and courage to persevere. *No Stone Unturned* is a MUST to read and proof that a person should never abandon a dream, because dreams really do come true. —*Debra*

Nadean Stone was challenged for 44 years in her efforts to find her birth parents. She was constantly thwarted by the Canadian Political System which asserted that because she was never legally adopted, she had no legal rights to any information about her heritage. But she never gave up. Her determination and perseverance drove her to pursue one avenue after another until she was, at last, successful. Facing constant adversity and painful personal situations, *No Stone Unturned* will capture your imagination, entertain you, bring you to tears, and garner your enduring admiration of Nadean. A riveting story from an exquisite writer. —*Carolyn M*

This book reads like a riveting first-person work of fiction, as one cannot believe that this story really happened to someone! And yet it did happen to Nadean, and therefore the book was a true page-turner. I couldn't put it down until I was finished. Nadean persevered through so much personal and bureaucratic adversity that would bury a lesser person. Thank you Nadean for sharing your story! —*Laurie S*

What an incredible book this is. I couldn't put it down. It weaves the tragic and the beautiful together into an amazing story of perseverance. I can't recommend it enough—Nadean really illustrates the power of the human spirit. —*Valerie*

This book surprised me. The cover does not give it justice, even though it is a real photo of the author. This true story is riveting. I could not put it down. Nadean Stone went through trials and tribulations that most of us only see in movies. It caused me to appreciate my family stability. I highly recommend this book. —*Mary A*

No Stone Unturned

A REMARKABLE JOURNEY TO IDENTITY

Nadean Stone

No Stone Unturned: A Remarkable Journey to Identity

Copyright © 2019, 2021 by Nadean Stone

No part of this book may be used or reproduced in any manner whatsoever without written permission except in the case of brief quotations embodied in critical articles or reviews. This book is a work of non-fiction. However, some names, businesses, organizations, and places have been changed.

ISBN: 9798734226964 Paperback

All rights reserved.
First edition 2019
Second edition 2021

Printed in the United States of America

10 9 8 7 6 5 4 3 2 1

Research for back cover statistic regarding the number of unmarried mothers forced into giving their babies up for adoption provided by Valerie Andrews: Andrews, Valerie J. White. *Unwed Mother: The Adoption Mandate in Postwar Canada*. Demeter Press, Toronto, 2018.

www.nadeanstone.com

For Andrew

Contents

"A mother's love for her child is like no other love. To be able to put that feeling aside because you want the best for your child is the most unselfish thing I know." —Mary, American Adoptions Birth Mother

"Never ever, ever give up." —Charles Schulz

"As soon as I saw you, I knew an adventure was going to happen." —Winnie the Pooh

Author's Note

To write this book, Fran Mires and I returned to St. Gustave, where we interviewed and videotaped most of the people involved in my story. Some who spoke to us on the condition of anonymity are today successful business leaders, politicians and judges. I changed the names of all. I reviewed letters, personal notes, emails, texts, and court documents and culled my memory to recall events as they transpired in the creation of the manuscript.

Prologue

In the early morning of August 4, 2017, our 28th wedding anniversary, I woke up alone in bed, sobbing. Bill opened the door, walked into the room and sat on the edge of the bed.

"Happy anniversary, darling." He looked more closely at my face. "What's wrong?"

"I was dreaming of him again."

The previous six days of extensive travel had been an unending roller coaster of raised hopes and subsequent disappointments. I was emotionally and physically exhausted.

"You know, Bill, sometimes when I think of Nadean, I truly believe that I am not her. She is over there and I am watching her in shock, awe and amazement. There is no way that I could have gone through what that woman has endured and survived it all with any level of sanity."

Bill gently cupped my small face in his enormous hands and looked deeply into my eyes.

"Who said you're sane?"

That comment elicited the response he was seeking.

Between unbridled peals of laughter and the continuing flow of tears, I said, "It can't end here, Bill. Some good has to come out of all of this. But if it has to end here, I will be okay as long as you love me."

Chapter 1

A Coin Toss

Many illegitimate newborns in Canada were sold or illegally given away by the Catholic Church and other institutions in the 1950s. On December 18, 1952, I became one of those babies. Six days after my birth, my mother signed documents relinquishing all rights to me and instructing Mother Superior Dympna to find adoptive parents. She then boarded an afternoon train in Blind River, Ontario, on Christmas Eve and left me behind at St. Joseph's Hospital.

Sid and Rita Russell were a young, accomplished couple living in Sault Ste. Marie, Ontario, eighty-four miles from Blind River. Rita was stunningly beautiful; Sid was charming and handsome.

They owned a grocery store called Russell's Confectionery, a bowling alley, and a beautiful 200-year-old home called "The Old Stone House," which was subsequently declared a historical monument and is now a museum.

The Russells were desperate for a child since their son, Beverley, died at birth at the family farm in Blind River in 1941. Rita's mother, Mary Tessier, who lived at the family farm with her husband, Henri, and his brother Omer, approached Mother Superior Dympna at St. Joseph's Hospital inquiring if any children needed a home. At the time, St. Joseph's was known to have a ward on the third floor for unwed mothers. Young, unmarried women traveled from many towns in Ontario to live with the nuns in the convent for several months, work at the home for the aged to pay for their room and board, and give their babies up for adoption.

On January 11, 1953, Sid, Rita, Rita's younger brother, Nestor, and Antoinette, his wife, left the farm in Blind River to drive back to Sault Ste. Marie after spending the weekend with their large family.

Nestor and Antoinette, twenty-year-old newlyweds, were in shock as they listened to Sid and Rita talking about a baby girl who was at St. Joseph's Hospital and available for adoption.

No one had spoken about a baby that weekend and now Sid and Rita were discussing whether they should go back to the hospital and take the child.

• • •

"Let's stop the car and talk about it," Sid said to Rita. "You have breast cancer and had operations and radium treatment. We don't know what is going to happen. How can we take such a risk with a baby?"

"Sid, I really want a baby. I am strong. I know that if God gives this baby to us then he is going to let me live long enough to raise it."

Rita begged Sid to turn back toward the hospital.

"Let's flip a coin," Sid said. "Heads we go back for the baby, tails we continue home."

The coin landed on heads, so they turned the car around and headed back toward the hospital. In the two seconds it took, my life's trajectory was determined by the toss of a coin.

Half an hour after Sid and Rita entered St. Joseph's Hospital, the couple emerged with Mother Superior Dympna and a baby wrapped in a blanket.

"This is our baby girl," Rita said to Nestor and Antoinette as she climbed into the front seat.

As the group left the hospital, they noticed a young woman standing by the windows on the upper floor watching their departure. She was in shadow. They couldn't make out her features. This was a practice of the nuns, to have a young woman appear in the distance to make the adoptive parents believe it was the child's mother. The nuns thought it would give comfort to the new parents.

They returned to the farm, where Mary helped them cut up cotton material to make diapers and blankets. Rita named me Nadean—she had found the name in a novel and liked it.

Upon arrival in Sault Ste. Marie, Rita's sisters were concerned and upset that the hospital had given her a baby.

"Rita, how can the hospital do this when you are so sick?" Rita's sister Phyllis said.

Rita did not reply and instead, set about making my nursery.

"That is the homeliest baby I have ever seen! She has huge eyes and is so skinny. She looks like a hungry bird," Rita's sister Roberta said, which made Rita cry.

Over the next two years, Rita flew to Toronto, Montreal, and Dallas, Texas, looking for cures for her breast cancer. She underwent radium treatments and had a double mastectomy. As her condition worsened and the entire family was consumed with her illness, no one thought to question or complete my adoption papers.

As Rita's illness progressed, the cancer spread from her breast to her lungs and she became more weak and unable to care for me. Her brothers and sisters set up shifts during the day and after work so one of them would always be present to care for Rita and me. My routine was chaotic. I would not sleep regular hours.

Nestor later told me "On many nights I would walk with you on my shoulder to get you to sleep. When I looked down into your face, you would always be wide awake looking up at me with those huge brown eyes."

During the last nine months of Rita's illness, I was sent to live with Rita's sister Phyllis and her husband, James, as Sid and the family needed to care for Rita. Sid, who loved Rita passionately, became increasingly depressed and began to drink heavily.

Fearing for my future, Rita prepared a will leaving me to her mother, Mary, to be raised on the family farm in Blind River. Sid was upset, but resigned.

He knew he could never win in a court of law against his mother-in-law, who would battle vigorously for me.

Rita died on Valentine's Day, 1955, at the age of thirty-six, two years after taking me. In two years, I lost two mothers.

The wake was held on the farm that Rita had loved so much. Her casket was placed in the living room for viewing and many mourners visited the family to pay their respects. She was remembered fondly by many. The townspeople reminisced and told stories about Mrs. Tessier driving into town with her horse and carriage, her four attractive daughters riding beside and behind her, Rita being the most beautiful.

Men admired them from afar but dared not approach, as Mrs. Tessier was known as a fierce woman who was excessively protective of her daughters.

My aunts recalled me sitting on the floor near the casket and banging my forehead on the floor until my nose bled. After the funeral, Sid said his good-byes and left the farm.

After Rita's passing, Mary took me back to the hospital and introduced me to Mother Superior.

"Sister Dympna, my daughter Rita has died. This is Nadean, the child you gave to her two years ago. Rita left her to me to be raised on the farm. I just want you to know that I have raised nine children, but Nadean will be loved and cared for and I will do my best to raise her like the others. Can you tell me anything about her mother and father?"

"Mrs. Tessier, I am so sorry for your loss. Nadean's mother is from Yugoslavia. She worked at St. Joseph's Hospital in North Bay. The reason she gave Nadean away is that her mother was coming over from the old country and she did not want her mother to know she had had a child. She has gone back to North Bay. I should also tell you that if Nadean looks anything like her birth mother, then she will resemble your daughter Rita. In taking Rita away from you, God has given this child to you to raise. You have been blessed with this wonderful gift."

Mary was sixty years old.

Chapter 2

How to Set a Rabbit Snare

My first memory of the farmhouse is of arising on an early winter morning, standing at the top of the stairs, and staring down into the glazed-over eyes of a large gray Canadian wolf. It stood rigid on the landing at the bottom of the stairs, atop scattered logs. Its lips were pulled back in a gruesome snarl revealing enormous bared teeth.

I don't remember shouting or screaming, but suddenly, my grandmother and great-uncle appeared on the landing next to the wolf. They were smiling.

"Don't be afraid, Nadean," Grandma said. "It's dead; it won't hurt you."

"*Viens, mon petit*," Mon Oncle said, which is French for "Come, my little one."

Mon Oncle stepped over the wolf, climbed up the stairs, and scooped me up into his arms. He carried me over to Grandma, who sat in a rocking chair next to a large window that looked out onto a snow-covered field. "Your mother, Rita, has gone to Heaven with Jesus, Nadean," Grandma said as she clutched me to her bosom. "She was very sick and left you with us to be raised.

"You don't need to be afraid of that wolf. It is frozen. Mon Oncle is a trapper. He caught the wolf in one of his traps out there on the ridge. Can you see the ridge way over there? Can you see the foxes running? Well, that is what he does. He traps animals and after they thaw out, he skins them and sells their pelts. We are trappers and farmers. You are going to live on the farm with us now and we are going to take care of you."

I remember looking out the window, seeing a fox running on the ridge and thinking I had arrived in another world. I was in shock and confused! I did not know these people. I was bereft and sensed that I was about to embark on a new journey in a strange world.

5

That summer Sid visited me for the first time since Rita's passing.

He brought a navy-blue-and-white sailor suit, white socks, blue-and-white saddle shoes, a toothbrush and toothpaste.

He held me over the kitchen sink, showed me how to brush my teeth and said, "You must do this every day."

Afterward, he sat with Grandma and they spoke for a long time. He took a photo of me standing in front of a dog's house with a puppy in my arm. He hugged and kissed me when he left. I would not see Sid again for many years.

I grew to love my Grandma; Papere, my grandfather; and Mon Oncle, Papere's brother. All were in their sixties, and it must have been a shock for them to take on the care of a small child.

Mon Oncle made small snowshoes for me and together we visited his traps daily in winter checking for beaver, rabbits, muskrats and weasels. He showed me how he set traps in the snow.

"You see here, Mon Petit," he said as he showed me how to set the trap, "I place the snare for the rabbit where we see rabbit tracks. That means he is going to come back this way and when he does, we will catch him in the trap. This is how we place it, just under the snow, on the tracks."

He set the traps for beavers, muskrats and weasels at the edge of the frozen lakes. When I became tired he placed me on the sleigh he pulled, next to the animals he collected from the traps. I loved following Mon Oncle. His life was so exciting to a child!

Papere worked as a supervisor for the Division of Highways, building roads, so would be away from the farm during the week. Papere spoke fluent French and some English, so was always able to find work supervising men in either bush camps or on the building of railroads and roads. Grandma took care of the farm house and Mon Oncle took care of the horses, cows, chickens, pigs, ducks and the three large gardens. It was a division of responsibility that worked. They owned 160 acres of land.

In summer, Mon Oncle would place me behind the yoke on top of the harnessed workhorse, Pete. He trudged behind in his rubber boots and held the plow with both hands as it moved with the horse.

"Hold on to the reins, Nadean, and make sure Pete stays straight in the rows."

The long reins were slung over his shoulders in case Pete bolted. I was so happy to have this huge responsibility of making sure the rows in the garden patch were straight.

Grandma took in laundry from American families who owned cottages on Lake Lauzon, a few miles from the farm. She, Mon Oncle, and Joseph, her youngest son, opened up and cleaned the cottages in early summer and closed them in the fall. And they also sold chopped wood and blocks of ice to the Americans. Grandma was a trusted resource for so many families who left the keys to their cottages with her as they departed each fall.

The seasons followed a predictable nature: trapping in the winter, feeding and watering all the barn animals in the morning and at night, cleaning out their stalls, planting the gardens in spring, and haying in the summer. We had no electricity or running water and no indoor plumbing. Water was supplied to the kitchen by a pump handle over the sink that drew water from a well near the house. Light was provided at night by kerosene lanterns. There was an outhouse a short distance from the house, and we used chamber pots at night.

Grandma dressed me in knee-length bloomer underpants until my aunts insisted that she change to more modern clothes.

I loved the weekends because my aunts, uncles and cousins visited the farm. In summer, the men worked in the fields cutting and bringing in hay for the animals and the women worked in the gardens and prepared large cooked breakfasts, lunches and suppers. We had huge gatherings of twenty to thirty people for meals.

After the dishes were cleared and washed and the kitchen swept, the adults moved the chairs out of the way so there would be room to dance. Some of the family played guitars, fiddles and harmonicas while others tap-danced and smoked their pipes and cigarettes. There was much laughter and teasing, and French and English were spoken equally.

I loved the haying season, as my cousin Charles and I would run in from the fields to be the first to reach the farm house. Whoever arrived first would have the honor of carrying the jug of Kool-Aid back to the barn for the men, while the other carried the glasses.

Just because I was two years older and faster did not mean that I would always win the race as I was horribly pigeon-toed and would often fall flat on my face, much to Charles' amusement.

The family would tell stories to me about my mother Rita. "Nadean, she adopted you because she wanted you and she loved you so much. She was the kindest and most beautiful woman." They grieved her loss immensely, but found comfort in having her daughter.

Aunt Leona, Rita's closest sister and best friend, missed Rita especially and thought everything she did was fabulous. She would hold me on her lap, talk about Rita, and then sing *How Much Is That Doggie in the Window?*

"Nadean, one time when your mother and I were teenagers, we entered a singing contest as the Tessier Sisters. We were dressed identically in blue-and-white sailor suits. As we arrived on stage, I panicked and could not even open my mouth to sing, so your mother sang the song alone. She saved us. She was so special!" Leona laughed and cried in relating this story.

During the long winter months when it was cold and dark so early in the day, Grandma and I would sit at the kitchen table by the light of the kerosene lamp and she would read to me from her Bible.

She had me memorize long passages. As time passed she taught me how to read, write, spell, count, and do sums.

One year after Sid's visit, a car stopped at the gate to the farm. A strange man climbed out and beckoned me to his car. I was playing on the swing near the house. He was holding a doll. As I started toward the car, Grandma ran from the house and screamed at me to stop. She carried a rifle.

She turned toward the man, raised the gun to her shoulder, and shouted, "Get off my property now or I will shoot!"

The man climbed into his car and sped away from the farm. Grandma took my hand and walked me back to the house.

"Nadean, never speak to strangers. Always hide if they approach you and never get into a car with anyone you don't know," she said as she looked into my eyes.

My grandmother always believed that the man at the gate was sent by Sid to kidnap me.

Chapter 3

Leona and Kurt

When I was five, Grandma decided I should start school. As there were no school buses that traveled to the farm district from Blind River, Grandma decided that during the school year I would live in Sault Ste. Marie with Aunt Leona, her husband, Kurt, and their adopted daughter, Christina, who was four years younger than I. I would return to the farm on weekends, holidays, and the summer months.

We interviewed at St. Thomas Catholic School and the principal, Sister Kenneth, told Grandma that I was too advanced to be placed in kindergarten.

"Mrs. Tessier," Sister Kenneth said, "Nadean knows her prayers, can read and write, spell, count, and do math. Even though she is only five years old, we should place her in first grade."

I hated living with Leona and Kurt. I missed Grandma, Papere and Mon Oncle so much, I cried myself to sleep every night. I would lie in bed and try to imagine the worst possible thing that could happen to me and wonder if I would survive the pain. I thought that if I could imagine the worst and still survive the pain, I would live.

"God, can I live if I lose Papere?" I cried.

"God, can I live if I lose Mon Oncle?" I cried more. When I finally asked God if I could live if I lost Grandma, I was inconsolable. The pain of losing Grandma was too great; I knew I would die of grief.

I found the city loud and overwhelming after the farm. When Alec, the boy next door, took me bicycle riding and a car passed on the street, I drove the bike into the ditch and hid. Alec stood above, looking perplexed.

I shared what Grandma had told me: "Never get into cars with strangers, because they will kidnap you and I will never see you again."

"Don't worry," Alec said. "I will walk with you to school every day and I will protect you."

While Leona did construction work on their new home, as well as the landscaping and other chores within and outside the house, her handsome and charismatic husband was a delivery driver for Labatt's beer company.

We were alone one Sunday and Kurt made a delicious Western sandwich for me. As I ate my sandwich, he stood in the kitchen with his leg cocked up on the stool, holding a cigarette between his fingers, and told me about his time in the Canadian army.

"I was a cook during the war—a good one. That is where I learned to make such good meals," he said.

However, he neglected to share that he had also gone AWOL, was caught, arrested, and put in military prison in Montreal until the end of the war. Aunt Leona lived in Montreal for a few years so she could be near him while he served his time.

Although he could be pleasant and funny when sober, Kurt was nasty and mean when drunk and I never trusted him. He thought the children were toys and would throw us in the air and catch us. One time as I came down, he missed catching me and I banged my head on the coffee table. It bled, but was not bad enough to require stitches. Leona cut my hair, cleaned the wound, bandaged it up, and I went to school the next day.

After two years of living with them, Leona took me aside and told me she and Kurt were adopting a little boy named Richard and she needed my cooperation.

"Nadean, the Children's Aid worker will be coming to our house and is going to ask you questions about living with us. It is very important that you tell her you are happy here and we take good care of you. If you do this, she will give the baby to us. If you don't, I won't get Richard, and I want a baby boy so much."

The Children's Aid worker arrived dressed in a lovely suit and long coat, carrying her handbag and official notebook. She asked if she could meet with me alone, away from Aunt Leona, so we went into the living room.

"Nadean, do you understand the word adoption?"

"Yes, I do. I am adopted."

"Good. Your Aunt Leona and Uncle Kurt adopted Christina three years ago and now they want to adopt a little boy. I work with the Children's Aid Society and we visit homes to make sure that the babies will be happy where we place them. We want them to be with good families. Do you understand?"

"Yes."

"Good. You have lived with your Aunt Leona and Uncle Kurt for two years now. Are you happy living here with them? Do they treat you well? Would a little baby boy be happy here?"

I wanted to shout, cry, and scream at her, "No, don't give a baby boy to them. It will be a mistake."

But Aunt Leona had taken me in when I had nowhere to go for school and she cared for me. So, with all the strength I could muster, I lied.

"Yes, I am happy here," I said to the CAS worker. "They are good to me and a baby will be happy here!"

Richard arrived a few weeks later.

One Easter Sunday I sat on a stool at the kitchen counter while Leona stood at the stove flipping pancakes. I was dressed in a brand-new black-and-white pleated dress and shiny black patent leather shoes.

Kurt, hung over as usual, came into the kitchen and demanded to know why I was eating pancakes before church if I was going to take Communion. I froze just as I was about to place the fork in my mouth. Pancake and maple syrup dripped onto the plate.

Leona smiled and looked at Kurt.

"She faints in church if she has no food in her stomach; all that incense makes her sick. Go ahead and eat, Nadean. Jesus will have a soft blanket to land on when he reaches your tummy!"

Kurt and Leona began to argue. I dropped my fork as Kurt grabbed the frying pan off the stove burner, raised it in the air and slammed it down, shattering the burner. He chased Leona around the house with the pan held high.

"Leona, I am going to fucking kill you!" he screamed. I ran to the telephone in the hallway and dialed zero.

"Please send the police! My Uncle Kurt is going to kill my Aunt Leona," I said to the operator.

The operator asked for my name and address and before I replied, I saw a shadow at my side and felt Kurt's presence. I looked up at him and he grabbed the receiver from my hand.

"Hello, we have no problems here. Nothing is wrong. My niece is just hysterical," he said to the operator.

He hung up the phone and looked down into my face with rage.

"If you ever call the police again, I will break your back," he said as he grabbed my shoulders.

I bent over and threw up all over my new dress and black patent leather shoes. We didn't go to Mass that Easter Sunday.

When I was eight, Aunt Leona told me that my father Sid had called. He had remarried a woman called Wilma and he wanted to bring her to Sault Ste. Marie and Blind River to introduce her to me and the family. Sid had been best friends with Kurt so it was reasonable that they would stay with us. Wilma, a blonde, was opposite in looks to my mother. She was friendly to me and Sid was warm and charming.

However, they were strangers to me. I tried to be polite but was not overly warm or affectionate with them, as I did not want Wilma to want me.

On Saturday morning, we all drove to the farm to spend the weekend with Grandma, Papere and Mon Oncle. Some of Grandma's children drove down from Sault Ste. Marie on Sunday to meet Wilma and share in the family gathering. I was petrified that Grandma was going to give me back to Sid and his new wife because, in my child's mind, I couldn't think there'd be any other reason for their visit.

There was much joking and reminiscing for Wilma's sake. Grandma was the consummate hostess. The adults ate at the large table in the main kitchen and the children sat at another table in the summer room nearby. We could not hear the adults' conversation.

At five that afternoon, the family members climbed into their cars for the drive back to Sault Ste. Marie.

I watched as Sid and Wilma said their good-byes to Grandma, Papere and Mon Oncle and then walked up to me. They hugged me, said good-bye, and started their trip back to Toronto.

As I got back into the car with Leona and Kurt, I said to Leona, "I am so glad Grandma did not let me go with them."

"Nadean, that would never have happened. Your mother Rita willed you to Grandma, and her dying wish was that you would be raised by her. Grandma would never have let you go."

While I was with Leona and Kurt, Mon Oncle developed shingles.

Everything at the farm as I had known it changed.

Mon Oncle was bedridden for weeks and suffered greatly from the pain, as the shingles were on his face, his right eye, and on his head. We were all afraid that he might die. Grandma and Papere decided to sell most of the cattle, many of the horses, and kept just a few animals on the farm.

My horse, Bluebird, was a big, gray, dappled beauty. I was still living with Kurt and Leona, and Bluebird would not respond to any of the other family members when they tried to make him climb onto the truck to take him away from the farm.

Aunt Roberta told me afterward, "Nadean, I remembered how you would coax him to do things with you, so I talked to him like you would and he got onto the truck." It saddened me that Bluebird had to be sold, but I knew it had to be done. Most of all, I was worried that Mon Uncle would die.

Mon Oncle did recover in time, but had endless headaches that were only relieved when he placed a steaming-hot washcloth over his eye and head. Because the headaches hampered Mon Oncle's ability to work, the farm never fully returned to the way it once was.

When Aunt Leona had a hysterectomy, Christina, Richard and I stayed with Uncle Joseph and Aunt Lois. The night before Leona's return from the hospital, we moved back in with Kurt.

That evening, after Kurt put Christina and Richard to bed, he sat in the living room with me on his lap.

"Why do you drink, Uncle Kurt?" I said. "Why do you hurt Aunt Leona?"

"I don't know," he said. "She gets angry and that drives me crazy."

"No, Uncle Kurt, she gets upset because you drink and you should stop. If you stop drinking she won't get angry."

Kurt began to cry and then stopped and stared at me. "You have a big mouth and are too smart for your age."

One night when Aunt Leona went to one of the regular school PTA meetings, Kurt and I were alone in the living room.

"We are going to play a game called wrestling and you need to try to get away," he said.

Kurt placed me on my back on the floor and lowered himself onto me.

"Uncle Kurt, I can't breathe. You are too heavy. You are hurting me! I don't want to play," I said as I struggled to get away.

This seemed to excite him more and he tightened his grip on me. Just then, I heard a voice, lifted my head, and looked backward.

Christina stood on the top step of the drop-down living room. "Daddy, I heard a noise and I woke up."

"Christina, go back to bed. Nadean and I are just wrestling," Kurt said.

After Christina left, Kurt picked me up and carried me back to the bed I shared with her. He laid me down on the bed and knelt beside it.

"I am so sorry, Nadean. Nothing happened. I promise I will never play that game again. You must not tell anyone," he whispered into my ear.

Kurt rested his head on my small chest and started to cry. "It's okay," I said, "but you must never do that again."

Too young to fully understand what happened or the fact that Christina saved me, I told no one about the incident with Kurt. I did realize, however, that I had to do everything in my power to get away.

Chapter 4

Grandma Fights the School Board

In the summer of 1961, I returned to the farm for the summer holidays. Finally feeling safe, I was overjoyed to be back with Grandma, Papere and Mon Oncle.

On the morning after my return, Grandma dressed me in a pair of shorts and looked at my legs.

"Nadean, how did you get those bruises on your legs?"

"Kurt hit me," I said as I stared into her eyes.

Her face blanched and her eyes widened as she stared at my legs. "Nadean, you will never go back to live with Leona and Kurt," she said.

We never spoke of it again.

Grandma refused to pay her separate Catholic school taxes and was sued by the school board that summer.

With the attorney she hired, Grandma stood before the judge and explained that her daughter Rita died six years before and I was willed to her. She went on to say that I had to live with Leona and Kurt in Sault Ste. Marie for four years because there was no school bus in Blind River to take me to school.

"I have the tax money right here, Your Honor," she said as she pulled an envelope containing cash out of her handbag and held it up to the judge. "It is time to bring Nadean back to live with me. So, when the school board sends a bus to take her to school, I will pay my taxes."

The judge looked at my grandmother and asked to speak to her attorney and opposing counsel in his chambers. They all returned to the courtroom a few minutes later.

"Mrs. Tessier, beginning this fall, a school bus will be sent to take Nadean to school every day. Case dismissed," the judge said.

That fall, a big bright yellow school bus stopped at the gate to the farm. Grandma stood beside me as the door opened and the driver, Mr. Bell, introduced himself.

"Hello, Nadean, I have heard all about you. We are going to be good friends. You are going to be the only student that I drive to school every day."

Grandma released my hand and I climbed aboard and sat directly behind Mr. Bell.

"Take good care of my grandchild," she said as the bus doors closed. Mr. Bell and I became great friends. Every day as I sat behind him holding on to the railing, I told him of my challenges at school and life on the farm. He would look at me in the mirror above his head and always expressed interest in my endless stories. For my first two years back in Blind River, I was the only student on the bus. After I climbed aboard, Mr. Bell would turn the bus around at the gate to the farm and we would drive back to town. As word spread of the new school bus route, more families moved into the farm district and in time, the bus became full of students. I would ride with Mr. Bell until I was eighteen and left for university.

The following summer, many relatives visited the farm during hay season to help take in the hay.

One day my cousin and I got into a fight and after she bit my arm, I bit her back.

"You are just an illegitimate bastard . . . a spoiled brat! You don't belong in the family. All the cousins hate you!" she said.

I ran to the porch and sat down on the bench next to Papere, who was smoking his pipe. I clutched his shirt and sobbed as I told him what my cousin said to me.

"Forget them, it does not matter! They are so stupid," he said as he held me in his arms, close to his chest.

In complete and utter desolation, I felt that I would never belong, never have a real home or a family of my own and that I would always be unwanted.

One day after I returned home from school, Grandma told me a detective had visited the farm. She said he told her he had been hired to do research on my birth. He asked her many questions and said he was going to the hospital that afternoon to see what records he could find. Grandma said the detective asked her if I was happy on the farm and she said I was very happy. Grandma said the detective would not tell her who hired him.

The next day, Grandma said the detective had returned and informed her that there were no files of my birth on record at the hospital.

Aunt Roberta was always as curious about my birth parents as I was and we often discussed trying to find my birth mother. Grandma was vehemently against us attempting a search, so I always wondered if the detective incident was true or if Grandma made it up to discourage me from attempting to locate my biological mother.

When I was twelve years old, Papere was diagnosed with stomach cancer and Grandma seemed to crumble emotionally. She and the family decided not to tell him how serious his illness was. Grandma had great difficulty coping with his diagnosis, so I took over the chores of running a household. Since we didn't have a car, I did grocery shopping on weekends when Uncle Joseph or another one of her children would visit.

When many of my friends were going out, I was doing the laundry with the old wringer washing machine and two washtubs, making up the beds, vacuuming, and washing and waxing floors.

Two years later, on May 22, 1967, Papere passed away. Grandma and his children sat in the front row at the funeral home during the viewing. The sons-in-law, daughters-in-law and cousins sat in the back of the room.

"Nadean, go up there and sit beside Grandma. You belong up there with her and her children, not back here with us," my Aunty Antoinette said.

I walked to the front row and sat next to Grandma; she sobbed uncontrollably. I felt her visceral pain as she longed for the love of her life, and I too began to cry.

After Papere died, Grandma suffered with bouts of angina. On many nights when she could not breathe, I called the ambulance and paced while she gasped for air until the medics arrived and placed an oxygen mask on her face. Then we traveled the great distance into town to the hospital, where she stayed for days until well enough to return home to the farm.

"Don't worry, Nadean," Grandma often said, "I am going to live until you are eighteen to see you through school. Then God can take me, but not before."

Chapter 5

Graduation and University

In 1909, at the age of fourteen, my grandmother was forced to drop out of school and take a clerk job earning $8.00 per month to help support her family. My grandmother was an exceptionally bright student, especially in math, a subject few girls were expected to excel in at that time, and the nuns at Grandma's school begged her mother to reconsider.

When my grandmother was raising me, she often voiced her regret that she was unable to finish school and become a teacher. Grandma told me that I needed to study hard and get an education because if I ever had children, I'd be able to support my family if my husband died. As such, school became my salvation.

My teachers seemed to take a special interest in me and encouraged me in my studies. When I was in grade school and new math was introduced, I was elected to take part in special studies to ascertain my level of comprehension of this cutting edge (at the time) math.

Upon high school graduation, I was designated an Ontario Scholar and awarded bursaries (grants) and scholarships to the six universities where I applied. I settled on Windsor University.

"Nadean, don't worry," Grandma said, "I am going to live long enough now to see you through university. Then God can take me, but not before."

None of my high school friends chose the small Windsor University, so I knew no one when Aunt Roberta drove me and my trunk to school that fall. I was immensely lonely, missed Grandma, Mon Oncle, the family gatherings on weekends, and my animals on the farm. I cried during my phone conversations with Aunt Leona and Aunt Roberta and they encouraged me to stay.

One overcast winter day, I was walking to class and noticed a man's long brown leather coat swinging in the breeze as he crossed the green. He had wavy black hair with long sideburns and I thought of Heathcliff in *Wuthering Heights*. I watched as this handsome young man, who with his dark and brooding features resembled the singer Engelbert Humperdinck, passed me without making eye contact. I often thought of Heathcliff, as I nicknamed him, and saw him around campus.

After completing our homework, my friends and I would often go to the gym during the winter months.

While watching a water polo game one afternoon, we met a student named Kevin, who was from St. Gustave. He invited us to a party the West Indian students from Windsor were hosting at the men's residence in Huron Hall. Kevin informed us that he would send a car to the girls' residence to pick us up. On that Friday night, a red Monte Carlo with black leather interior pulled up at Laurier Hall.

As we entered the party, Kevin approached and told us to help ourselves to the food and drinks and showed us where they were setting up the music. I turned to look at a young man making connections on the reel-to-reel music system and was over the moon when he turned to face me and I saw it was my Heathcliff.

I walked over to the music table and when *Sweet City Woman* started to play, he introduced himself as Juan Rivero and asked me to dance.

After hours of eating, drinking and dancing, Juan announced that he was leaving the party and offered my friends and I a ride back to our residence. As he dropped us off, Juan asked me if I would be interested in going to the library with him that week. We had our first date a few days later. Juan had helped form a band of West Indian student musicians and was the lead singer and guitarist. I loved listening to them at their practice sessions. Their obvious delight and joyfulness in their playing was infectious to someone as reserved as I.

Juan, who graduated from Bristol University in England with a degree in law but did not take the English Bar Exam, came to Windsor to complete the university's graduate program in business. His plan was to transfer all credits to the Canadian Chartered Accountancy program and then return to St. Gustave as an accountant. Juan's father, Guillermo, and his mother, Alice, lived in Rio de Janeiro, Brazil, and were St. Gustave and St. Eustace's ambassador and ambassadress to Brazil. Juan's brother, Roberto, who was studying law in England, also planned on returning to St. Gustave when his studies were completed.

"The family's goal is for my father to return to St. Gustave and become Prime Minister. If that does not happen, Roberto will run for office and once elected, I will become his Minister of Finance," Juan said.

During the next three months we dated exclusively, but did not become serious.

I returned to the farm in May with no commitments given by either of us, but within days of my return, Juan called and asked if he could come to Blind River to see me during the week he had off between semesters.

I booked a room for him at a small hotel along a lake in Algoma Mills, two miles from Blind River.

We spent our days exploring the countryside and the farm and our evenings at dinners and the movies. As we walked the fields at the farm, Juan was amazed that the animals followed me everywhere, and he called me the Pied Piper.

"As a child I spent many years alone on this farm during the week," I said. "I had no friends. Only cousins on the weekends. So, the animals became my best friends. I spent hours with them. Some of them I raised from birth."

As the sun set one evening, Mon Oncle, Grandma, Juan and I sat in the kitchen talking. Juan took his guitar out of its case, sat down in the chair next to Grandma and began to sing. All of us were taken with his charm and graciousness. As I watched him sing to my grandmother, I knew that this was a man to whom I could give my heart!

Juan asked me to drive back to Windsor with him and to stay for a few days on campus. Along the way we stopped at a few hotels but the price for one night was high.

"I am really sorry. I don't have enough money for this hotel. One day we still stay in the most exclusive and beautiful hotels. You will never suffer from a lack of money. I promise," he said.

"It is okay," I said. "Money does not matter to me."

Chapter 6

St. Gustave and Windsor

That summer, Juan's family returned to their weekend home on Manos, a small island off St. Gustave, and I was invited to join him.

Juan's mother, Alice, a slim, blonde beauty originally from Montreal, and his father, Guillermo, a handsome man of Hispanic descent, were both welcoming and gracious. Roberto, Juan's brother, along with Carlotta, his nineteen-year-old sister, and her twin brother, Andres, had already arrived and were settled into the house. I met Lillian, known as Miss Lil, their nanny, who was very kind to me.

Alice and Guillermo hosted parties for extended family and friends and I fell in love with the country and its people. We swam, water skied, boated, explored St. Gustave and its many beaches and had dinners at the homes of friends and at restaurants in Port Espania, the capital.

Before Juan and I left St. Gustave, Andres' car slid on a rain-slicked road and overturned as he was coming home one evening from a date. While he managed to climb out of the back window with minor cuts and scrapes, his car was totaled.

That fall Juan started working with Peat Marwick, an accounting firm in Toronto. I switched my second-year studies from a major in French at Windsor University to fashion design at Sheridan College in Toronto because I could not bear the 230-mile separation between Juan and I.

I spent the first two weeks at Sheridan renting a room from a professor and his family and was very unhappy. I did not like living with the professor and his family, did not enjoy my new course of study, and found traveling around Toronto to be overwhelming.

One afternoon, my professor told the class how much he loved his former job as a mannequin dresser at Macy's in New York.

"If you enjoyed dressing the mannequins in New York so much, why are you teaching fashion at a college in Canada?" I asked.

"This is where the money is," he replied.

This struck me like a lightning bolt and I realized then that I needed to return to Windsor to complete my degree.

At the end of class that Friday afternoon, I walked to the administration office, advised them I was returning to Windsor, and signed all necessary transfer forms.

That evening I packed my bags and trunk and moved to my cousin Louise's house in Mississauga.

While I knew I had to do what was best for my future, when I called Juan and told him of my plans, we were both devastated. I did not know how we would be able to maintain a relationship while he worked long hours in Toronto and I attended school in Windsor.

However, there was no turning back for me and on Saturday night, I climbed aboard the 7:00 p.m. train to Windsor. As I stared out the train window at Juan standing on the platform, tears streamed down his face. Beyond consolation, I was barely able to raise my hand as the train departed the station and I watched him disappear.

I felt a gentle tap on my arm and looked at the man sitting beside me. "Your boyfriend?" he asked, as he looked out the window. "What happened?"

Between sobs, I told him about Juan, my decision to return to Windsor, and my fear that I was saying good-bye forever. He listened patiently and finally invited me for a drink in the bar car.

"I don't feel for a drink right now," I said.

"Well, I do, and you can have coffee."

As we sat in the bar car, he listened to more of my story and was very encouraging.

"Nadean, it will all work out, you just wait and see," he said. "My girlfriend is meeting me at the station and we will take you and your trunk back to Windsor."

Although I was two weeks late for the semester I was able to enroll in all of the classes required to complete my degree in French and have all of the scholarship and grant funds transferred back to Windsor. I decided to take two extra classes during both the fall and spring semesters and to attend intersession and summer school the following summer to enable me to complete my degree in two years instead of three.

As Juan was working long hours at Peat Marwick, I traveled on many weekends so we could be together. I signed up for car pool rides with students traveling to Toronto and started hitchhiking when there were no car pools.

On one occasion, I was picked up by a policeman in regular clothes who shared horror stories of students who had been kidnapped. He made me promise to stop, took me to a bus station, and gave me bus fare for the trip to Toronto. Although I returned to hitchhiking a couple of weeks later, I began to think more of the risks I was taking. When Air Canada offered a student standby rate of $11.00 one way, I traveled by air on weekends.

Every weekend as I arrived in Toronto, I jumped onto the subway and would count the stops until I could run through the door to Juan's apartment and into his arms.

After graduating from Windsor University in 1973, I decided to pursue an MBA in accounting and finance at McMaster University in Hamilton so I could qualify as a chartered accountant, like Juan. Business studies were a whole new language to me and I found the MBA program extremely challenging. In a class of fifty students, I was one of only seven women, was only twenty years old, and had very little life experience.

"Okay, Nadean," Grandma said when I began the MBA program, "now I am going to live long enough to see you through this university. Then God can take me, but not before."

When I left the farm for university, it was too difficult for Grandma and Mon Oncle to live on the farm alone during the winter months. They decided to move to Aunt Roberta's home in Sault Ste. Marie and returned to the farm in the spring. At Christmas of 1973, I flew to Sault Ste. Marie to spend the holidays with the family and Juan flew to Brazil to spend Christmas with his family.

When Juan returned from his holiday he presented me with a beautiful amethyst ring that had two diamonds on each side and asked me to marry him. I said yes and we moved in together and set our wedding date for December 14, 1974.

At the news of our engagement, Grandma shared her final commitment to me.

"I will live now until you are married, Nadean. I will know that you have someone to love and take care of you. It will be okay if God takes me then."

Chapter 7

The Wedding

On Saturday, December 14, 1974, on a beautiful sunny morning at a small Anglican church, St. Martin's in the Field, we were married. We had a small reception with champagne and appetizers at our apartment in High Park following the ceremony.

Andres and Juan's cousin Michael and his family attended from Juan's family. Aunt Roberta and Christina attended from my family. Grandma could not attend because she had an angina attack and was in the hospital again in Blind River.

Juan was devastated that his parents did not attend our wedding.

They had decided to remain in Brazil to await our arrival after our honeymoon and promised us a wedding reception at their residence and a family holiday together.

After giving my bouquet to Christina to carry to my grandmother, Juan and I boarded a plane for Salvador Bahia to begin our three-day honeymoon. We then traveled to the family residence in Brasilia, where we joined Guillermo, Alice, Roberto and his wife, Charlotte, Andres and Carlotta.

Alice was excited about the wedding reception she planned for us at their gorgeous home and I showed her the evening dress I purchased for the occasion.

"It's very pretty, Nadean," Alice said as she inspected my dress, "but it's not quite right. I think we need something else."

Alice took me, Charlotte and Carlotta shopping at her favorite boutique and chose a beautiful long white gown that only needed minor alterations.

"This is it," Alice said as she held the gown. "You will look beautiful in this dress, Nadean."

Three hundred guests attended our reception, including government officials and members of the diplomatic corps. A reporter was in attendance and the glamorous party was filmed. Weeks after our reception, clips of the event were shown as a news item prior to the feature presentation at the movie theater.

On Christmas Day, as we sat down with Juan's family for breakfast, their butler Raj announced that someone was calling from Canada for Miss Nadean.

"Hello, Nadean," Aunt Roberta said when I answered the telephone. "I am calling to tell you that Grandma died this morning at the hospital."

At that moment my whole world fell apart. I asked Aunt Roberta if I should try to fly back to Canada.

"No, Nadean. You said your good-byes to Grandma a few weeks ago and she was so happy to get your bouquet. You are a world away. It's Christmas Day. Everything is closed. By the time you get back, the funeral will be over. Stay with your husband and your new family. Try to be happy there."

Guillermo and Alice organized a private family Mass for me in Brasilia and we all attended. I struggled with overwhelming sadness and loneliness, yet tried to be as upbeat as I could manage on the outside. During a moment of absolute clarity I realized that Grandma kept her final promise to me: God took her eleven days after our wedding.

The entire family flew to Rio de Janeiro for the second week of the holiday and we stayed at a beautiful hotel on Copacabana Beach.

New Year's Eve was especially memorable. Brazilians traditionally dress in white on New Year's Eve, go to the beach carrying lit candles, and make offerings during a ceremony honoring Iemanja, Goddess of the Sea. They toss gifts of flowers and other items into the sea. If the Goddess accepts their gifts they will have a prosperous year. If their gifts are returned on the incoming tide, the year will not be as prosperous.

After dinner Juan and I walked along Ipanema Beach holding hands and gazing as the Brazilians threw their gifts out to sea. It was a brilliant moonlit night and the locals along with many children were so happy. They joyfully handed flowers to us and gestured to us to throw them into the sea. We stood on Ipanema Beach, held one another closely, and welcomed in the New Year.

When we returned to Toronto after our holiday, Aunt Roberta informed me that my grandmother's will was going to be read at an attorney's office in Sault Ste. Marie and I needed to be present for the reading.

"Why?" I said. "Can't you go and just tell me what it says? I have just returned to work after a two-week holiday. I will have to ask for a special consideration. Do I really need to be there?"

"Nadean, this is important. You need to be here," she said.

The following week, I sat in the lawyer's office with Aunt Roberta, Aunt Phyllis, Aunt Leona, Uncle Joseph, Aunt Lois, Uncle Nestor and Aunty Antoinette. There was a collective gasp from the group when the lawyer announced that Grandma left the entire 160-acre farm and house contents to me.

"How did this happen?" I said. "There must be a mistake."

I heard the expressions of disbelief and the beginnings of anger from the aunts and uncles. When everyone left the office but Aunt Roberta and me, I asked the attorney if he was sure these were my grandmother's wishes.

"Yes," he said.

Then I remembered a conversation with Grandma after one of her trips in the ambulance to the hospital when I was a teenager. She was concerned I would be neglected if she left the farm to her children when she died.

"I am worried that they will cut you out and not take care of you. I am worried too about Mon Oncle. Who will take care of him? Do you want the farm? If I leave it to you, will you take care of it and take care of Mon Oncle if I die before him?"

"Grandma, you know that I love the farm. I don't care who you leave it to. I will always make sure that Mon Oncle is taken care of."

In the next few weeks, the family splintered over her will. Sides were taken and four of her children supported me and three vehemently disagreed with Grandma's wishes. I was torn over what to do and Aunt Roberta was in the middle of it, as she helped Grandma hire the attorney in Sault Ste. Marie who drew up the will.

Roberta was convinced that Grandma misread the will while signing it and she meant to leave the farm to all of her children and me in equal shares. However, I knew that Grandma was too bright and careful to have made such an egregious mistake. She signed that will knowing full well its contents. However, she could not have foreseen its ramifications. I wrote individual letters to all of her children expressing my surprise at the contents of the will and asked them to communicate in writing their advice and wishes as to how to resolve it.

I said, "Based on your wishes, I will decide what is to be done."

Three of her children sent vile, horrific letters in response, expressing their outrage and anger toward me.

"You are an ungrateful spoiled bastard who does not belong in our family."

"You are an illegitimate, a nothing who has stolen our birthright, our inheritance and our mother's love. You were always Mother's favorite."

Page after page, their hatred toward me poured out, and I was inconsolable.

After much heartbreak, consultations with an attorney, and discussions with Juan, I realized that if I left the farm in equal shares to each of the children they would never be able to agree on anything, as they were so polarized by their hatred toward me and now toward each other.

Against my attorney's advice, but with Juan's support, I sold the 160-acre farm to Uncle Joseph for $1.00, requesting that while he owned it, other members of the family should have access to it. Mon Oncle was given a life tenancy, which meant that he could live on the farm until his health prevented it or he passed away. In my mind, the farm had gone back to the family, where it belonged, and I was done.

Chapter 8

St. Gustave, Nassau, and the Cayman Islands

From our very first date, Juan expressed his desire to return to the West Indies. He hated the winters in Canada and wanted to be in a warmer climate and closer to his family.

The partners at Peat Marwick understood and supported his desire to move to one of their offices in any of the islands. In June of 1975, they subsidized an exploratory trip so we could determine where we felt most comfortable. Since I was working with Price Waterhouse, I arranged to meet with partners in the islands, where Price had an office. We arrived on a Saturday night for one week in St. Gustave. Juan had chosen the Bougainvillea Inn, a small, local hotel, so I could experience the local culture.

There was no hot water available at the hotel for bathing and Juan warned me not to drink any tap water on the island. Juan's cousins Miguel and Alain were anxious to show me the best of St. Gustave, and the day after our arrival we all set off for Macron Beach, a three- hour drive from Port Espania.

I loved the quiet of Macron, its empty beach, soft sand and coconut trees. I went for a swim and as I came out of the water, I walked toward Juan and his cousins and fainted. Juan and Miguel revived me and we headed back to the hotel. Upon arrival, I started vomiting and was unable to leave the Bougainvillea that evening. I had used tap water to brush my teeth and had the beginnings of gastroenteritis from the tainted water.

As the days progressed and we met with potential employers and friends, I ate nothing and drank only bottled soda water with bitters. By Wednesday night I was weak from lack of food and was scheduled for my final interview with the partners at Price Waterhouse at a dinner on Friday evening.

"Juan, I need a doctor. I am going to go to the General Hospital."

"You can't go to the General Hospital," he said. "None of our family goes there for help. You need to see a private physician."

But Juan hadn't lived on the island since he was eleven years old and didn't know any doctors. I called the General Hospital and explained my situation. By the grace of God, I was transferred to a doctor in the emergency room who was from Canada. He told me to get to the hospital immediately and that he'd be watching for me so I wouldn't have to wait in line. Dr. Miller stood at the entrance, as promised, and ushered me into the hospital while Juan waited outside. The doctor examined me and gave me some strong medicine to take until I felt better.

Juan met with the partners at Peat Marwick during the week and they offered him a position in St. Gustave with the promise of a partnership in two years if all went well.

By Friday I was feeling a little better and looking forward to my interview with the partners at Price. The partners reserved a table for ten at a lovely Italian restaurant in the hills above Port Espania.

As the meal ended and I took a final sip of wine, my stomach started to rebel. I excused myself and went to the ladies' room. When I had not reappeared after twenty minutes, the partners' wives came looking for me and found me hanging over the toilet.

"Please ask Juan to come for me," I said. "I need to leave now."

Juan had to stop frequently on the drive back to the hotel so I could vomit, and by 3:00 a.m., I was lying on the bathroom floor, unable to move. Juan located the telephone number of a doctor and was instructed to take me to a nursing home immediately. The doctor would meet us there.

When we arrived, the nurses offered me neither a chair nor a wheelchair, so I laid down on the floor to the entrance and didn't move. Juan was mortified.

"You are Mrs. Rivero and you need to stand up!" he said. "You can't lie there on the floor like that."

Finally, the doctor arrived and he and Juan carried me to a bed. I was given an IV drip and was discharged the following evening, ten pounds lighter.

We boarded our plane to Nassau on Sunday morning and as it soared above St. Gustave, Juan apologized for the horrendous week.

"After all you've been through, could you ever possibly think of coming back here to live?"

"Of course, darling," I said. "It could not possibly get any worse."

Guillermo, Alice, Roberto, Charlotte, Carlotta and Andres joined us in Nassau. Juan and I went through additional interviews with the partners at Peat and Price and spent the rest of the time with the family at the beach, visiting friends and shopping.

We decided to cancel our flights to the Caymans and choose between Nassau and St. Gustave. After discussions with Alice and Guillermo, it was clear that St. Gustave was not only the best decision, it was the only decision.

Chapter 9

An Edible Fruit

We arrived in St. Gustave on June 6, 1976. Miguel and Alain, anxious to help us get settled, took us around Port Espania looking for apartments. We found a beautiful 20-unit complex at the top of Lady Chaucer Hill. Going down the hill, in a tiered-step fashion, each of the two units per floor had an open patio with stunning views of the city and the sea beyond.

Deana Lewis, wife of a well-known English architect, Jeffrey Lewis, gave us the tour and described the amenities at the complex.

Deana, a very pretty black woman, spoke with a strong English accent and lived in a large home next door to the complex. As she continued to rattle on about the building's features, I noticed the pool.

"Deana, why is the pool empty?"

"It *fullin*," she said.

There was a sharp cackle of laughter behind me, followed by a cough, as Juan, Alain and Miguel tried to contain themselves.

"I'm sorry, Deana," I said and shook my head, "I don't understand."

"Deana meant that the pool is filling up, Nadean," Miguel said, and smirked.

I had not realized that she had broken into slang.

After we agreed to take the apartment and climbed into the car, the three men broke out in hysterics. Juan turned to me and smiled.

"Nadean, you will experience this throughout the country," he said. "We call it Yankee talk. The locals go to the airport to see a friend off to the US or England and come back trying very hard to speak with an American or English accent. But it never fails that they trip themselves up and get caught, just like she did. This is an exaggeration of course, but the locals really like to 'put on the dog.'"

While Juan began working with Peat Marwick, I was hired to set up the Institute of Chartered Accountants for the accounting profession in the country. The Institute, the governing body for the profession, was similar to the American Bar Association for attorneys. I hired a staff of three and registered local students for classes and exams in the UK, organized seminar luncheons and annual dinners, published a bi-annual magazine, and managed the finances of the Institute.

Visiting the country as a tourist and actually living in a third-world country was a huge adjustment for me. The locals did not seem stressed or pressed to do anything.

I always said that "Tuesday could fall on Thursday and no one would care."

Two months after our arrival, Roberto and Charlotte arrived from England and opened a legal practice in Port Espania. At Roberto and Juan's urging, Guillermo and Alice resigned from the diplomatic corps and returned in 1977.

The boys, anxious to become involved in business with their father and hoping his contacts would open doors for them, continued to pursue their political dreams.

Shortly after their return, Alice and Guillermo had an altercation. Juan went to their home and spent hours talking to Alice. When he returned late in the afternoon he said all had been settled, but he was upset.

"What happened?" I asked.

"I can't talk about it, but at the end my mother looked at me and said, "I hope I never come up against you because you are ruthless.""

Juan was visibly hurt by his mother's admonition.

"Juan, she doesn't really know you anymore. You went away to boarding school when you were only eleven years old. Many years have passed since then and you only visited on holiday. She is wrong—you could never deliberately hurt anyone."

Our life consisted of glamorous dinners; cocktail parties given by the diplomatic corps, the president, and prime minister; art gallery artist showings and fashion shows; parties at the family's weekend home and at the island homes of friends; and flying by private plane to the exotic islands.

Guillermo and Alice were a gorgeous, glamorous couple. When Queen Elizabeth and Prince Phillip visited in celebration of the country's independence, Guillermo and Alice were asked by the prime minister to escort them around the island and to the government's celebrations and many festivities.

The family was interviewed and photographed for *Town & Country* magazine. At one of our many Sunday parties, the US attorney general was taken by boat to our island home, where Alice and Guillermo were entertaining President Sir Eliot Clarkson. When the Pope visited, Guillermo and Alice were invited to attend a small private meeting with him.

Alice often said, "We prefer to live in St. Gustave, where we are big fish in a small sea. We would never be happy living in Canada or the US. They are too large and we would be small fish in a big sea."

And I came to understand her statement when I met my Canadian member of Parliament, who was on a trade mission at a cocktail party at the Canadian High Commission.

The practical realities of living in a third-world country, however, were always present. We had no telephone. When we first arrived, there was a pay phone at the apartment complex next to the laundry room, but it was stolen soon after.

There were frequent electrical outages and insufficient water for the complex. The complex was above the 200-foot water mark, so the water pumping station in Port Espania was unable to pump water up the hillside to our complex. We ran out of water daily as the maids did laundry and cleaned apartments. Juan and I would return home from work to no water for cooking or bathing.

The landlord paid the water company to carry truck-borne water and empty it into the tanks, but it would be gone the following day. Some goods that were in short supply, like potatoes, were often sold at black-market prices. Chicken and cheddar cheese were frequently missing from the grocery shelves. These were the harsh realities for everyday citizens.

Juan and I bought two large plastic garbage containers that we placed in the second bedroom of the apartment. We filled them with water and used it for bathing, cooking and flushing toilets. This unique reservoir system became a lifesaver. I carried laundry to my in-laws' residence and did it there.

On two occasions, our apartment was flooded because the water truck had arrived while we were at work and our maid had left the water tap open. We had to hire a company to remove the water from the carpets, and it took days to dry out the apartment. On the second occasion, the tenant below us, a Japanese businessman, was flooded as well due to our taps being left open. He was furious!

We flew to Miami to take a break and to explore the possibility of moving to America. While there, we saw a local TV story about St. Gustave becoming a Republic.

Juan said, "Things will start to improve in St. Gustave. We need to go back."

I joined the Canadian Women's Club, a charitable organization, and became vice president, and then president.

I was asked to model for a high-end, exclusive boutique owned by Geraldine, the wife of a senator in the ruling party, the People's United Party (PUP). A photographer captured me modeling at one of the small intimate shows at her boutique and my photo appeared in *The Leader* newspaper. Juan called from work, saying "Nadean, you can't imagine! One of the newspaper boys on the corner was holding up a *Leader* and waving it in the air as I was driving to work. I looked and your picture is taking up the whole page on the cover. You look beautiful."

Rodriguez Auto, a large local company, was introducing a new car called the Laurel and needed an impressive advertising campaign for its national launch. I was approached by its advertising company and asked to appear in a nationally televised commercial, playing the part of the beautiful wife of a man who has everything but the Laurel. The campaign was a huge success, and Rodriguez Auto took many thousand-dollar deposits on the vehicle prior to its availability.

We continued to attend fabulous dinners and cocktail parties given by Alice, other members of the diplomatic corps, and the president. Gaj Singh II, Maharaja of Jodhpur, and his wife were two of many impressive guests.

When elections took place in 1978, Guillermo, Roberto, and Juan campaigned nightly for the PUP. The PUP won the election again and were in power until 1986.

In 1978, Juan's law school friend Jonathan visited us from England. We organized flights to St. Eustace and stayed at a beautiful golf resort called the Mount Jerome Hotel.

As we walked along the beach near Mount Jerome, Juan picked up a small green fruit from the sand and said, "Hey this is a Dunks. It's a local fruit."

I asked if it was edible and Juan told me it was so I took a large bite. Jonathan took a very small bite and spat it out immediately. At first the taste was pleasant and sweet and then a strong burning sensation began. "Juan," I said, "I don't think this is an edible fruit. My mouth is burning."

We raced back to the hotel. I held up the fruit as we approached the desk and asked if it was edible.

"Oh, God, Madam, no!" the front desk clerk said as he shook his head. "That is a manchineel, it's poisonous! You can't eat that!"

"Well, I just did! What do I do now?"

"Madam, we don't know. We've never seen anyone eat one."

We rushed to our rooms and Juan called Dr. Hilton in St. Gustave.

"Well, I have never actually had a patient eat one," Dr. Hilton said, "but it is poisonous and you need to get her to a hospital immediately. Her esophagus is going to develop blisters, swell, and her breathing will become labored. Eventually, it will be impossible for her to breathe. If she doesn't get treated immediately, she will die."

"We need to get you to emergency or you could die," Juan said.

The three of us rushed out of the hotel and Juan grabbed a taxi driver. "My wife just ate a manchineel. Please take us to the hospital emergency room right away. Drive as fast as you can!"

"Everything is burning," I said as I sat in the back of the cab. "I'm having difficulty breathing. My chest hurts."

"Oh God, I've killed my wife."

The driver sped up and it became a perilous journey as the driver drove around many winding bends for miles, across the island toward the hospital.

I started to perspire as I panicked and my breathing became more difficult. Juan held my hand as I tried to expand my chest and grab more air.

The emergency staff at the hospital responded immediately as Juan explained what happened.

They grabbed a milky alkaline substance and told Jonathan and me to drink all of it. And then they ordered me to drink a second one.

"I still can't breathe and my throat is burning," I said to Juan when we arrived back at the hotel.

"Come into the bathroom and make yourself throw up," Juan said. When I couldn't, Juan called Dr. Hilton again.

"She needs more medical treatment," Dr. Hilton said. "I am going to call Dr. Ramsingh in Bacchus Bay. I will explain what is happening. Go to his office now."

Before we left, Juan called Dr. Ramsingh as well to explain the urgency of our visit.

"I am scheduled to give a lecture at the Red Cross and you need to get here by 5:00 p.m.," Dr. Ramsingh said.

As we began another hair-raising drive, I had to stop along the way so I could vomit and use the bathroom at numerous hotels.

We arrived as Dr. Ramsingh was locking up his office. He injected me with cortisone and we began the arduous drive back to Mount Jerome, stopping every couple of miles for me to be sick and use the bathroom.

At one of our stops we discovered a beautiful hotel run by Mr. Carmichael. He had established a nightly custom of donning a long-sleeved white shirt, black bow tie, and black trousers and inviting his guests to share cocktails while he played the piano on the veranda. Despite being so terribly sick, I found him to be utterly charming and vowed to return when I was well again.

The medicine finally worked and upon our return to Mount Jerome, I collapsed in bed. The next morning, we discovered that the top layer of my tongue had peeled off.

I experienced stomach issues for many months thereafter.

Chapter 10
Disenchantment and Change

Juan became unhappy with Peat Marwick. After working with the firm for two years, the partners were not ready to offer him a partnership so he resigned, joined Roberto's law practice, and hired a young woman called Francis as his secretary. He was required to return to the University of the West Indies to obtain his law qualification to practice in the country.

A few months after joining Roberto's practice, Juan came home from work one day and said, "Nadean, there is a rumor going around that one of the Rivero men is having an affair, but it's not me," Juan said. "It's Roberto. I just want you to know in case you hear anything."

I was taken aback, yet wanted to believe him, so I ignored the rumors. It didn't take long for Juan to realize that working in a partnership with his brother Roberto would never succeed. After observing their interactions, I realized that two strong men with enormously competing egos could not possibly work in the same office. Juan felt rootless. After six months with Roberto, he resigned from the firm, left law school, and opened his own chartered accountancy practice, taking Francis with him. I would discover years later that it was Juan who was having an affair with her.

When the movie *Kramer vs Kramer* was released about a custody battle over a young boy, I found the court case and its outcome heart-wrenching. Sobbing uncontrollably in the cinema, I turned to Juan.

"Whatever happens to us, let's promise we'll never fight over our child, please?"

Despite having no running water, we decided to host a cocktail party at our flat. The guests were young and attractive. I was especially pleased when members of the Bacardi and Fernandes families, competitors in the rum trade, arrived and asked for rum and Coke.

I had set out high-grade rum from both houses. I had also spent the previous weekend recording hit tunes from the radio, the Bee Gees and Lionel Ritchie, on reel-to-reel tapes. Guests danced on our balcony under the stars, and looked down the valley and out to sea. It was an enchanting night. The party was a huge success. Between songs, Juan and I ran to the bathroom to empty buckets of water into the toilet tank. After the party, thank-you letters and calls arrived for days.

In 1979, Guillermo was awarded the country's highest honor, the St. Gustave Cross.

The award would have been a knighthood, had the country remained a British colony rather than becoming a republic.

Alice and Guillermo were vacationing in Canada when the formal award ceremony was scheduled to take place, so Juan and I attended in their place. The ceremony was held at the president's residence. Dress was formal and the event was covered by television and print media. Juan looked especially handsome as he walked to the podium to receive his father's award from the president of the republic. He was featured on television news the next evening.

In June 1979, we finally moved from our apartment on Lady Chaucer Hill to Grandview.

The townhouse development was on the site of the old golf clubhouse, on a hill in a semicircular formation with valley walls on each side. It looked down onto the capital city and the harbor. Once again, our home had spectacular views of the valley and sea beyond. It had two patios, one covered and one open, and its own small swimming pool.

Juan installed a large water tank on the perimeter of the property to accommodate shortages. We applied for and were given our own telephone. Electricity outages and food shortages continued, but we were ecstatic with our new home, which was situated on a hill slightly above and next door to Alice and Guillermo's large house.

In 1980 we were presented with much joy with the impending birth of our first child.

Juan and I were thrilled with the news. I stopped drinking alcohol, ate well, drank whole milk, and exercised daily so the baby would be healthy. I gained forty-one pounds and Juan told me I never looked more beautiful.

"I would love a little boy just like you," I told him. "But I will be happy with a girl as long as it is healthy."

Years later I discovered that Guillermo told Juan and Roberto that I became pregnant so Juan would stop his affair with Francis. I had suspicions about an affair, but refused to believe Juan would do such a thing. And I was far too naïve and trusting to have thought up such a scheme.

After thirty-six hours of labor, I gave birth to a beautiful baby boy at Stewart Maternity Clinic. Stewart's is a midwifery clinic where the doctor is called just before delivery is expected.

We named our eight-pound, twelve-ounce boy Andrew Alberto Guillermo Rivero, names from his father, grandfather, and both of his uncles. He was the first male grandchild and Juan and I were overjoyed. Andres and his wife, Edna, flew down from Canada for Andrew's christening. The night before the ceremony, family members gathered at Alice and Guillermo's house for formal family photos.

Andrew was christened on Easter Sunday by the bishop of the Anglican Church during a small, private ceremony. Alice organized a lovely lunch on their patio after the ceremony. The bishop was invited to join us.

"This is the happiest day of my life," I said as I raised my glass for a toast. "I have everything I have ever wished for. I am a wife and mother. I finally have a family and a child. I could not be happier."

They were taken aback, as I seldom expressed such outward emotion, but all were pleased.

Every evening after Juan came home from work, we placed Andrew in his carriage and walked in the neighborhood with Coco, our blond cocker spaniel and our cat, Abercrombie. Late one evening as the sun started to set, we both looked at Andrew and almost simultaneously realized how deep our love was for this child.

"I have never loved another human as much as this child," I said to Juan with tears in my eyes. "I could not bear it if anything ever happens to him. We can't have just one child. We must have more children."

Juan agreed.

A few months after Andrew's birth, Juan learned that Ernst and Young, a big-six accounting firm in the United States, was looking to merge with a local accounting firm in our country to expand its international presence. E&Y interviewed numerous firms and reduced the selection of potential candidates to two, Juan Rivero and Co. and David Marshall and Co. Juan wanted the international connection as much as David did. David's firm had been in existence longer, but both were well-positioned for such a merger.

"Ernst and Young are sending a partner from the New York office to meet with me and David," Juan said to me. "They will visit our offices, review the qualifications of our staff, our current client base and our ability to assist with the growth of business for them locally. How can we be sure that my firm is chosen for this merger?"

I told him not to worry. We would develop a plan for whatever time the partner had allotted for us and we would "totally wow" this guy.

I suggested that he, his father and Roberto take the partner on Roberto's 50-foot boat down the islands to the family home for a half day. They could swim and fish. I would organize food and drinks. When they returned in the afternoon, they were to leave the partner at his hotel to rest and change, then pick him up for a cocktail party at our house that evening.

I pulled out all the stops for the party—great catered food, drinks, waiters to serve, an impressive guest list of leading businessmen, politicians, and the president and his wife. Everyone had been informed of the importance of this evening for Juan and me. They all played their parts to perfection.

A few weeks later we received the news that Ernst and Young would be merging with Juan Rivero and Co. Announcements were made in the local newspapers and Juan was overjoyed.

The other candidate, David Marshall, shared with me years later that he knew he had a really good chance going up against Juan since both firms had similar qualifications and backgrounds.

"However," he said, "I had more experience and a larger firm so I stood a better chance. Then I factored you in and knew I could not win. You would do everything in your power to see that Juan got that merger. You would pull out all the stops to impress that partner and you did. Kudos to you."

In August 1981, during a routine postnatal exam, Dr. Trina Barnett replaced Dr. Ralph Hilton, who was on vacation.

"Nadean, do you need to empty your bladder?" the doctor asked during my pelvic exam.

"No, why?"

"I am feeling a growth on your left ovary that is as large as a grapefruit. Do me a favor, empty your bladder and come back. I'll look at it again." When she discovered the growth remained, I looked at her for a moment before I asked the dreaded question.

"What do you think? The big C?"

"Not necessarily," she said. "Ninety percent of cases are benign. Of the remaining ten percent, most are fluid rather than tissue-filled. Only three percent of tissue-filled tumors are malignant."

I was sent home with medication and asked to come back in two weeks for an appointment with Dr. Hilton.

"Nadean, it's still there and very large," Dr. Hilton said when I returned for my exam. "I recommend surgery."

"Dr. Hilton, how could this be?" I said. "I have had no symptoms except for a slight swelling of the lower abdomen at the end of the day after eating and thought I still had weight to lose from the pregnancy. How could it get to be this size without being detected?"

"It was hidden by the pregnancy."

Surgery was scheduled for the following Tuesday at Stewart Maternity Clinic, where I had given birth eight months earlier.

Dr. Hilton informed the family that he was able to get all of the tumor but while excising it, the tumor burst inside my abdominal cavity and the results would take a few days.

On Saturday morning Juan and Andrew visited me at Stewart. "Juan, do you have my results yet? Surgery was four days ago," I said. "I have not heard yet," he mumbled.

"If it was you here in this bed, I would be asking the doctor!" I said. "They must have the results by now. We need to know."

Juan called Dr. Hilton and was asked to contact Guillermo and come to the doctor's house immediately.

"The tumor is malignant. Her chances are fifty–fifty," Dr. Hilton said. Juan was devastated.

Juan, Andrew, Alice and Guillermo returned to the nursing home and waited outside the room when Dr. Hilton entered. He repeated what he'd told Juan: although it was rare for a person so young, I had ovarian cancer and my chances were 50-50.

While I sobbed from the hospital bed, Dr. Hilton recommended that I immediately seek treatment in the United States or Canada.

As they all stood at the end of my bed, Juan with Andrew in his arms, I saw the parallels: my adoptive mother, Rita, died after a three-year fight with cancer, when I was two. If cancer took me quickly, I might live only another two years and Andrew would be without a mother.

I looked at my son and silently begged for God's help. "Please, God, let me live until Andrew is eighteen. If you take me then, it will be okay. He will have enough of my values and morals by then."

Like my grandmother, I too made a pact with God for the life of my child.

Chapter 11

Toronto General

We left Stewart Maternity Clinic that afternoon. I was in the back seat with Andrew while Juan drove. The rage and grief I felt exploded from me as I screamed, "Why me? I'm only twenty-eight! I'm only twenty-eight!"

Juan remained silent. There was no answer. I've never again asked why I was chosen.

The following week, Alice and Guillermo made calls to hospitals in the US and Canada as they sought advice for my treatment. Friends and family heard the news of my illness and visited with words of love and concern.

"Nadean, Princess Margaret Hospital in Toronto is a cancer research center and one of the best in Canada. Perhaps you should return home to Canada for treatment," a member of the Canadian Women's Club said.

I became very weak and required someone to be with me in case I fell while showering.

"We've made calls," Alice said as she waited outside my shower stall while I bathed. "The doctors at Mount Sinai in New York say they will do exploratory surgery on you and test the results. It is a very good hospital. You know, the Shah of Iran was treated there."

I felt the cool water on my face and as my tears fell, I replied, "But, Alice, the Shah died."

Between Andrew's birth, in December 1980, and September 1981 he and I had been inseparable. I breast-fed him for nine months. Now I would be snatched away and sent sixteen hundred miles away to Canada. I was grief-stricken over our impending separation and fearful I would not return.

After many consultations with numerous hospitals, it was decided that Alice, Juan and I would fly to Toronto and seek further diagnosis and treatment at Toronto General Hospital.

The night before our departure, a professional photographer arrived and took photos of Andrew, Juan and me. We didn't know if and when I would return.

We stayed with Juan's brother Andres and his wife, Edna, in Oakville, an hour's drive from Toronto.

We met with Dr. Gare, head of the gynecology and obstetrics department, and he informed us that the pathology slides they received were promising.

"There are malignant cells mixed with highly differentiated benign cells," Dr. Gare said. "However, when the tumor was excised it burst, and I'm concerned that there might be free-floating malignant cells in your abdominal cavity. I recommend we do a complete hysterectomy. While I am inside, I will inject a saline solution into the abdominal cavity, then draw all of it out.

"While in there, I will also take biopsies of your major organs to ensure that the disease has not spread. As there were malignant cells on the outside of the ovary, I am concerned that they could have touched your other organs. We will follow the surgery with radium treatment."

Alice, Juan and I were stunned and tried to absorb this latest shock. "Dr. Gare," I said, "why can't you go in, not do a hysterectomy, but do all of the other tests? Then depending on the results, go back in and do the hysterectomy if necessary?"

"You had major surgery just two weeks ago. We can't go in, close you up and then go in again so soon. It will be too hard for you to recover." He took me to an examination room and as he examined my stomach, I started to cry.

"Dr. Gare, I have only one child. I want more children. I am an only child. I don't want that for my son."

"I know it is a difficult decision, but it is what I recommend."

When we returned to his office he looked at all three of us and asked us what we wanted to do. I looked around his office at his many family photos and made one last effort.

"Dr. Gare, you have a beautiful wife and three lovely children in those photos. We want more children. If it was your wife sitting here in front of you, what would you tell her?"

He remained silent for a few seconds as he stared at me.

"If it was my wife in front of me," he said, "I would say this to her: You can choose not to have the surgery. You can go home and try for another child, which might take two years. However, eventually you will be back here and when you do, your chances won't be as good. The cancer could have spread. My advice to you is that life is short. Live to raise your son."

"Why can't I have chemotherapy instead of a hysterectomy, as that will enable me to have more children?"

"From all indications, your disease is local and isolated to your abdominal cavity. Chemotherapy is like using an atomic bomb to treat an ant. It affects the entire body. Radium treatment is limited to the diseased area."

Alice and Juan remained silent as Dr. Gare and I volleyed back and forth on the merits of the two treatments.

Finally, I realized I had no choice in the matter.

"Dr. Gare, I will do the surgery. Please organize to have it done as soon as possible."

The surgery was scheduled for two days later and I was in the hospital for ten days. Test results arrived throughout the week following surgery. Each morning, Dr. Gare and Dr. Gregorich, his assistant during surgery, entered my room with glowing smiles on their faces.

"Nadean, the test results are coming back negative, indicating no spreading of the disease to your major organs. The saline solution has returned negative, as well. It would appear that you are a stage one cancer patient, which is excellent. You might not need radium treatment."

My adoptive father, Sid, and his wife, Wilma, visited. I had found them nine years before and introduced them to Juan when we were dating. Sid looked handsome in his suit, and Wilma tossed her beautiful mink coat onto the end of my bed.

During their visit I asked Sid if he and Rita ever completed adoption forms for me.

"No, Nadean," he said. "We were so consumed with your Mum's illness, we didn't even think of it. We assumed that the hospital or Children's Aid would organize the papers. I don't know if they were ever completed. No one got in touch with us to ask about it."

As the week progressed, I became visibly upset with the doctors' daily reports. My reaction perplexed them.

"I did not need the hysterectomy!" I said. "The right ovary and my organs are all clean."

The doctors looked at me in shock. They felt they had saved my life and I was unappreciative.

As a precaution, Dr. Gare had removed the omentum, a piece of fatty tissue that sits just under the stomach lining. It is often removed when women undergo a tummy tuck. The omentum serves no real purpose and is usually removed during a hysterectomy.

Nine days after my surgery, Dr. Gare entered my room looking much more serious than he had to this point. He paused a moment before he spoke. "Nadean, the final test result just arrived," he said. "The lab found a microscopic cluster of malignant cells inside the omentum. They had lodged there when the tumor burst during your first surgery. Your condition has now been elevated to stage four cancer and you will need to undergo radium treatments."

When I asked both the doctors and the nurses who visited my room if I was going to live, they would not answer me.

Juan returned home one week after my surgery to be with Andrew, and Alice stayed with me. She traveled every day from Oakville to sit with me and was a great source of strength during this fearful period.

Upon my release, I returned to Andres and Edna's home to await further tests and treatment at Princess Margaret Hospital.

Dr. Gare called two weeks after my release. We talked about my upcoming treatment at Princess Margaret, the possible long-term effects and prognosis, and the requirement that I start taking estrogen pills to counter the effects of premature-onset menopause.

"Nadean, what saved you was early detection by Dr. Barnett, and then your diagnosis and treatment. Ovarian cancer is the silent killer. Many women do not see their gynecologists on an annual basis for an internal exam.

"Some older women who are larger and heavier than you have extended abdomens, which are concealing tumors on their ovaries or fallopian tubes. They think they are just heavy. As a result, the tumor can go undetected for years, growing silently. There are virtually no symptoms until the tumor becomes so large that the patient begins to experience pain. By that time, it is usually too late. By then the tumor is extensive in size, and the cancer has spread to other organs, such as the omentum or the breast.

"That is why the statistics are so dismal, 50–50. A positive outcome is really dependent on early detection. You were fortunate that Dr. Hilton had scheduled a postnatal exam after Andrew's birth. Your cancer is local in nature. I am confident that once you complete the radium treatments, you will live a long life and be there to raise Andrew."

Dr. Gare was correct in his initial diagnosis and recommended treatment. I had beaten the odds. A regular postnatal exam by a newly qualified ob-gyn saved me. Dr. Hilton had missed finding the tumor before my pregnancy and after Andrew's birth. My survival was nothing short of a miracle.

"You were correct in your recommendations, Dr. Gare. I'm sorry that I doubted you. I was desperate to have more children. Thank you so much for saving my life."

We had become close in a few short weeks and experienced such highs and lows together, we were reluctant to hang up.

"Good-bye, Dr. Gare," I said as I started to cry.

"Good-bye, Nadean. Enjoy your husband and son. Live your life to the fullest."

Chapter 12

Princess Margaret

As Alice and I entered the first floor of Princess Margaret Hospital for further tests, diagnosis and recommended treatment, I thought I had entered Dante's Inferno.

Patients were lined up in beds along the hallway awaiting radium treatment or transport to their rooms. Some were quiet and listless; some moaned softly with pain. Dressed in hospital gowns with IV drips suspended above their heads, some had partially shaved heads with large blue X marks. Some were missing parts of their noses and cheeks. Their faces were partially bandaged up. Some slowly shuffled along in the hallway toward the elevators, pushing their IV stands.

The attending nurses were patient, cheerful, kind, professional and caring among all this horror. The contrast was startling. The nurses were accustomed to it; I was not. It was shocking to me. These poor people were fighting for their lives and looked much sicker than I. My disease was internal and hidden. Theirs was front and center.

I had numerous tests and MRIs and finally met with Dr. Bishop, who recommended that I take a course of radium treatments every day, Monday through Friday, for a period of six weeks. My body was tattooed in a diamond pattern in front and back from my chest to my lower abdomen. This would enable the technicians to position the machine within the tattooed area so as not to damage my internal organs.

We delayed the start of treatment because the radium machine broke and needed to be repaired. There was only one machine, so my treatments started two weeks later than planned. I missed Andrew and Juan terribly, but had no choice. I was committed to beating this disease.

Aunts Roberta, Leona and Antoinette called regularly with words of encouragement. Each had formed prayer groups with their friends, some of whom I had never met. They met daily to offer up prayers for my recovery. Many people cared so much.

Travel became more difficult as I grew weaker, so the family decided I should move to Toronto to live with Juan's cousin Michael's wife, Katherine, and her two sons. Katherine had lost Michael four months previously in a car accident. Although still grieving, she was happy for my company and the adult distraction during the evenings and on weekends. Katherine, a chartered accountant, worked during the day for a large firm.

For the first week of treatment, I was able to travel alone to the hospital via bus and subway. However, as the treatments progressed and I became increasingly sick with vomiting and diarrhea, travel became enormously challenging. I never knew when I would suffer an attack.

On one occasion I had to ask the subway conductor to stop the subway, as I was not feeling well. He stopped the train and took me to a bathroom in the underground. He was very kind. He waited outside for me.

"Are you pregnant?" he said with a smile as I emerged from the bathroom.

"Thank you for asking, but no. I'm not pregnant. I have cancer and the radium treatments make me sick. That is where I am going now, to Princess Margaret for radium."

He took my arm and gently guided me back to the subway train. As I sat down on the bench, I looked up and smiled at him. He looked sadder than I.

After this incident, Katherine called Aunt Roberta in Sault Ste. Marie. "Roberta, I am calling because I need your help. Nadean is becoming weaker every day and I am worried about her traveling alone to the hospital. It is a long trip and I am afraid she might pass out. She has lost a lot of weight. The treatments are taking a huge toll on her body. She has constant vomiting and diarrhea. I have to work and can't take her to the hospital."

"Katherine, thank you for calling. I am going to ask my sister Leona to go to Toronto to stay with you. She can take care of Nadean. I will send money as well, so they can take taxis to the hospital every day. Do you think this will help?"

Aunt Leona's arrival was a godsend. She took charge of my welfare and cooked meals so that I could eat healthily. My appointments were scheduled for noon each day. I learned by experimenting that if I ate nothing for four hours prior to treatment and nothing for four hours after treatment, I would not vomit.

Aunt Leona and I traveled by taxi to the hospital each day. She too was initially shocked upon seeing the patients in the hallway, but grew accustomed to it. We sat in a large room with other patients waiting to be called into the radium area. We shared a small chuckle in anticipation as we waited. When we sat closely together and my name was called and I stood, the other patients always looked at Aunt Leona in surprise.

She was in her sixties, extremely thin, and had many deeply etched lines in her face after years of smoking and enduring various heart ailments. She was the one who looked sick, but I was the one going in for radium treatments.

Every Friday afternoon the nurses took a blood test.

"Your white count is below acceptable levels, Nadean," they said. "When you come back on Monday we are going to test you again. You can't have treatment with such a low count. If your white count has not risen to within the acceptable range by Monday, we will have to give you a blood transfusion."

I took their threats as a personal challenge. If I succumbed to a blood transfusion, then the disease was in control. If I could go the entire six-week period without a transfusion, then I was in control and beating the disease. All weekend, Aunt Leona made nutritious meals and I consumed as much as I could. Every Monday I was tested and passed.

"We don't know what you are doing, but yours is an outstanding improvement. We have never seen such a consistently quick recovery over a period of two days by any patient. And you have learned to control the vomiting. What are you doing?"

"I could write a pamphlet for you about how to minimize the side effects of radium. First advise the patients to fast during the four hours before and four hours after their scheduled radium time. This will stop the vomiting, as they will have no food in their stomach. The vomiting weakens us. Outside of that eight-hour window, consume as much healthy food as possible. In addition, over the weekend, when they are not receiving radium, eat substantial meals often during the day, homemade soups, spinach, veggies, pastas and lots of protein, like steak. This will raise the white blood count to acceptable levels by Monday."

The treatments had to continue uninterrupted during Christmas week, so Juan and Andrew flew up to be with me. I was overjoyed to see them. We stayed with Katherine and they traveled with me daily to the hospital. I could not wait to return to a normal life.

During the six weeks of treatments I never had a blood transfusion.

It was later discovered that Canada had not been testing for AIDS in 1981 and 1982. Over a thousand healthy patients were infected with the disease due to tainted blood transfusions administered during that time.

God and Aunt Leona had saved me from the possibility of contracting that potentially fatal disease.

Chapter 13

Home Again

On January 26, 1982, four months after I had left, I flew back to my family.

I was taken in a wheelchair from the tarmac to the arrivals area, where Andrew, Juan, Alice and Guillermo were waiting. I weighed only 105 pounds, my recovery was slow, and I felt weak and tired most of the time, but I was overjoyed to be home. As I had been thrown into premature-onset menopause, I started taking estrogen and vitamins and iron pills for energy.

I tried desperately to return to a normal life as wife and mother. Juan became frustrated with my seeming lack of progress and expressed his concern.

On a planned weekend family trip to the island home, I felt so weak that we drove first to Dr. Hilton's home so he could examine me. My blood pressure was 80/50.

"You are dead. You have just not rolled over," Dr. Hilton said when he looked up from his stethoscope.

I smiled. Juan did not.

We continued on to the weekend home with Juan grumbling to me and his parents.

On Andrew's second birthday, in December 1982, Juan and I agreed to start potty training. The differences in our parenting value systems started to surface with this decision.

Juan constantly expressed his disappointment in the speed of my recovery to me and to his parents. Dr. Hilton advised that the two surgeries, radium treatment, and early-onset menopause took a huge toll on my body, and it would take many months of recovery.

In January 1983, we enrolled Andrew in a small Montessori school in the mornings so he would have social interaction with other children. Charlotte, Roberto's wife, and I also spent time together, as her daughter Carrie was Andrew's age.

As my mornings were free, I decided to push my recovery and join Charlotte at the Poitier Brothers gym class.

The classes were held in a large converted two-car garage with no air conditioning, under a galvanized roof. The classes were conducted in sweltering heat. The brothers were informed of my condition.

"Just do as much as you can," they said. "If you feel weak, stop, march in place or sit down."

As the months passed, I started to regain my strength. However, on one occasion the heat was so intense that I collapsed to the floor. I couldn't drive, and Charlotte took me home. Juan was upset, and I tried to explain that I took the challenging classes to make myself stronger.

Once Andrew was fully in the "terrible twos" stage, Juan and I began to disagree on discipline. He accused me of being inconsistent and told me that instead of going to the gym, I should stay in bed and rest.

We disagreed about everything with respect to Andrew. I was a more liberal, but cautious parent, and our sharply contrasting value systems and opinions emerged.

I forbade Andrew to walk behind Guillermo's push lawn mower with Guillermo as I thought it dangerous. Juan thought it was cute and said I was unnecessarily overprotective.

In August 1984, Juan asked me and Andrew to travel with him to St. Eustace on Roberto's boat for a long weekend. Charlotte was not going with her three children and I decided to stay home with Andrew. I told Juan that the sea crossing could be rough and the boat would be tossed about. I also knew there would be a lot of drinking and I was worried about Andrew's safety on the boat.

Andrew was only three. One of my friends had recently lost her three-year-old daughter down the islands, when the child fell off a jetty into the sea. Another friend had recently lost her three-year-old son in a swimming pool accident as well. Attending the funerals of those young children was heartbreaking.

Upon his return from St. Eustace, Juan seemed less patient with me and even more critical of my parenting skills.

One evening, a dear friend, Peter Lakeman, joined us for dinner. Peter and his wife had moved to the US and he was back in St. Gustave visiting family. During the meal, Juan was irritable and impatient. I tried to lighten the mood by talking about the latest happenings in the country, some of which were very funny.

At one point in the conversation, Juan turned to me and narrowed his eyes.

"You are a failure as a wife and a woman. No man will ever want you again. You have nothing to offer anyone. You can't even have a child."

There was stunned silence for many moments.

"Juan," Peter said, "how can you say such cruel things to your wife and in front of me? You two need counseling immediately or this marriage is over!"

Peter stood from the table to leave and looked at me.

"I am so sorry," he said. "I really hope you can work things out."

After Peter left, I began to cry and asked Juan what was troubling him. I took his hand and tried to soothe his anger. He had never spoken to me in such a cruel manner, with so much venom. Juan refused to speak to me and went upstairs to bed. We never spoke of the incident.

• • •

On September 24, I organized a party at the weekend island home to celebrate Juan's birthday. Family and friends were invited and enjoyed the day swimming, eating and drinking. Juan was physically present, but not emotionally engaged.

In late September, the phone began to ring frequently at our house. I could always hear children's voices in the background and someone breathing before the person hung up.

I told Juan about the calls and asked if he knew who was calling.

"There is someone else," he said. "I met her in St. Eustace on Roberto's boat."

"Is this serious?" I said, and took a deep breath.

"We are still figuring it out."

I asked him to move out, which he did, moving into an apartment that Roberto kept for his girlfriends.

Juan visited Andrew each evening, but remained in Roberto's apartment. I was desperate, frantic and lonely.

"I apologize for asking you to leave," I said. "I am so sorry. We can work this out and have a good life again. Please come back to us. I will work at making you happy again, at making things better for us. We have a beautiful child. We cannot let our marriage fail."

On October 8, 1984, Juan visited again after dinner and sat on a chair in our bedroom. Andrew was on the bed against my pillow and I sat on a bench at the end of the bed.

"The woman I have met is Chantal Singh, a native of France," Juan said. "She is married to Arjun and has lived in their family compound in Savannah as a virtual prisoner. She does not drive and was severely depressed when I met her.

"Recently, I rescued her at night, in darkness from the family compound. Although she has had numerous lovers who promised to assist her financially, none of them have kept their promises. I am prepared to look after her and she has agreed to leave her children, an eight-year-old girl, Simone, and a five-year-old boy, Silvain, behind with her husband.

"We just spent three days together at the Hilton hotel before she flew back to France. However, she is going to return and live with me. I also committed to her that I would leave Andrew behind with you. We are going to start a new life together, just the two of us."

His words were astounding and I could not believe the story or that he was sharing it in front of our three-year-old son.

How could any mother or father agree to leave their child behind?

Chapter 14

On My Own

Between October and December 1984, I was inconsolable. Andrew lost the family unit and I felt responsible and guilty. I thought that if only I had not asked Juan to leave, our little family would still be intact; if I had been a better wife, we would still be together.

The pain I felt for Andrew's loss was more acute than the pain I felt for myself. After putting Andrew to bed at night, I would sit downstairs in the living room, play mournful music like Barry Manilow, and sob. As there was no air conditioning downstairs, the windows and sliding glass doors were always open and I'm sure I gave the neighbors an earful. I couldn't sleep and tossed and turned until 2:00 a.m., most nights.

I woke up exhausted in the morning in time to bathe Andrew, have breakfast, and take him to his Montessori school. Once again, I lost weight due to a lack of appetite. Aunts Roberta and Leona called frequently with words of consolation and encouragement and they were concerned that the stress would impact my health.

I befriended Laura Rivero, who had been married to Jason, Juan's first cousin. When Laura took her two children, Karley and Alex, and left Jason, I supported her through the separation and divorce. I continued to invite her to family gatherings and encouraged her return to work.

Laura was beautiful. She had been a British West Indian Airways flight attendant before she married Jason, who was a BWIA pilot. People always joked that the acronym BWIA stood for either Britain's Worst Investment Anywhere or, But Will It Arrive?

Laura told me about an article published in the newspaper that I hadn't seen, describing a prominent politician's son who left his sick wife for his mistress and that the wife remained at the family home and was inconsolable.

In order to establish some semblance of normalcy in our lives, I hired an attorney, Samantha Wilson, to create a separation agreement that provided Andrew with a consistent visitation schedule between our two homes. Juan initially agreed to the conditions of the agreement and then proceeded to violate all of them.

Although he no longer lived with us, Juan arrived at Grandview whenever he wished and asked to take Andrew with him.

"We need to abide by the conditions of the agreement, Juan. It is the only way that Andrew will settle into a routine," I said.

"I am going to visit every night and read to Andrew," Juan said. "I pay for this house, so I can visit my son whenever I want to."

"Juan, we are trying to settle into a routine that we can live with. Your constant violation of the visitation schedule is disrupting to Andrew and to me."

"I don't give a damn about you!" he said.

Samantha recommended we seek counseling from a child psychologist, Allyson Harwood. She felt that Juan might respect a doctor and learn to abide by the agreement, if he could be made to understand that it would be helpful to Andrew. Juan visited Allyson and agreed that her counseling might help our son.

Andrew, upset over the separation and acting out, started counseling with Allyson and I joined an adult parenting group. Juan insisted that Andrew call Chantal "Mom," and I objected to no avail.

One afternoon Juan came over, again, outside of the agreed-upon schedule.

"I want to take Andrew with me to my house. I don't give a damn about the agreement."

"You can't do this," I said. "You need to take him when it is permitted."

We stood in the doorway of Andrew's bedroom, near the landing on the second floor. With Andrew in his arms, Juan tried to pass me and I blocked his path to the stairs. While he held Andrew in his left arm, he grabbed me by the neck with his right hand, pushed me up against the wall, and tried to choke me.

"I am going to break you financially!" he said as he had me pinned to the wall. "I am going to kill you!"

I held on to the top of the railing and fought him to grab Andrew. We struggled and I wouldn't back down. Finally, he released my neck and put Andrew down on the landing.

"I will ruin you!" he said as he stormed out of the house.

Andrew was frightened. I took him in my arms to my bedroom and held him closely to my chest as I cried quietly, until he settled down.

"Daddy didn't mean it, Andrew," I said as I rocked him. "Now that we are not living together, we need to have a plan that we follow. You will live with me during the week and spend time with your father on the weekends." Fifteen years later, Andrew shared with his girlfriend that he witnessed his father choke and threaten to kill me.

Alice and Guillermo continued to support me emotionally, but were caught in a conundrum. They loved their son, did not approve of what he did or how he treated me, but were powerless to have any impact on him.

"Nadean, it's time to start working at getting better emotionally. You need to stop crying every night. People will not want to be around you if you are constantly crying. You need to start making a life for yourself without Juan. He is not coming back," Guillermo said.

Even though he meant to be kind and it was hurtful, it was also a wake-up call: I needed to be strong for Andrew and me.

I had not worked since giving birth to Andrew, which was followed by my illness and slow recovery. I decided it was time to find a job that would provide freedom to be with Andrew in the afternoons.

Price Waterhouse hired me to work five days per week until 2:00 p.m., which enabled me to be at home with Andrew. It would not provide much income, but it did give me the flexibility I required.

Juan, Andrew and I established a routine that worked when Juan did not violate the terms. Andrew saw Allyson weekly and I continued with my parenting group.

Life as a single woman on a small island held many challenges.

Juan, his mistress and I could not be invited to the same social events, and social events were an important and significant aspect of life there. As he had more money and power and came from a highly respected political family, Juan continued to receive invitations from our political friends. I no longer received invitations and was terribly lonely. It was time to make new friends and carve out a life on my own as a single mother.

Betty McNaughton, Andrew's pediatrician, invited me to dinner one evening and introduced me to Isabel Harrison.

"Nadean, I thought you might like to meet Isabel. Isabel is single, sails with the All-Girls Sailing Crew, and I thought the two of you might become friends," Betty said.

The three of us had a lovely dinner but as I listened to Isabel expound on her life, work and friends, I thought, No way will we ever be friends. Too out there for me; too wacky. Isabel had wild, unruly and unkempt hair. She was loud and drank Betty and me under the table.

Whereas I was so straightlaced and conservative, she was the ultimate liberal in all things.

Not long after I met Isabel, my friend Barbara, who was owner and skipper of the boat Isabel sailed on, invited me to join her sailing group. As Juan had Andrew every other weekend, I was thrilled to join the All-Girls Sailing Crew, the first all-female racing crew in the Caribbean.

The group consisted of six or seven women who sailed Bellatrix, a thirty-three-foot Beneteau. Men were not allowed on board. I knew nothing about sailing and was not a good or confident swimmer, but did not care. Isabel was on board when I arrived. My role as a new crew member was to raise and lower the backstay at the back of the boat when instructed to do so by Barbara.

On my first sail, the sea was rough and it was pouring rain. I had no foul weather gear other than a thin, plastic rain covering that Andrew and I bought at Disney World. I was soaked, and cold and tears ran down my already wet face as I stood with the women looking out to sea at the many boats racing ahead and behind us. I had never felt so alone.

A few months later, Barbara, a competitive skipper, asked me to join the crew in Barbados for a sailing regatta. The girls would be the only all-female crew.

Barbara's husband, Eugene, had his own boat and we competed against him and all the other boats captained by men. I became a more competent sailor and was elevated to pulling in the sheets after we tacked. I hauled in the sheet, placed it over the winch, and tightened it down.

When I arrived in Barbados, Barbara advised that she had teamed up all single people in cabanas, as we had to share rooms. After an orientation meeting at the yacht club for all participants, the sailors had a fabulous dinner of local Barbadian food, then returned to our rooms for rest, as we had an early start the next day.

I grabbed my bag, walked to my cabana and discovered that I had been teamed up with Isabel.

She was sitting up in bed when I walked into the cabana. The air conditioning blasted frigid air and I changed into my nightgown. Isabel looked up at me as I began to remove my makeup.

"Do you always bring all that makeup stuff with you?" she asked.

"Yes, absolutely. I put makeup on every day and take it off at night."

"I don't wear makeup."

"Really? I never would have guessed. You might think of trying it."

"Just to let you know, I get very hot at night so I took the bed nearest the air conditioning and turned it on to the highest level. Is that okay?"

"Actually, I am always cold, so I don't like AC blowing on me. You are more than welcome to your bed. However, I would prefer if you would turn it down a bit as I am freezing."

"Can't do that or I won't sleep. I get so hot, that sometimes during the night, I even throw my nightgown off, so don't be surprised if you find me totally naked in the morning."

"Well, that will be a joyful wakeup for me. Okay, I will sleep with my dressing gown on."

"And she has a dressing gown, too. You really do put a lot of effort into your looks. Do you know that during a regatta, I don't even wash my hair or comb it?"

"Why am I not surprised? It looks it."

As I settled into bed and opened my book, I felt Isabel staring at me and I tried to ignore her.

"Do you read a lot of books?" she asked.

"Every night. It is the only way I can go to sleep."

"I don't read—I can't concentrate," Isabel said.

"You should try it. It will expand your mind."

I could feel her eyes on me. She wanted to talk; I wanted to read. "Well, I am going to turn off the light so I can go to sleep now," I said when I was finished reading.

"I don't fall asleep until 1:00 or 2:00 in the morning. I have to watch TV 'til then."

"I can't sleep with the TV on. We have an early rise, as we need to get the boat ready. I have to buy the food and drinks, so I need to get some sleep."

"Well, if I can't watch TV, then I will just have to sit here and read a book. What are you reading? Maybe I can read that until I can fall asleep."

"Eureka, here you go! I'll cover my head with the duvet to sleep. I am freezing cold anyway, so it will keep me warm."

"Goodnight, Nadean."

And that was how our friendship started. Who could have foreseen with this amusing, unpromising start that Isabel, who was totally opposite to me in every way, would become one of my dearest friends? Isabel was a fun, nutty character who loved to drink. No one could understand the attraction one had for the other. She came into my life when I desperately needed a friend who would provide fun, joy, entertainment and make me laugh.

I was stable, predictable and cautious; she was over-the-top crazy!

Isabel was the yang, the bright, positive light, to my yin.

The sailing team welcomed me, were kind, and in time, became an amazingly supportive group. Over the next four years, I took sailing classes at the Yachting Association, became a competent sailor, raced on weekends, and competed in regattas throughout the Caribbean. We won numerous races.

Laura, Isabel and I went out often with Allen, Dougie and Bruce to the Yachting Association, nightclubs, parties, Carnival fetes, and organized dinners at our homes and spent weekends down the islands. Allen and Laura had dated previously, but were now friends. Dougie and Bruce were accountants whom I met through the Institute of Chartered Accountants.

Bruce and I dated for a few months. He was a lovely man, but I ended the relationship. I did not find anyone whom I could love as I had loved Juan. In addition, I had a child to consider.

I would not become seriously involved with any man who could not be a good, kind, positive stepfather to Andrew. Bruce would have been a wonderful stepfather, but my feelings for him were not deep enough.

Andrew started St. Andrew's school in September 1986. Juan and I continued our visitation and sharing arrangement. Juan continued to belittle my parenting skills and my character in front of Andrew and anyone who would listen. He tried to align himself with Andrew's teachers against me, but they maintained a neutral position. I chose not to speak negatively about Juan in front of Andrew. I felt that it was extremely harmful to him and expressed my concerns to Juan. He replied that he didn't give a damn about me.

Andrew acted out and said he didn't want to go to school. I insisted he go and took him when he was with me. On Monday mornings, after a weekend with his father, if Andrew said he didn't want to go to school, Juan let him stay home. Juan felt Andrew should not have to do anything he didn't want to do, which perpetuated the arguing and conflict between us.

"Name your price, Nadean," Juan said. "I want Andrew to live with me. I will give you anything for Andrew. If you don't, I will ruin you financially."

"I can't be bought at any price, Juan."

Chapter 15

Jeremy and Donna

In February of 1987, Barbara called and asked me for a favor. "Nadean, my friends Jeremy and Donna Kavanagh have a single friend visiting from the United States. They are having a party for him and have asked me to find a single woman to round out the table at dinner. I told them about you and they asked me to invite you to dinner. Would you be interested?"

As I had a nonexistent dating life, I told Barbara I would go to the party and asked for the details.

It occurred to me that once I met this couple and their friends, I could return the invitation, thereby enlarging my circle of friends. It was customary to have friends over to help entertain one's house guests. The host and hostess would organize a party soon after the guest's arrival.

Then throughout the house guest's visit, their friends would, in turn, organize parties for the house guest. In addition, a hostess would ensure that there was an even number of people at the table. One man for one woman. As their guest was single, Jeremy and Donna were anxious to find a single woman to help entertain him.

"Nadean, why don't you sit here next to Bill," Donna said when I arrived at their party.

Bill turned away from the young blonde woman he was speaking to, looked at me, and smiled as Donna introduced us. As the evening progressed, however, Bill virtually ignored me, despite numerous efforts to engage him in a conversation. He spoke often to the lovely young woman who sat on his other side.

I would discover later that her name was Sarah and she was Donna and

Jeremy's son Brian's girlfriend from Canada. Brian and Sarah would marry three years later. Bill was being polite to their potential daughter-in-law, but that evening, I wasn't aware of this.

I was totally perplexed by Bill's behavior as I am never ignored, especially by men. The extent of his interest in me that evening was his offer of some roast chicken when we were in line together at the buffet table. I concluded that I wasn't attractive to Bill. He hadn't even given me a chance to be interesting or boring.

I did not know any of the other guests except for Janice and Stephen. Janice sailed with me on the all-girls crew, so I spent time with them. At the end of the evening, Donna asked Jeremy to follow me home so that I would arrive safely. Jeremy asked Bill to join him for the trip.

"Bill, why don't you go with Nadean and I will follow in my car," Jeremy said when we arrived at our cars.

Bill did not look pleased, but acquiesced.

I couldn't wait for the twenty-minute trip to be over.

When I am nervous, I talk nonstop. I told him how I came to live in the country, pointed out the significance and history of each historical building we passed, the vegetable market where I shopped, Kavok restaurant, which served Polynesian cuisine, Hi-Lo grocery, and the road that led up to Andrew's school.

Bill said nothing and I was more than a little relieved when we pulled into my parking lot.

"Donna, Janice and Stephen are taking me to the beach tomorrow," Bill said when we got out of my car. "If you are free maybe you would like to come with us?"

"Thanks, I am sorry, but I have plans."

"Well, I will be here for the next week, so if you are passing by Jeremy and Donna's place, drop in."

Oh, please, I thought.

"Thank you, but that will be unlikely." I turned to my host. "Thank you for a lovely evening, Jeremy. Good-bye."

I discovered later that when I arrived at Jeremy and Donna's house, Bill thought my husband must be parking the car and would be joining us. When my husband did not materialize, he realized that Donna had invited me as a guest for him. He became annoyed at not being informed, so ignored me.

However, during the following week, whenever he attended a dinner party at one of Donna and Jeremy's friends, there would be an attractive single female present to round out the table. Only then did he discover that this was a custom, and he began to enjoy their company.

I would later find out about a conversation that Donna had with Bill over breakfast one morning during his visit: "Bill, you've been here a week. You have met some lovely women at the dinners. It's Friday. Why don't you think of asking one of these women out for dinner?"

"Donna, I did not come here to hook up with any woman."

"No one said you had to take one home with you. Didn't any of these women appeal to you?"

"I really didn't give the one I met on the first night a chance. She sure talked a lot. But maybe I could give her a call."

"Nadean," Donna said. "She is lovely. Do it. Call her now."

Bill called my house and was told by Helen, our housekeeper, that I had left to take Andrew to school.

Bill and Jeremy were both in the pool design and construction business, so whenever Bill visited the country, he joined Jeremy on his construction sites. They enjoyed their time together discussing design and construction challenges and solutions.

Later that afternoon at the home of one of Jeremy's customers, the wife emerged from the house to say there was a phone call for Mr. Kavanagh.

Jeremy took the call and returned to tell Bill the call was for him. It was Donna.

"Bill, I know you wanted to ask Nadean out for dinner and I knew Jeremy would keep you out on construction sites all day and you wouldn't have a chance to call Nadean. So, I called her and asked her to go out to dinner with you tonight!"

If Bill was upset before, he was furious now. However, he did not wish to offend his hostess.

"Donna, this is not the way I do things. I will call her when I get back to your house. What did she say?"

"She said to call her."

That evening Bill called and apologized for Donna.

"Actually," I said, "it was quite funny. I would be happy to go out for dinner. We didn't get off to a great start at Donna and Jeremy's, so perhaps we can start over."

I told Bill about a Carnival fete coming up that was hosted by Veni Chez Moi, a local restaurant.

"There will be over a thousand people attending. Tickets are really hard to come by. But after Donna called, I called Rebecca and Amanda, the owners of the restaurant, and they are holding two tickets for me. We can swing by there for the tickets and then go to dinner. Is that okay? It's a fabulous party. Drinks, great local food, and dancing to calypso music. You will be glad you went. It is a real Carnival experience."

When we arrived at Veni Chez Moi, it was swinging.

I moved around the restaurant and introduced Bill to friends. I told Rebecca that we had another event, so we needed to leave. She took us into the back room, opened a small wall vault, and took out the two tickets.

Bill couldn't believe the tickets were so preciously guarded.

I was a little tipsy from the drinks and very little food and as we walked down the steps, I slipped and toppled forward. I was able to prevent a full-frontal fall and landed on my hands and knees at the bottom of the stairs. My blue denim skirt had flown up into the air and landed in a perfect semicircle on the ground around me. I was embarrassed and laughing so hard, I couldn't get up.

"Are you okay?" Bill said as he ran down the stairs.

He placed his arms under mine and lifted me easily and gently from the ground.

"Well, this is an unforgettable start for a dinner date," I said.

Our reservation was at Il Giardino. Bill was interesting, intelligent, funny and charming. He told me about his life and business in Vermont. He had been a Boy Scout, attaining Life Scout level and the God and Country Award. He had considered pursuing a ministerial degree but changed to linguistics in college.

For a number of years, first as a teenager and then as a young adult, he worked at and then ran a Christian camp for emotionally disturbed children. He had known Jeremy and Donna since 1977 and had visited the country a few times with his spouse. Bill had been married and divorced twice. Neither of his wives had wanted children. That was the reason for the breakup of his first marriage. His second wife had an affair with her boss, which ended that marriage.

"I would give everything up in my life, my business, my home in Vermont for love."

"That is interesting, but you can't live on love if you have lost everything," I said.

"Are you unhappy with the meal?" the waiter asked as he approached our table. "We can prepare something else for you."

"No, why do you ask?" Bill said.

"You haven't eaten anything on your plate."

We looked down and realized that we had been so engrossed in our conversation, we had taken only a few bites before we stopped. The food was ice-cold.

After dinner we went to a nightclub to listen to local musicians. At the end of our date, we said good night with a quick kiss.

The Veni Chez Moi Carnival fete was great fun. Laura and Isabel were eager to meet this new man in my life and found him to be charming and attractive.

Bill left two days later with no commitments from either of us.

We both suspected that this new friendship had the potential to develop into a relationship, but where could it go?

Bill had a business and lived in Vermont; I lived 2,234 miles away. It was 1987—there were no cell phones or email. Long-distance calls were expensive, and snail mail took ten or more days to arrive.

Chapter 16

Veni Chez Moi

A day after Bill left the country, I ran into Sarah and Brian at Eastmall. "Nadean," Brian said, "have you heard from Bill?"

"Not yet," I said.

That report was quickly relayed to Donna, who called Bill that evening to tell him of the conversation. Bill took my *Not yet* comment as an indication that I had an expectation he would stay in touch. He called and wrote letters. I wrote back.

Bill decided to return in April, before the start of his busy season in the pool construction business. In early May his company would begin opening swimming pools for the summer, meeting with potential customers, and bidding on and designing new pools.

After two months of long-distance phone calls and letter writing, the pressure on both of us to form a relationship was enormous. We barely knew each other, and had no idea what kind of future we might face. Bill arrived with many gifts for me, and toys and clothes for Andrew. He was kind, thoughtful and eager.

I found our expectations after a long-distance affair to be overwhelming. I thought I was crazy to attempt a relationship with Bill as I didn't really know him and was convinced it couldn't go anywhere. I pulled back. Bill was hurt and disappointed.

"Look, this isn't going anywhere. I will continue to stay at Donna's for the rest of the week; then I'm going home. Let's just forget about this. It's not going to work," Bill said.

"I agree, Bill. I am so sorry. Before you go though, let me take you to lunch at Veni Chez Moi. I promised you a meal there. Amanda is a Cordon Bleu chef and the food is superb. Please, it is the least I can do."

"Okay, that would be nice," Bill said.

We did not see each other until the day of the planned lunch. "Madam, Mr. Stone is here to take you to lunch," Helen announced over the intercom.

"Helen, I am still getting ready. Andrew is playing in his bedroom. Please take Mr. Stone upstairs to Andrew's room and they can talk while I finish getting ready."

When I finally left my bedroom and arrived at the landing near Andrew's, I stood quietly and watched the scene unfolding before me.

Bill knelt on the floor and talked to Andrew, who looked up at him with great interest. They were putting Lego pieces together and Bill told him about the model railroads he and his father used to build when he was a boy in Vermont.

This handsome man was totally focused on my son and he, on Bill. In that moment I realized this was a truly good man, one who could have a positive influence on Andrew and who would be kind and caring toward him.

We walked downstairs, and Bill and I dropped Andrew off at his father's condo on our way to lunch.

Amanda and Rebecca could not have been more attentive, describing their many offerings and telling us how each dish was prepared and cooked. We selected the baked king-fish with an appropriate wine. The meal was superb. I was relaxed and enjoying the company of this lovely, engaging man.

Our relationship started that day.

Bill was anxious for me to visit Vermont. He had just built and moved into his new home on ten acres of land on the island of South Hero on Lake Champlain.

I flew into Montreal on a Friday and waited for him to arrive. He had bought and picked up a red Audi Quattro convertible that afternoon and driven up from Burlington. Our first weekend together was at the Four

Seasons in Montreal with sightseeing during the day.

We drove back to Burlington on Sunday, Mother's Day, and met his mother, Arlene, for dinner at Sirloin Saloon.

I met his sisters, Debbie and Cindy, the following day, and his friends Sparky, Dave and Laurie as well. Sparky had a heating and air conditioning company and had helped Bill with the construction of his house. Dave worked with IBM as a software engineer. Laurie was a teacher.

Bill and Dave were racquetball partners and competed in tournaments at the Racquet's Edge Fitness Club. I took aerobic classes with Laurie while the guys played.

Bill and I hiked Mount Mansfield, visited Ben and Jerry's, the Von Trapp Lodge and other local attractions, attended the Apple Island Circus performance with Dave and Laurie, and had fabulous dinners together and with his friends. It was a lovely week that allowed us to become more accustomed to one another and to grow in our relationship. Bill did everything to make my week with him comfortable, fun and memorable.

Our last dinner was at Wally's Fish House. I got food poisoning, was violently ill all night and missed my flight to New York the following morning. I spent most of the day in bed recovering and left the next day. I was going to stay with Juan's sister, Carlotta, for a few days in Manhattan before returning home. Although my marriage to Juan had ended, his family continued to care for me, invite me to dinners not attended by Juan and Chantal, and to involve themselves in my life with Andrew.

When Bill's busy season was over after the Thanksgiving weekend, he began to spend more time with me and eventually rented an apartment and ran his business remotely.

He tried to start a hotel project in St. Eustace. He had investors, and he and a US architect visited the beach site and drew up plans. He was confident that he could spend significant amounts of time in the country and still be on top of his business in Vermont. I was apprehensive.

The Canadian Women's Club was holding its annual fund-raising dinner, so I invited Alice and Guillermo to join Bill and me at a table. Bill was his usual considerate, charming self, and both of my former in-laws enjoyed his company immensely. The evening went well.

The following weekend, I had use of the family home on Manos so I invited Alice, Guillermo, Laura and Isabel to join Bill, Andrew and me for lunch on Sunday. Helen was with us, as well. Everyone was enjoying the sun and swimming until Andrew slipped on the mossy boat ramp and slid into the water.

Helen had been standing nearby watching him. She ran onto the ramp, slipped and fell backward, banging her head on the concrete. Bill rushed to her, gently picked her up, and as she leaned on him, walked her back to the house. We put her to bed and Bill took a facecloth with ice and held it to her head. Alice and Guillermo were impressed with his caring and attentiveness.

Andrew was unhurt and Helen recovered enough for all of us to get into the boat later that afternoon and head back to the mainland. Helen rested that night and the following day and was back to her usual pleasant self by Tuesday. She was a kind and caring woman who would have done anything for Andrew. She read her Bible to him in the afternoons and helped him with his homework.

I worked, and although Helen was my housekeeper, I joked that she was my wife. I earned the income and she ran the household. We were a great team, and Andrew flourished under her love and guidance.

Helen had her own bedroom and bathroom in our home. The bedroom had two bunk beds and on many occasions, her best friend Kathleen stayed over and visited with her. They had birthdays one day apart so we celebrated them together. I would make the cake and Andrew and his friends would sing happy birthday to the ladies. Whenever I entertained, Kathleen would help serve the appetizers and dinner, clean up afterward, and stay the night with

Helen. Both ladies were very fond of Bill, who brought treats from the States.

Diwali is the Hindu festival of lights celebrated every year in autumn. It dates back to ancient times in India, as a festival after the summer harvest. It is an official holiday in the country.

It spiritually signifies the victory of light over darkness, good over evil, knowledge over ignorance, and hope over despair. Its celebration includes millions of lights shining on housetops, outside doors and windows, and around temples and other buildings in the communities and countries where it is observed.

Hindu families light up diyas (lamps and candles) inside and outside their home. Bill, Andrew, Helen, Kathleen and I climbed into my car and drove around the residential areas looking at the lights. Andrew sat in back between Helen and Kathleen. Afterward, we would go for ice cream. We all enjoyed this time together, and Andrew especially loved the evening. As we drove home, I thanked God for my little family.

Several weeks later, Juan once again visited our home unannounced. I protested that he could not just drop in whenever he wanted, as it was enormously disrupting. Andrew and his friend, Albert, were playing with Legos in the living room. We started to argue.

"Please leave, Juan. This is upsetting to all of us. The boys don't need to hear this."

Juan grabbed me by the neck, pushed me across the room, pinned me against the wall and choked me. I pulled at his arms, but he was too strong for me. My eyes were bulging and I looked at the boys, who were too startled to move.

"You are an incompetent mother and a failure as a woman!" Juan screamed. "You are so stupid! I'm going to ruin you financially. I'm going to bury you."

Juan released me and marched out of the townhouse.

I tried to hide my fear from the boys and asked Helen to take them for a swim in our pool. I called Samantha and Allyson and scheduled appointments the following day.

"You are divorced now," Samantha said, "and there are agreements in place for visitation. He has no right to come to your home without permission."

Samantha prepared letters to Roberto, who was acting as Juan's attorney, protesting his behavior and urging restraint.

"I want you and Juan to join a family group counseling session once a week at night," Allyson said. "I think it might help Juan learn appropriate behavior. Also, I think you should start writing letters to each other as you are unable to communicate in a nonconfrontational manner."

Juan and I joined the group. He tried to be in control and on his best behavior, but could not resist criticizing my parenting skills in front of the members. After a few weeks of this pattern of behavior, Allyson described our relationship to all present as unequal and unbalanced.

Instead of an adult-to-adult relationship, ours had devolved into a parent-child relationship, with Juan being the parent.

"Nadean, you are totally intimidated by Juan," Allyson said. "He sees you as weak. You do not stand up for your beliefs, or fight for yourself or what you want, which reinforces his perception of you as weak and solidifies the parent-child scenario. He totally dominates you."

"Yes," I said, "I know that I need to stand up for myself and I will try." Inwardly I believed that it wouldn't matter what I said—Juan would disagree with everything I said because he had no respect for me. I was too worn out to even try.

Chapter 17

Australia

In 1988, I was offered a position with Barbados Mutual Company as the manager of their investment portfolio. I would work part-time, but the increase in compensation would be significant.

"I am going to fly to the Cayman Islands to investigate emigration and employment opportunities there," Juan said when he visited me at my new office.

"Why?"

"The economy here is terrible and I might do better there."

"But what about your family here?"

"I have to do what is best for my family. For Chantal, you and Andrew."

"Juan, we are no longer a family. You have started your new family with Chantal. That was what you wanted."

"Yes, but Andrew and you will always be part of my family."

A week later he called me to let me know that the Caymans were out and he was now thinking about Australia.

"Australia?" I said incredulously. "Why there?"

"It is a big country and Sydney is a fabulous city. There are lots of large accounting firms, and with my experience I should be able to join one as a partner."

"What does Chantal think about this? What about her children? How can she leave them behind?"

"Chantal says she will go with me anywhere that I choose."

I was not totally surprised at this turn of events, as I experienced Juan's frustration with his career prior to his starting his accounting firm. Whenever

Juan was not making enough money, he would become frustrated and unhappy and start thinking about a change in career.

In May 1988, Juan applied for emigration to Australia.

Australia had a points system in which applicants were required to complete forms detailing their education and work experience.

The applicants would be assessed and graded according to the skill set they had to offer and the needs of the country. A minimum point limit for emigration to Australia was seventy-five points.

Juan asked for private counseling sessions with Allyson in which he described his frustration with living and working in the country and his desire to emigrate to Australia. He told Allyson that he wanted Andrew and me to emigrate with him and Chantal.

"I have absolutely no desire to live in Australia," I said. "If I move there, I will not know anyone other than Juan and Chantal. I would be giving up all of my friends. I will have to start my life all over again. I am in a great relationship with Bill and I would be giving that up, as well. It is a crazy idea! Juan is pressing me to complete the application forms. He comes to my office and calls me regularly."

Allyson smiled. She had learned how manipulative Juan could be from the parenting group sessions and her private meetings with him.

"What do you want to do, Nadean?" Allyson said.

"I want to do what is best for Andrew. That is the most important thing to me."

"Well, if Andrew's welfare is paramount for you, what do you think you should do?"

"Are you telling me that I should apply for emigration to Australia?"

"I cannot tell you what to do, Nadean. I can only express to you my opinion as a child psychologist, that whatever happens to you and Juan, what is best for Andrew is that you are both together in the same country. That truly is what is best for him."

"Then, I really have no choice, do I? I have to sacrifice my happiness and all that I have achieved here. This is not a happy solution for me, Allyson. I am really disheartened."

"Nadean, life is not easy. Sometimes we have to make hard choices for the happiness of others."

We discussed the pros and cons and I continued to argue.

"Okay, I will do it," I finally said as I began to cry, "but I am doing so with great reluctance."

When Juan called again, I told him my decision.

"Allyson believes it is in Andrew's best interests if we are in the same country, so I will complete the forms for Australia."

"I knew you would come around! You will see, Nadean. We will all be happy in Australia. I am talking to a few firms and things are looking really positive. You love sailing. You can join a crew there."

Laura expressed her opinion on this latest development in her usual straightforward manner. "Are you crazy? Look at what Juan has put you through since you separated and divorced. What will happen once he gets you in Australia and you don't have us to support you emotionally? I think this is a very bad decision. You mustn't go," Laura said.

Bill listened to the discussions quietly, but was not surprised. He knew the depth of my love for Andrew and that he always came first. Ours was an unbreakable bond.

As luck would have it, the last race of the sailing season was the President's Cup in May. The girls' sailing crew won handily. The winds were good and Barbara's tactics were spot-on.

As we sailed into the Yachting Association at the end of the race, all of the competing men were standing on their boats shouting, whooping and clapping us into the slip.

The president of St. Gustave, Sir Eliot Clarkson, presented us with the cup. I had looked forward to the sailing crew's Sundays together for the past four years. Sailing and the women's crew had become my salvation, and if Australia accepted me, I would be leaving them.

Bill was in Vermont when we won the race. He ordered huge bouquets of flowers, which I delivered to the crew. It was both a happy and a sad time for me.

Juan and I had been exchanging letters at Allyson's urging for months. His letters to me, which had been critical and patronizing, now ceased. He just called and visited my office whenever he wished to talk about Australia and our life there together.

Andrew and I flew up to Vermont for two weeks in July. Bill had allowed a local farmer, Tim, who lived on land next to his, to plant corn in his fields.

The stalks were high and Andrew would run in the field in his red rubber boots with Bill's dog, Mildred, a basset hound, chasing him. We could not see his head, just the stalks moving as they ran. Andrew loved the freedom, enjoyed Ben and Jerry's, climbing Mount Mansfield with us, and Dave and his son, Daniel. We had a lovely week together.

Juan called while we were in Vermont to tell me that things were progressing nicely with his Australia plans. It was the last thing I wanted to hear.

"Nadean, I am seeing such a positive development in Andrew during the two weeks he has been away in the US," Alice said upon our return. "He has matured so much in such a short space of time, seems much more settled, calm and to be in control and at peace with himself."

I met my sister-in-law, Charlotte, coming out of Allyson's offices. Charlotte had just dropped Carrie off for an appointment with Wanda Perez. Carrie, a very bright child was dyslexic and the lessons with Wanda helped with her reading. I was about to enter for my appointment with Allyson.

"Nadean, I just found out that Roberto has a mistress," Charlotte said. "He keeps an apartment here in St. Gustave and his mistress is living in it. Do you know anything about this?"

"No, Charlotte, this is the first I am hearing about it."

"Are you absolutely sure, Nadean? I need to know."

"Yes, absolutely. I had no idea about any apartment."

"Did you know he had a mistress?"

"Charlotte, I really don't want to go there. Things could happen that you might come to regret."

"What do you mean? Did you know he had a mistress? Nadean, I need to know."

"Charlotte, I do not know for sure. I heard rumors and that is all. Truly. I have no proof. Just gossip, and you know what talk here is like."

"Well, I know the address of the apartment and I want to go there to see for myself. Once I know for sure, then I will decide what to do. Can you help me?"

"How?"

"I don't have a key to get in. I checked Roberto's desk at home and can't find one. What can I do?"

"Do you really want to get inside that apartment?"

"Yes."

"No matter what you find?"

"No matter what I find."

"Then call a locksmith. Tell him that you are Mrs. Rivero, the wife of Senator Roberto Rivero. You have misplaced the key to your apartment. Your husband is in court and you can't disturb him. You need to get into the apartment. Ask him to come and open the door for you."

"Do you think that will work? Will he believe me?"

"Yes, of course. You are a member of a highly recognized and respected political family. Your husband is a senator in the government. He will not question you. Just be careful. Go in, look and leave. Don't get caught there. Promise?"

"Yes."

"Good luck then. Let me know what happens."

Charlotte took her friend Jennie with her. Upon entering the apartment, they found it to be nicely decorated. The fridge was well-stocked with champagne, caviar, lovely imported cheeses, shrimp and steaks.

The walk-in closet had beautiful designer clothes from the United States and the drawers in the cupboard held gorgeous Victoria's Secret lingerie, perfume bottles and jewelry.

And Charlotte went crazy. She and Jennie opened and emptied the champagne bottles into the sink. They tore open all the packaged cheeses, shrimp and steaks. They threw the food into the kitchen sink and poured the perfume onto them. They grabbed scissors and cut up all of the designer clothing and the lingerie. They placed the remnants in the laundry sink and threw bleach on the once-beautiful garments. They were spent and exhausted, but Charlotte had the proof she needed.

In the days that followed, the rumor mill was at its highest: Roberto had a girlfriend! Someone broke into her apartment that was paid for by Roberto and laid waste to it. Everything had been destroyed. The girlfriend had returned to the US, as she was terrified. The police had not been called in.

Everyone was asking who could have behaved in such an irrational manner.

A week later, Roberto and Charlotte hosted a birthday party for Guillermo at their home. It was a fabulous affair, and Charlotte played the role of dutiful daughter-in-law and gracious senator's wife to the hilt. The next day she asked Roberto to leave their home. Alice and Guillermo appeared to be in shock. I gave Charlotte tremendous kudos for knowing about Roberto's affair and still standing at that party, greeting all the political guests and playing the part of the happy wife, in full knowledge that she was going to ask him to leave the next day. What a performance.

The calls started the day after Guillermo's party.

"Did you know about this, Nadean?" Alice asked. "Did you tell Charlotte about Roberto's girlfriend?"

"No, Alice, I did not. Charlotte suspected and when she asked me if it was true, I hesitated but could not lie. I told her I had heard rumors but did not have any proof."

"How will you feel, Nadean, if they separate and divorce as a result of this? It will be your fault."

"No it won't, Alice. Roberto has been cheating on her for years and you all knew about it. Charlotte suspected but she could never prove it. I told her of the rumors and she found the proof. Whatever happens is what was meant to be. I just hope she is smarter than I was."

"What do you mean by that?"

"Nothing, Alice, just me rambling on."

A few months after taking up residency in St. Gustave and managing his company remotely, Bill discovered that the manager and assistant he trusted to run his business were stealing money from his company. They had not paid his company's federal matching income taxes during his long absences and he was now responsible to repay those, while also trying to recover his losses and save his company.

In addition, he had partnered with his friend Sam on a commercial building project. He and Sam had taken a loan with a local bank to fund the project. They had agreed to buy key man insurance on themselves to cover their commitment to the bank in the event that one of them died. Sam did die, and Bill discovered that Sam had not purchased his key man insurance. As the project was no longer going forward, Bill was now responsible for repaying the bank for their large loan.

He tried desperately for months to save his company but could not meet all of the financial obligations. He declared business bankruptcy, closed his company, sold his house to pay his debts, and started looking for a job. He had lost the company he started on a shoestring seventeen years earlier.

It was one of the lowest points in his life.

"I am going to be okay, Nadean. We're going to make it. I will find a job and start over. It won't be easy but I am only forty-one and have many years ahead to recoup. But I need to know that you are with me." I had no idea how we could make this work going forward and felt responsible. If he had not been chasing me, he would have known what was happening with his company and not lost everything. I thought back to our first dinner together at Il Giardino, when he said he would give up everything for love. Well, it had come to pass.

What a sad time for both of us. I could not see how it would work out, but I couldn't abandon this good man who loved me and was kind and caring toward everyone, especially Andrew.

"Of course, I will stay with you," I said. "I will support you. We will make it work."

Chapter 18

Orlando

The Cub Scouts at Andrew's school needed an Akela to assume a leadership role for the upcoming school year. I was asked by the school principal to take on this responsibility and agreed. The Cubmaster was a lovely older gentleman named Mr. Montgomery, whose patient and gentle manner endeared him to the boys. It was great fun being with all these eager little ones.

Andrew was so proud of his mother. We had pack meetings at the school and I organized the first overnight camping trip that the troop had ever taken. A few fathers volunteered to accompany us and we camped at a former cocoa plantation in the hills.

We unpacked and then the boys, fathers and I built a campfire to cook our dinner. After dinner we sat around the campfire and sang songs.

The boys slept in sleeping bags on the second floor of the cocoa house, where cocoa leaves had once been placed to dry before being cut up and packaged.

Their fathers and I sat up playing cards till midnight. I was so happy for this amazing experience with my young charges and these generous men. The next day we cooked breakfast, hiked and explored the surrounding hills and swam on the beach nearby.

Bill visited us when he could and always attended the pack meetings. Having achieved a high level in scouting, Bill was competent in many of the skills that the boys needed to obtain their badges such as photography, mastering chess, and building model planes and was eager to share and help with the boys' development.

In November, Juan was informed that he had been accepted into Australia.

He couldn't wait to visit my office and share his good news.

"My application has been approved!" he said. "I got the seventy-five points, and a large accounting firm offered me a partnership upon arrival in Sydney. They will hold the offer for three months. Now all we need is for your application to be approved."

I tried to hide my devastation.

"How will Chantal get accepted? She won't make the seventy-five points."

Juan planned for every contingency. "We are going to get married. Once we are married, she will be allowed in."

A few days later we received the news that I had not met the minimum requirements and scored only seventy of the seventy-five points needed.

Unbeknownst to me, Bill had also applied to Australia and was approved. If I made the grade, Bill was going to follow me.

Juan was bitterly disappointed and asked me to travel to Australia in December.

"I'll pay for your trip. If you can find a job, then the government will regularize your status and let you live there with me, Chantal and Andrew."

Because Allyson advised that this was the best outcome for Andrew, I reluctantly agreed, even though I would miss Andrew's birthday on December 10, his school concert, and our Cub Scout holiday party, which I had organized and was hosting.

The day before my planned departure for Australia, Juan called. "The High Commission called me and said that even if you are able to find a job in Australia, your status will never be regularized as you don't have enough points!"

My relief with the outcome was short-lived, as Juan would not give up.

"I know what the Commission said, but this is a great opportunity for all of us. Come with me to Australia on a tourist visa. I will support you financially until your status is regularized," he said.

"Juan, that idea is preposterous. I have done everything that you asked and there is no way that I am going to get into that country legally. I cannot do anything more. I know you are disappointed, but I am done with Australia."

Juan was so angry he did not speak to me without resorting to vile, abusive language. We then had to return to letter writing as our only form of communication, and his critical, patronizing letters and behavior resumed with increased intensity.

He refused to change visitation weekends so Andrew could spend my December 18 birthday weekend with me, so I spent it with only Bill, Laura and Isabel.

One week later, I invited Bill and all family members, including Juan, Chantal and her son, Silvain, to our house for breakfast on Christmas Day. I wanted to take the high road and ensure that we were all civilized, for the sake of the children.

Laura, her children and Isabel joined us and Andrew was thrilled that we came together as a large family in his home.

"Nadean, I could not believe it," Isabel said. "I watched you take your lovely Wedgwood platter and hold it next to Chantal so she could serve herself and I thought you have gone mad! I would have broken that platter on her head."

"I did it for the children, Isabel. We need to put Australia behind us and move forward."

After breakfast, Bill walked Alice back to her house, a couple of hundred yards away.

"Bill," Alice said as he was about to leave, "you would be a good influence on Andrew, a good stepfather. I can see that you would be good for Andrew."

Bill told me that he wanted to visit Juan at his office to talk about Andrew and me. Now that Australia was off the table, he felt that we needed to be respectful and civil to one another. I forewarned him that it would be a futile exercise, but he was insistent. Bill always thought the best of people, so he could not imagine that they would not respond in kind.

During their meeting, Bill told Juan that he was not trying to take his place with Andrew.

"You're right," Juan said with a smirk. "That won't ever happen."

Bill's bankruptcy was discharged at the end of December. He procured a position with a swimming industry manufacturer and was scheduled to start his employment as sales manager in Orlando, Florida, on January 2, 1989.

As Bill was now an employee, he no longer had as much flexibility for vacation and personal time to spend with us.

On January 7, 1989, Isabel and I drove to Juan's condo to pick Andrew up for my scheduled weekend with him. When Juan opened the door, I saw the anger on his face and he refused to bring Andrew to the door. "Juan, this is my weekend," I said. "You need to bring him to me now."

"Andrew doesn't want to go with you."

"That is a lie. You manipulate him and his feelings. I insist that you bring him now, Juan!"

"I hate the very sight and smell of you," he said. "You are a drain on me emotionally and financially. You are a bloody fool, a fool. I can't stand you and wish you would get out of my life for good!"

After more verbal volleys back and forth, he finally backed down and brought Andrew, who was then completely distraught, to the door. Isabel, who had only heard my recounting of Juan's behavior, was in shock after witnessing it for the first time.

As Chantal could only get into Australia legally through marriage and Juan refused to give up on that goal, their wedding ceremony was scheduled for January 21, 1989, on the patio at Alice's house.

Although it was to be my weekend with Andrew, Juan called to ask if Andrew could spend the time with his family to share in the joy of this festive occasion and if he could be picked up on Thursday to be involved in the excitement of the preparations.

"Of course," I said.

"I can no longer provide any financial support for Andrew or you as I am getting married. You will have to figure out how to make ends meet," Juan said when he came to get Andrew.

As Alice's patio was a hundred yards from my bedroom window and I had no desire to be anywhere near that fateful event, Isabel organized a lovely dinner at her house for Charlotte, Laura and me—the former Rivero wives.

Andrew had a school break in February, so Juan, Chantal, Silvain and Andrew spent the week in Pompano Beach, Florida, at Alice and Guillermo's apartment in Palm-Aire. I flew to Orlando to be with Bill. The house he rented was modern and large with a lovely landscaped garden and pool, beautifully furnished and in a great school district called Wekiva.

As Australia had fallen through, Juan suggested that we all look at immigrating to the US. In the span of one month, he returned to the civil version of Juan.

At Juan's request, I made an appointment with an immigration attorney in Orlando to discuss immigration requirements for Juan, Chantal and me. I also called the CPA Institute to inquire about the requirements for him to practice in the United States.

On Monday, Bill and I visited elementary schools in the Wekiva area. We met with a couple of principals, took tours of the schools, and I selected the one I thought would be best for Andrew and close to Bill's house.

"I am meeting with accountancy firms in the morning," Juan said when he called. "I have no problem with you marrying Bill. I believe Andrew should grow up in a two-parent family and I have to admit that Bill is a good influence on Andrew. If we all live in the United States, I can see Andrew on weekends."

I was astounded. Juan and I had never discussed any of this and I had not had any conversations with Bill in this regard.

"What did he say?" Bill asked when I hung up. "He just gave us permission to get married!"

We were no longer surprised by anything Juan said or did. Just two days later, Juan called again.

"I can't make enough money to live well in the US. We all have to return to St. Gustave. If you don't promise right now that you will return to the country and stay, I will tell Andrew tomorrow morning you are breaking up the family, that you are removing him from his father and his loss is entirely your fault."

I knew that Juan was ruthless enough to carry through with his threat. I realized in that moment that I was a prisoner and would only be free if I was willing to abandon my son.

"I will go back," I said.

With this capitulation on my part, Juan resumed his angry tirades and harsh treatment toward me.

I spent Easter weekend with Bill in Orlando.

At Joseph's, a lovely romantic restaurant, Bill asked me to marry him. "Bill, you know that I love you," I said. "But I can't accept. I will never be able to leave the country. I am a prisoner on that island unless I leave Andrew behind, which I will never do."

Our lovely romantic evening ended with great sadness and heavy hearts.

As I now needed to support Andrew and myself financially, I accepted full-time employment with Barbados Mutual. The position came with a new car, which was much appreciated. According to our divorce agreement, Juan was required to replace my car every five years, and he never did.

When he found out I was receiving a company car, Juan snuck into Grandview, used his extra car key for my old car, drove it from the premises, sold it, and kept the proceeds. Juan continued to visit me at my office and sometimes stayed a half hour or longer, to discuss emigration anywhere he thought he could make a living.

"Australia will hold the job I was offered for another year," he said.

"Juan, how can you possibly leave your family behind here?" I said, and sighed.

His answer, cold and heartless, was one I could not have anticipated. I tried to conceal my shock and in that moment, it all became clear to me. I knew he could read my face. He tried to cover his statement with his usual smile and charm, but it was too late: I finally saw his true character and I was done with him.

"It's time for me to leave, Juan. I need to get home," I said.

He insisted on walking me to my car, trying to rebound all the while. I remained quiet, no longer even remotely interested in hearing his plans, ever again.

Two movies came out to which Bill and I had completely different reactions: *The Good Mother*, about a woman who loses custody of her daughter, and *The War of the Roses*, in which a divorcing couple fight over their family home. The dark humor, cruelty and bizarre behavior in *The War of the Roses* made Bill laugh. I cried during both and he didn't understand my reaction.

"*The Good Mother* is what I'm afraid of. *The War of the Roses* is my life."

Chapter 19

A Hike in the Mountains

On a glorious sunny Sunday morning in June, Bill, Andrew, Silvain and I joined a group of twenty people from my gym for a hike in the mountains.

As we walked inland and arrived at the base, our leader, Peter, suggested we leave our cameras and backpacks behind, as the hike up would be challenging.

We would be climbing up a narrow dry gorge, holding on to rocks and trees for support. The boys were excited and Bill and I were enjoying the prospect of a beautiful sunny day together. A young couple agreed to stay behind to guard the cameras and packs.

As we started our climb up the gorge, the incline became progressively steeper. A light rain started to fall. As it was warm rain, we found it refreshing and continued upward.

However, after a half-hour, the rain became much heavier. The climbers looked at one another and we talked about continuing or turning back to base.

"It isn't bad. I'm going to continue on up," Peter said. The other climbers agreed to follow Peter.

"I am worried about this, Bill," I said. "The boys are not experienced climbers. This is the start of the rainy season and it could become much worse. I think we should turn back."

Bill agreed, and as we started back down the gorge, holding on to trees and carefully climbing over rocks, the rains became torrential. We stopped in the crevice of a rock formation to catch our breath and let the boys rest. It was gushing rain now and the wind had picked up.

We huddled together inside the rock formation and Bill and I peered out and looked up the gorge. As the torrential water blasted down, trees and branches tumbled down the incline.

I was very worried about how we were going to get the boys safely back down the mountain. I knew that if we stayed in the crevice, we could be swept down with the rain and debris as the water increased in volume and intensity. I tried to keep the fear out of my eyes and looked to Bill for guidance. The boys found it exciting. They had no idea of the danger we were in.

"Nadean, I think I can make it down the gorge if I take one of you at a time," Bill said. "The gorge is narrow. If each of you hold on to my shoulders and grab my waist with your legs, I can grab on to the trees and rocks on the sides and make it down to base camp. I will then climb back up for the next one."

"But, Bill," I said, "there are trees and logs falling down the gorge. What if one hits you or the boys on your way down?" The danger and uncertainty were overwhelming.

"We have to try. If we wait and the rain becomes more powerful, we will lose our footing here. I will not be able to get all three of you down at the same time. We need to make a decision now and go for it."

"Nadean, who do I take first?" Bill asked.

I looked at the boys, who were listening and watching me. I thought of Chantal, who had no idea that her son was in such danger. How could I lose her son and then have to tell her it was my fault?

"Take Silvain first," I said. "Andrew and I will wait for you to come back."

We looked at one another and knew this plan could fail miserably. Andrew and I might go tumbling down the gorge after Bill left with Silvain.

"Okay, Silvain," Bill said. "Climb on my back, put your arms around my neck, and grab your wrists with your hands. Put your legs around my waist and place one foot over the other. No matter what happens, don't let go. We might end up underwater, but I will get you back up. Just hold on and we will make it."

Silvain grabbed on to Bill, and Andrew and I watched as Bill held on to the trees to start his descent. A huge gush of water came pouring down the gorge. Bill lost his grip and, in an instant, disappeared underwater. Andrew and I held on to one another as we waited, hoping for their safety and Bill's return.

We continued to watch logs sliding down the gorge and I couldn't imagine how Bill and Silvain would survive the onslaught.

It seemed like an interminable time, but finally we saw Bill's head appear above the water. He scrambled back up the gorge, grabbing on to whatever handhold he could find on the walls.

"Silvain and I went underwater a few times," Bill said upon his return. "There is a huge flood down at the bottom. The young couple who stayed behind tied all of our stuff in trees. The stream we walked across this morning to get to the base is now six feet high and very wide. The water from the gorge is flowing at a high rate. There is no way out. The boys will never make it across.

"We will have to wait at the base for the rain to stop and the water to recede enough to get across to the cars. Silvain is with the young couple. Okay, Andrew, you're next."

Andrew held on to Bill's neck. He was younger and smaller than Silvain, so not as strong. Bill took one last look at me and started down with my child. They disappeared around a bend in the gorge.

I waited and prayed to God for their survival. It seemed like forever, but Bill returned for me. I could see that he was tired, but exhilarated.

"They are both safe, Nadean. Your turn."

Without delay, I held on to his neck and we started our descent. Within minutes, Bill lost his footing again and we disappeared underwater. We surfaced and continued down. He grabbed branches and rocks when he could.

Sometimes, he slipped and we slid down. Eventually, we arrived at the bottom in six feet of water. He swam to the side of the stream and we climbed out. The stream flowed fast as the rain continued to fall. The only people we saw were the young couple we left behind. We didn't know where Peter and the other hikers were.

Bill took out his penknife and cut banana branches. The six of us huddled together in the grass beside the stream with the branches over our heads. The rain pelted us. We were all drenched and cold. The mosquitoes started to attack us. We had no bug spray, no drinking water and no food.

When we left that morning we anticipated a one-hour drive to the mountain, an hour hike in and out, and a drive back in time for lunch. It was past noon and I knew Helen would be worried about us.

The hikers returned at different times. They looked shaken and scared.

"Nadean, I was so worried about you and the boys," said Elizabeth, one of the hikers, upon her return. "I am so glad you stopped when you did and turned around. You won't believe how bad it became for us. Peter should have known better than to continue up that gorge. As we got closer to the top of the mountain, the gush of water became more intense. Logs and trees were sliding by, next to us.

"We should never have been up there. My girlfriend and I thought we were going to die. We decided to turn around and try to climb back down. Some in the group were continuing up. Then the water became so strong we lost our footing and just came tumbling down the gorge. All of the hikers started falling. As we were turned around in the water, we saw people falling from the top of the gorge. We all got tangled and caught up together. We went underwater and came back up. People were screaming. I was praying that you and the boys had arrived safely."

"I am so glad to see you and the boys," said Jim, another hiker, when he returned to base. "Joan and I have two teenage daughters at home. No one even knows where we are on this hike. As we tumbled down the gorge and went underwater, Joan grabbed me by the neck. I had to make a split-minute decision. I pushed her away and screamed at her to swim hard. One of us had to survive or our children would be without parents. I did not know which one of us would make it, but one of us had to. I did not know if she made it until we reached the stream here and I saw her climb out of the water. It was dreadful, really dreadful! I thought it was over for us."

When all of the hikers were accounted for, the men decided to form a human chain across the stream and pass the women and children along to the other side.

The first attempt was disastrous. The water was flowing so fast that they could not hold their wrists together and remain upright. The chain kept breaking apart. I refused to allow the boys to try crossing. We were going to stay on the grass until Bill and I could take them across ourselves, even if we had to carry them.

The rain stopped and we waited hours for the water in the stream to recede. By the time we were able to cross, it was 5:00 p.m. and we had an hour until dark. Bill and I waded across first with the boys, and were the first to get to our car. We climbed in joyfully and started our drive home.

We had traveled less than a mile from the stream when we came to a huge mahogany tree that had fallen across the road. The tree and the mud that had slid down the hillside blocked our path. We were the lead car, so all cars stopped behind us. The men gathered together and tried to figure out a plan of escape.

The length and circumference of the tree was huge, and it could not be moved. Bill saw a lean-to off in the distance and walked over to see if someone could help us. An Indian workman said he used the hut for hunting on weekends. He had an old axe that he gave to Bill.

Bill started chopping the tree in half in the middle section. The axe was old and kept falling apart. Bill asked the hikers for cloth to tie the handle to the axe. None of the male hikers offered to help him. It took an hour or so, but he got through the log.

We all gathered on one side and pushed one-half of the log to the side of the road so our cars could pass. Bill kept the axe with us.

This happened two more times.

The third time we came across a tree in the road, the women hikers shouted, "For God's sake, will you men help him? Can't you see he is exhausted? He can't cut that tree by himself!"

A couple of men stepped forward and took turns relieving Bill. The third and last tree was a real challenge, as there was so much mud on the road. It was now close to 7:30 p.m. and all of the women hikers were frustrated and anxious to be free of this ordeal.

I walked up to Bill and started to move mud from the road with my hands. The other women followed suit and then the men chipped in. The third tree was finally cut in half.

However, there was so much mud on the road we were not sure if my car would get through it.

"Just floor it," I said. "I don't care about the car. I just want to get these boys home."

Bill reversed my car, slammed on the accelerator, and we hurtled toward the mud slide. The car got stuck. No one else could pass us, as we were the lead car. Everyone stood in front of my car and pushed us backward. The women and men removed more mud from the road with their hands. Bill and I started again and this time, my car made it through.

We finally arrived home at 9:00 p.m. Helen was beside herself with worry. She had not called anyone, because she did not know where we had gone to hike.

The boys bathed, and we fed them and put them to bed. They had no idea how dangerous our ordeal had been. Bill's running shoes had literally fallen apart from climbing the jagged rocks in the stream and his swim up and down three times. We were both exhausted.

"Bill," I said, "thank you for saving the boys and me. We would never have got off that mountain tonight without you. You were amazing."

He had risked his life to save the three of us in the gorge and then, with superhuman strength, saved the entire group.

He was willing to give his life for my son and the son of another woman. Bill, the American foreigner, had taken charge of survival and escape for the entire group.

We were in my bathroom, looking at one another in the large vanity mirror. He had just come out of the shower after removing tons of mud from his hair and clothes.

"If you ask me to marry you again, I will accept. I don't care what happens," I said, and smiled.

"Will you marry me?"

"Yes."

The next morning when we awoke, all of us, including Helen, went outside and examined my car and assessed the damage. There were a few scratches to the body, but what was so amazing was the amount of mud that covered the car, up to and including the windows. It was a huge mess. The boys thought it funny.

Bill and I realized how precarious our situation had been. We took pictures. Helen didn't believe our story until she saw the car! Andrew and I referred to Bill as "MacGyver" after that experience, as he could fix anything!

Chapter 20

Our Wedding

Bill and I told Andrew of our engagement and pending marriage. He was delighted.

"Juan, I think we should prepare a custody sharing agreement," I said when I told him our news. "Andrew will live with me and Bill in Orlando and visit during the holidays and summer."

He agreed, but delayed signing the agreement that Samantha had prepared.

Charlotte was organizing her trip to England with her three girls for the summer. I advised her to go and not return, or she and her girls would be in the same fix that I was in. They left at the end of June and never returned.

After Charlotte's departure, I met with Allyson for my weekly one-on-one appointment. I told her that Juan was refusing to sign the custody-sharing agreement.

"It is too bad that you did not just leave the country with Andrew and fight the battle in the US," Allyson said.

"I could never have done that, Allyson, as it would have destroyed Andrew. I have to do things the proper way, even if it means staying here after our wedding. Guillermo is the one who started that crazy kidnapping story, saying I would take Andrew out of the country and never return. He told that to Charlotte when he took her to the airport at Easter. He said that was my plan. Well, he was wrong. I would never kidnap Andrew."

"I know that," Allyson said. "I have observed you to be open, honest, direct and without guile. Andrew's schoolwork has improved under your care. You should feel proud. You are a good mother."

On July 4, Helen appeared in my bedroom and asked to speak to me. "Madam, do not trust Mr. Juan," she said.

"Helen, why do you say that?"

"Madam, this is a letter that Mr. Juan gave to me. He offered me $10,000 and a visa to the US if I will swear an affidavit that you mistreat Andrew."

Helen showed the letter to me. It was on Juan's company letterhead and the offer was as she described.

"Helen, may I keep this letter? I need to show it to my attorneys."

"Yes, of course, Madam," she said. "Madam, Mr. Juan is an evil, evil man. Please be careful."

"It will be okay, Helen, don't worry. We will work things out."

On July 7, I sent Andrew to his father's condo. Our wedding was set for Friday, August 4, and we were scheduled to depart for the US on Sunday, August 6.

Juan promised to return Andrew to me prior to our wedding so Andrew could share in our happiness, as I had done for his wedding in January.

On July 29, Juan asked if he and Chantal could visit Grandview to measure for curtains, as they planned to move back in after we left. I acquiesced and Helen greeted them at the door and escorted them around the ground floor of our unit.

Helen looked at me afterward and shook her head. "Unbelievable, Madam," was all she said.

Juan refused to return Andrew to me prior to our wedding. I was not surprised at his meanness and cruelty.

He said he would bring Andrew to the courthouse on the day of the wedding.

Bill's flight was delayed due to a hurricane, so he spent Wednesday night in Puerto Rico. Laura, Isabel and I were worried that he wouldn't be able to fly in by Thursday, the day before our wedding.

Thursday, August 3, I went to my dressmaker, Yongmei, to pick up my suit for the courthouse ceremony and my dress for the evening reception.

As she made the final adjustments to the dress, I burst into tears. "Nadean, what is wrong? It is bad luck to cry the day before your wedding."

"Yongmei, you have no idea. I know everything is going to go wrong. Juan won't let Andrew come back to me and the wedding is tomorrow. I know he is going to ruin my wedding."

"Nadean, you must believe it will work out. You must stop crying. Really, you need to be positive."

I continued to sob as she removed pins and finished the details. Helen, Isabel and I left Grandview for the courthouse on Friday, August 4. The wedding was scheduled for 11:00 a.m., and Isabel drove. Helen surprised me with a small bouquet, as I had not even thought of flowers in my grief over not having Andrew with us.

"Lady in Red" played on the radio, and Helen sang as Isabel drove us to the courthouse.

Laura, Karley, Alex, Bill, Jeremy and Donna met us at the courthouse. Suddenly, Juan appeared with Andrew.

"Andrew can go in for the ceremony," he said.

The ceremony was tense and perfunctory. Bill was joyous; I merely went through the motions. Even on that special day, Juan still controlled me. After the ceremony, we stood outside the courtroom and took a few photos. No one looked truly happy except Bill. He had no idea what awaited us.

Juan stood nearby watching as we took photos.

"We are going to lunch now and we are going to take Andrew with us," Bill said to Juan as I took Andrew's hand.

"No," Juan said.

Bill put his hand on Juan's chest to protest and two bodyguards appeared behind Juan.

Everything that followed unfolded in slow motion. I told Bill to stop, knowing the guards would attack him if instructed to do so by Juan. Bill and Juan started to argue. Juan grabbed Andrew's other hand and pulled him away from me. Juan, Andrew and the bodyguards ran up the street. Laura and Isabel gave chase.

I held my hand to my mouth, speechless, shocked and unable to move. Bill stood next to me.

Laura and Isabel caught up with Juan and begged him to let Andrew accompany us to the wedding lunch and reception that evening.

"Never!" Juan said. "I don't give a damn about the wedding."

Laura and Isabel returned to us and related their conversation with Juan.

"We are going to see my barrister," I said. "Perhaps he can do something. You both go on to the lunch. Bill and I will meet you there." Instead of joining our friends at our wedding lunch, Bill and I met with my barrister, Raymond Martinez, a former attorney general of the country.

"You cannot do anything at this time as this period is still legally within Juan's visitation with Andrew," Raymond said after he reviewed our custody agreement.

Reluctantly we left my barrister's office and joined our wedding guests, who were waiting at the restaurant for us. Laura and Isabel drove to Alice's house that afternoon and begged her and Guillermo to intervene so Andrew could attend the reception that evening.

"Not unless Nadean gives Andrew's Canadian passport to Juan," Alice said.

They called me from Alice's house and I told them that would never happen. Laura and Isabel spent hours pleading with them before they had to go to Roy and Betty McNaughton's house to decorate it for our reception.

I thought about a time, years before, when Alice said to me, "Blood is thicker than water. No matter what happens in life, I will always side with my children."

Although Alice liked me and Bill, she would not support us even if she disapproved of her children's actions.

We all tried to be joyful at the reception, which was lovely. Laura and Isabel decorated the McNaughton house beautifully. Bill genuinely seemed to be happy. I acted the part, but was enormously sad and fearful. The morning after our wedding, Juan appeared at Grandview at seven o'clock and stood before the sliding glass doors on the patio. He banged on the glass to wake us and repeatedly shouted *Hello!*

Bill went downstairs to confront Juan.

"You need to vacate this house immediately," Juan said to Bill. "Nadean no longer has any rights in this country. She gave those rights away when she got married."

If Bill could have found the key to the wrought iron that protected the glass doors, he would have opened them and choked Juan.

Unsure of my rights in the country, I called the shipper and asked if he would come to Grandview that day and pack our things for shipment to the US. His men spent Saturday and Sunday packing our furniture.

After the packers left late Sunday afternoon, Bill and I stood in the kitchen. I was enormously sad to be leaving the home I knew for ten years and leaving my cat, Abercrombie, and dog, Coco, behind.

As Bill and I talked, we heard a noise in the living room and saw Guillermo running from my house back to his. He had been listening to our conversation.

As I did not have Andrew, I would not leave St. Gustave for the US. Laura and her children flew to England on Sunday for a three-week vacation and I moved into her guest room. Bill left for America the next day and I began my married life alone, homeless, afraid, with neither a job nor a car; upon setting our wedding date, I had resigned from Barbados Mutual and returned my company car. Worst of all, I was without Andrew.

I spent the next three weeks meeting with my attorneys, Samantha, Raymond and Joyce Thompson, a second barrister who had joined our team.

Bill and Aunt Roberta called with words of encouragement.

I had no idea how long it would take to resolve the situation and was unable to make plans.

I tried to see Andrew, but Juan would not permit it.

Samantha finally filed an emergency appeal to the court, which was in recess for the summer. On August 29, three and a half weeks after our wedding, an emergency session was declared by the court.

Justice Alfred Warner, a retired Supreme Court Justice, was called in to hear our petition and preside over the matter. After hearing arguments from both sides (Juan was represented by his brother Roberto, a senator in the government, and his partner, Douglas), Justice Warner declared that Juan had kidnapped Andrew.

"The court orders Mr. Rivero to return the child, Andrew Rivero, to his mother, Mrs. Stone, at two o'clock this afternoon. As it would appear that this matter will probably go forward as a custody case, I would be available to preside as judge."

Attorneys for both sides met with each of us to discuss Justice Warner's offer. My attorneys were ecstatic and advised me to accept. Roberto also accepted Justice Warner's offer.

Outside the courtroom where the other party could not hear, my attorneys shared that Justice Warner was a highly respected and admired member of the judiciary. He was one judge they trusted implicitly. He was incorruptible and could not be bribed, unlike other judges in the country.

"Nadean, we are so lucky that he was selected to hear this appeal and that he has offered to preside over this case. He knows what lies ahead of us."

Andrew was returned to me that afternoon by Juan, who was decidedly unhappy. Andrew acted strangely toward me. He had been away from me for nearly two months and was not his usual affectionate, loving self. He responded to me in clipped tones.

A day later, friends gathered at Laura's for dinner. Laura said she needed a dessert from HiLo at Eastmall, so I offered to drive to the store in her car and pick it up.

Andrew asked if he could come with me. I found his request odd. There were many children playing at Laura's and he appeared to be enjoying their company. When we arrived at HiLo, I asked Andrew to stay close to me.

As I turned to pick up a cake from the counter, Andrew disappeared. I couldn't find him anywhere. I was in a panic. I rushed to the manager of HiLo and asked him to help find my son. He closed all doors to the store and ordered everyone to look for Andrew. He alerted security for the mall and we started walking the aisles and looking into the stores. I knew Juan was behind this. The manager let me use his phone to call Laura, who said she and Edward, a friend and attorney, would come immediately.

I ran frantically up and down the aisles of the mall on the first and second floors.

I finally found Laura and Edward at HiLo, and they had Andrew with them. I asked him what happened. He said, without conviction, that he got lost. Edward shared that when he and Laura drove around the perimeter of the mall, they saw Juan standing inside one of the entrances. They parked and walked into another entrance nearby, where they saw Andrew walking along without a care in the world. He appeared to be looking for someone. When they asked Andrew what he was doing, he said he was lost.

The next evening Laura took Andrew into her bedroom and questioned him.

He finally produced a wallet with $115.00 and Juan's business card with handwritten telephone numbers.

Andrew shared that by pre-arrangement, he and Juan had agreed that Andrew would deliberately run away at the first opportunity and call Juan to pick him up.

"Laura," I said, "I have to tell Samantha and Allyson. This is going to get much worse."

"Nadean, you can stay here as long as you need to."

• • •

On September 1, I took Andrew to meet with Allyson. She spent an hour with him and informed me subsequently that Andrew had been brainwashed, as if he were in a religious cult. He had suffered tremendous emotional damage by reason of the extended period he had been with Juan, nearly eight weeks.

The incident at Eastmall was a result of brainwashing, and up to then it had been a game to Andrew. As his attempt to run away failed, Andrew did not know what to do next. He was upset and angry with me. Our relationship had been severely damaged during his time with Juan. Andrew visited Allyson again four days later.

She reported that he was much changed, calmer and more at peace with himself.

Chapter 21

The Custody Battle

School started in September and Andrew returned to his classes. Barbados Mutual had not been able to find a replacement for me, so my former boss rehired me and returned my car. The courts would not even resume until October, so I worked, and Andrew and I lived with Laura, Alex and Karley. On the weekends, Andrew visited his father, per the original visitation agreement. Allyson and I worried about Juan's continuing influence on him.

Chantal became pregnant shortly after their wedding. The baby was due in November. Andrew told me, upon his return from Juan after his first weekend, that his father and Chantal were going to move to Australia after the baby was born.

Our court appearances started before Justice Warner in October. I had immense faith in his integrity and fairness. He was a giant of a man, well over six-foot-four, and possessed a manner that commanded respect.

My attorneys advised that the custody battle could take many months. I felt it best if Andrew and I lived on our own, so Patsy D'Agostino, a friend, lent her apartment to us. Located on the top floor of a large house owned by Mr. and Mrs. Benes, it would be the first of many places we lived.

It took forever for the case to proceed in the courts.

There were no court reporters, so the judge and all attorneys took slow, deliberate, copious notes and often reviewed and discussed their notes to ensure they were accurate. We would spend an hour in court and then not reconvene until the following week. I would leave work, walk to the courthouse, attend the session and return to work.

While walking to the courthouse one day, I came up behind Juan,

Roberto and Douglas They did not notice me. As I watched their backs, I felt extremely alone, powerless and very much afraid. How could I defeat these three men? I felt so small in comparison. I could only ask, "God give me courage."

On October 19, Andrew and I lay in my bed reading a bedtime story. I was in my nightgown and he in his pajamas. Suddenly, there was banging at the front door. As Andrew and I approached cautiously, I saw large dark men standing at the window next to the door.

One man held a document to the window.

"Open this door now!" he said. "We are policemen and we have a search warrant."

"How do I know you are really policemen?" I said. "I need to see the warrant. Please pass it through the window."

"No! If you don't open this door now, we are going to break it down."

The man held up a sledgehammer. Then I heard Mr. and Mrs. Benes on the stairs.

"Officer," Mr. Benes said, "you cannot break down that door! This is my house, and Mrs. Stone and her son are my tenants."

"We don't care," the officer said. "We have a search warrant and we are coming in whether you approve or not."

"Please, let me see the warrant," Mr. Benes said.

Mr. Benes looked at the document and looked at me through the window.

"Nadean, it looks legitimate. I think it best if you open the door." I held Andrew close to me and sensed this was a trap.

"I need to call my attorney first. Please wait a few minutes," I said.

I called Samantha and she told me to open the door, but make sure I kept her on the line. I unlocked and opened the door, and seven large, dark men in navy-blue sweaters, tams, and black pants rushed inside.

They tore the apartment apart while two other officers remained on the landing.

Mr. and Mrs. Benes pushed their way into the apartment, past the officers.

"I need to stay here with Mrs. Stone," Mr. Benes said. "My wife will take Andrew downstairs to our home. I don't want him to see this."

"Officer, if you tell me what you are looking for, please, I will help you find it. You should know that my ex-husband, Juan Rivero, and I are currently in a custody battle over our son. I think that your coming here tonight might be connected to this. You are being set up. Please let me help you. This is not my apartment and I can't let you destroy it. I was in court this morning and perhaps my former husband put something in my briefcase. I left it in the courtroom while I stepped out to talk to my attorneys," I said.

The lead officer told his men to stop and he turned to me.

"We are looking for a gun. It is against the law to own or carry guns."

"Ah," I said. "Please come with me. Let me show you."

They followed me into the bedroom and I pulled out the top drawer of a bedside table and withdrew a gun.

"Officer," I said, "last Thursday night when I was reading a story to my son, he opened this drawer and pulled out this gun. This apartment is owned by my friend, Patsy D'Agostino. She is letting us live here as we do not have a home at the moment. I told my son to put the gun away and I would call Aunty Patsy to ask her about it. My son went to his father's home this past weekend. I called Patsy, who told me that it is a toy gun. She keeps it in her drawer in case an intruder breaks into her apartment. She plans to use it to frighten the intruder."

The officer took the gun and examined it.

"Yes, it is a toy, but not even toy guns are allowed here, so we are going to take this."

Andrew and Mrs. Benes appeared in the bedroom.

"Mummy, I am so sorry," Andrew said as he cried. "I told Dad about the gun."

The officers were visibly upset as they realized they were duped.

I took the officers to the kitchen and invited them to sit down at the table. Andrew sat on my lap. Mr. and Mrs. Benes stood nearby.

"Officer," I said, "if you look at that search warrant I think you will find that it has been signed by Roberto Rivero. He is an attorney and a senator, and he is my former husband's brother. Roberto is also representing Juan in this custody battle."

The officer looked at the warrant and nodded. "Yes, it was signed by Rivero and Co., Solicitors."

The officer who was so puffed up with indignation in the beginning looked at me with sadness, understanding and remorse.

"I am so sorry to have put you and your son through this, Mrs. Stone. It was totally unnecessary."

The next day Juan appeared at Andrew's school.

"I did not tell the police, Andrew," Juan said. "It is not my fault. My attorneys did it. Don't tell your mother that you are on my side in this case."

Andrew's teacher waited for me when I picked him up after school to tell me Juan had visited the school and met with Andrew. Andrew climbed into the car and told me immediately about his father's visit and what his father had said.

I realized the stakes were getting higher. Juan was becoming more desperate. How could any loving father put his child through such a frightening experience, then lie to him and encourage him to lie to his mother?

I met with Samantha and she prepared a letter describing the frightening incident to Juan's attorneys, protested Juan's behavior, and requested restraint. A copy was filed with the court for review by Justice Warner.

Two weeks later I arranged with Juan to pick Andrew up from a Cub Scout gathering on a Saturday afternoon. Juan was supposed to meet me to hand Andrew over.

When I arrived at the club, I could not find Juan or Andrew. No one had seen my son.

I panicked because I thought Juan had kidnapped Andrew again, and I hit the breaking point. While driving down the hill from the club, I sped up as I approached a bridge over a small stream and slammed on my brakes just before impact. My car slid on the gravel, then stopped. I dropped my head on the steering wheel and emitted bone-chilling screams as I struck my head repeatedly on the steering wheel while I sobbed.

I did not notice the young couple who watched me from their car after they pulled up beside me.

"Is there anything I can do to help you?" the driver asked. "Can I take you somewhere?"

"No," I said. "No one can help me."

"Are you sure?"

"Yes, no one can solve my problems. There is no hope."

The couple waited for a bit and watched me cry. Then they slowly drove away and I drove back to Laura's house.

Laura called Juan numerous times and he finally picked up his phone. "I don't give a rat's ass if she is worried and frightened," Juan said to Laura. "Andrew is there. Find him."

I returned to the Cub Scout meeting and after asking many people for assistance, I found Andrew happily playing with his friends.

Our endless days in court went on for months.

The case was heard either once a week or every other week.

In November, after the birth of Chantal's daughter Anna, her older daughter, Simone, got into a fight with Andrew and slashed his thumb with a razor. My attorneys included this incident in a future court document.

Between August 1989 and May 1990, Andrew and I moved nine times, renting and borrowing apartments and cars from friends, but more often returning to Laura when we had nowhere else to go.

One apartment that we rented was horribly run down and depressing, but it was all that I could afford. My former in-laws and their families cut off all contact with me. Barbados Mutual, which knew that I would eventually leave the country, hired my replacement in November following a months-long search for the right candidate. When that happened, I had to leave my job permanently and again give up the company car.

An English couple offered to lend an old car that their teens used when they visited on holidays. I accepted, gladly.

As I pulled into Andrew's little private school pickup line with my "latest borrow," I saw Andrew standing in the distance searching for me.

When I pulled up next to him, he looked at the car with shock. I leaned over and pushed open the passenger door.

"Hello darling, climb in!" I said. "This is our newest borrow."

The tiny car had started out as a white vehicle. It had been in numerous accidents, so the trunk cover had been replaced with a black cover. The driver's door was dented and didn't open, so I had to climb in on the passenger side and scoot over the shift to the driver's seat. It had numerous dents all over the exterior. However, it had four wheels, the engine worked, and I was enormously grateful to have it.

"Mummy, you can't drive this kind of car," Andrew said as he climbed in. "You are a lady and must drive a nice car."

"Things are very hard for us right now, Andrew. We will get through this and one day we will have a nice car again. But for now, we need to be very thankful and happy with whatever God has provided to us."

My grandmother left $28,000 Canadian for me when she passed in 1974. The account consisted of funds she had received from the Canadian government on a monthly basis to care for me. She had carefully banked all of it for my future and she had also deposited her own money when she could afford to do so. I had not spent any of the money, saving it for an emergency. I used it to pay my attorneys. Bill and Aunt Roberta also sent money when they were able to, as I had no source of income.

Throughout this difficult period, Bill visited me for long weekends when he could, and Charlotte called from England occasionally with words of encouragement.

And I cried a river of tears.

"You are a white woman in a black country trying to take the son of a leading political family out of the country. Won't happen. You will never win," Juan said.

Sides were taken. Attorneys whom I did not know and had only seen occasionally in the courthouse would stop me on the street and ask how the case was going. They were sympathetic and encouraged me to be strong.

"Nadean, you have a great judge," one attorney said. "He is learned and wise. Place your faith in him."

Everyone knew about our case, but it was not covered in the press, thankfully. So many people expressed great sympathy for me, and provided constant support. The mothers of Andrew's schoolmates sent notes of encouragement to me in Andrew's lunch kit. They also sent written prayers and novenas. Everyone recognized that this battle was overwhelmingly against me by virtue of the family's political standing and Roberto's position as a senator.

Juan's attorneys had a list of arguments they presented against me:

– Nadean is adopted. She does not know what it is to have a family. She has no parents, brothers and sisters. Family is not as important to her.

– Andrew is a "Son of the soil." He has extended family in the country, uncles, cousins. Life is better for him here.

– Bill has incurable kidney disease (he does have kidney disease, but it is not incurable) and will die.

– Nadean had cancer and will not live long.

– Bill had a bankruptcy and can't support Nadean and Andrew.

– Juan has income to support Andrew in a lifestyle he is accustomed to.

– Chantal will be a good stepmother.

– Nadean is not a fit mother.

We countered every argument they presented with more forceful arguments.

There was a lot of ranting and prevaricating by Roberto and Douglas, who put on dramatic performances each day in court. My attorneys, in contrast, were serious and professional.

Chapter 22

The Testimony

Allyson, Andrew's child psychologist, was called to testify first.

"I have observed," she stated, "that the father manipulates Andrew, which is detrimental to Andrew's relationship with his mother. Juan is overly critical of Nadean in Andrew's presence and treats her with disrespect. He refers to her as a weak and incapable person. Nadean, on the other hand, always speaks positively about Juan to Andrew. I am concerned that Andrew's father will not honor any agreement if he is given custody of Andrew and that Nadean will never see her son again.

"Nadean is honest and without guile. She is a good mother and a good influence on Andrew. She is guided by high morals. She will follow any decision made by the court, even if it is harmful to her."

Chantal testified and admitted to the court that she too was adopted and is an only child. This countered Juan's attorney's initial argument about my lack of family influencing my parenting skills. Chantal's upbringing was similar to mine. How could she be a better parent? She also confirmed that her daughter Simone slashed Andrew's thumb with a razor during an argument.

"I don't get it," Samantha whispered into my ear, when Chantal concluded her testimony. "You are both beautiful with similar backgrounds. She is just a darker version of you."

Bill was called to the stand and Douglas treated him with enormous disrespect, referring to him as *Will-lly-am* Stone, drawing out his name. He tried to present Bill as sick, penniless and without the ability to provide an acceptable life for me and Andrew.

Our attorneys established that while he had been diagnosed with kidney disease, it had not progressed for years and his chances for a long life were good.

He had procured a position with an established company that provided a decent income. Together, he and I could provide adequately for Andrew.

Christmas Eve without Andrew was especially difficult for me. I sobbed uncontrollably during Mass. It was embarrassing to all sitting around me, but I was beyond embarrassment. I spent half of Christmas Day with Andrew and on Boxing Day, I flew to Ft. Lauderdale and spent a few days with Bill.

"I don't know who I want to live with," Andrew said to me in January. "I am tired of not having our own home or a bedroom. The case will not end soon, Mum. Dad says that after this judge, it is going to two more court cases."

It was then I realized that Juan was talking about the appeals court.

That could take another five years.

In April, Samantha invited me to dinner at her house. We had worked together over five years, beginning with my separation in 1984.

She was a gracious hostess, serving lovely wine and food. She recounted how she met her husband in England and came to live in St. Gustave.

After dinner, we sat on chairs beside one another and looked at the stars as we sipped our wine. It was a lovely treat for me to have such a peaceful evening.

However, my peace was shattered when Samantha turned to me and dropped a bomb.

"Nadean, you should get ready to consider moving to the US and leaving Andrew behind."

My jaw dropped and I shook my head.

"Wait, Samantha, do you think we are going to lose?"

"Nadean, you very well might. You see everything in black and white and life is not like that. There are gray areas, and you need to see the gray."

Frightened and furious, I turned toward her and stared into her eyes. In that moment, I realized that Samantha, while a good solicitor, was insecure, intimidated and fearful of Roberto, Douglas and Juan.

"Samantha, I know what is right and wrong, fair and unfair, just and unjust. What is happening here is not fair! It is trial by fear and intimidation. In this matter, I will never see the gray and I will never leave my son behind.

"Samantha, it's obvious that Roberto, Douglas and Juan are going for the jugular. You are my attorney and I need you to fight for me, to do the same. Go for the jugular."

I knew then that I had to make my testimony forceful. Testimony that sealed Juan's fate.

When I was called to the stand, I was apprehensive.

My only consolation over those long months was Justice Warner. I had faith that he would see through all of Roberto and Douglas's courtroom antics and banter to the salient arguments of the case. I knew Roberto and Douglas's weaknesses, and I knew I had to try not to let them intimidate me.

"Yes, Juan is a good father and loves his son," I said when Douglas presented me with the question.

"Mrs. Stone, if the court gives custody to Andrew's father, will you leave the country and move to the US?"

I tried to speak, but instead began to cry. I was unable to answer. Justice Warner asked if I was okay to continue. I took a deep breath and nodded.

"I love my son more than anything in life. I have faith in the court and sincerely hope that this will not happen. I love my husband, as well. However, if the court grants custody to Andrew's father I do not know what I will do. I will never leave my son behind."

"Does that mean you will leave your husband and stay in the country?"

"Mr. Phillips, I do not know what I will do. I cannot say, as it has not happened and I only pray that it doesn't."

The judge and my three attorneys were visibly upset by my crying. Douglas sat down and it was then Raymond's turn.

"Mrs. Stone," Raymond said, "you completed all the forms for a move to Australia so that Andrew could have his parents in the same country as recommended by his psychologist. When you were denied a visa to Australia you declared subsequently that you would not follow Andrew's father to Australia or anywhere else in the world. What caused you to change your mind?"

"Juan would visit me often at work and talk about Australia. When I did not score enough points to get in, he was frustrated and angry and continued to visit me and talk about other possible countries and islands in the West Indies. He was desperate to leave the country.

"At our last meeting I asked him, 'How can you possibly leave all of your family behind and move to a country where you have no family and know no one?' Juan's response was, 'My parents sent me off to boarding school in Canada when I was eleven years old. They never really loved me. I don't get along well with Roberto. We have a sibling rivalry. Andres, the only one I care about, lives in Canada. I seldom see Carlotta and I am not close to her anyway. I really have no family to care about or miss.'

"When he said those words to me, I was in shock and disbelief. I realized at that moment that if he cared so little about his own family, what did he truly care about me?

"I knew that if I followed him to Australia or anywhere else that I was completely on my own. If he became angry with me in another country and took Andrew away from me, I would have no recourse. No family, no friends. I would not survive it. That was when I saw his true character and decided that I would not follow him anywhere."

The judge and attorneys stared at me and Douglas chose not to ask any further questions. I was instructed to step down.

There was silence in the courtroom as the judge and attorneys took notes and I walked back to my seat. It felt as if the air had been sucked out of the room.

As I reached my chair and sat down, I looked up at Juan, who was directly across from me. He looked around to see that the judge and attorneys had their heads down and were still busy taking notes.

He smiled at me with a grotesque sneer. Juan then took his right hand and, still smiling, slashed it across his throat up to and above his head.

I gasped as I felt the color drain from my body, and all heads lifted. "Mrs. Stone, are you okay? What's wrong?" Judge Warner said.

I did not know what to say or do as they all stared at me. "It is okay," I said. "I am fine, your honor."

As we left the courtroom, my attorneys and I gathered on the sidewalk.

"Nadean," Samantha said, "we did not expect Douglas to ask that question about the court's decision, but when he did and you cried, it showed the judge the level of your love for Andrew. We cannot ask our clients ever to cry on the stand, so that was powerful.

"Also, your testimony about Juan, Australia and his family was brilliant. It is too bad Roberto wasn't here today to hear that. His partner will tell him, though. What happened when you gasped? What is wrong? You look pale."

I told them about Juan's reaction to my testimony.

"Thank God you said you were fine," Raymond said. "That was a threat on your life. If you had shared Juan's behavior with the court, the judge would have been forced to declare a mistrial and we would have had to start all over. Unbelievable!"

After court, I visited friends who owned a fabric store a few streets south of the courthouse. I had developed the habit of doing that as the case wore on. They were very protective of me and kind, even lending me cars when I was in need. When I arrived, the two brothers asked about my day, as usual.

When I described my testimony and Juan's reaction, both looked at me in horror.

"Nadean, you need to move out of your apartment tonight. Don't stay there alone and don't even go back. Move back to Laura. You can't be alone now. Juan will not do the deed himself, but he can hire someone for very little money to kill you. You need to take this seriously. He must be so angry right now that he is not reasonable. Move, and do it now!"

I called Laura from their shop and told her the latest developments. "Come over right now," Laura said. "Don't go back for your things. It is Friday. Andrew will be with Juan for the weekend. You need to be somewhere safe."

That night as the group of friends gathered at Laura's house and I related the incident in court, all were troubled and fearful for me. They were convinced that Juan was capable of hiring someone to kill me.

I was still processing all of it and was too stunned to accept this possibility. How did Juan and I ever progress to this level of animosity?

When Juan was finally called to the stand, he testified for two agonizingly long days. He was skewered, sliced and diced on the stand as my attorneys shredded his testimony. All of his lies began to unravel and he trapped himself. He had written numerous letters to me over the years, all of which I had kept. Those letters served to support my arguments and refuted his.

"Chantal was also adopted, but not until the age of eight," Raymond said. "She was an orphan for some time. Is that true?"

"Yes," Juan said.

What Juan and his attorneys did not realize was that Judge Warner and his wife adopted two children. With his statements, Juan's prejudice toward adoptees, at least toward me, was sealed.

Our attorneys informed the court that Juan had not supplied financial statements to support his allegations of financial capability.

"No, I have not filed tax returns for the last five years," Juan confessed.

"Mr. Rivero, you are a professional chartered accountant and have your own accounting firm. Do you file tax returns for your clients?" Raymond said.

"Yes."

"Then why have you not filed tax returns for yourself for five years? As a result of not filing tax returns you have not paid any taxes to the government, is that correct?"

"Yes."

The judge looked furious and my attorneys appeared to enjoy the line of questioning.

"Mr. Rivero," Raymond said, "perhaps your financial capabilities are not as you have declared. Are you truly able to support Andrew, your wife, the baby she just had, and her two other children?"

"Yes, I can support all of them."

"Then, Mr. Rivero, the court will need to see evidence of this financial ability. Will you be able to provide such evidence?'

"Yes."

"You are dismissed."

The next day, Juan returned to the stand.

"Since my testimony yesterday, I have filed five years of tax returns."

"Mr. Rivero, since yesterday you have been able to file five years of tax returns and pay your taxes?" Raymond asked, and shook his head.

"Yes," Juan said.

"How much did you pay in taxes?"

"Three thousand dollars."

There was silence in the courtroom as all took notes. It was a paltry sum.

"Mr. Rivero, does your divorce decree stipulate that you are required to replace Andrew's mother's car every five years?"

"Yes."

"But after seven years you did not do so and in this letter to Andrew's mother you write that you cannot afford to do so. Is this your letter to Mrs. Stone?"

"Yes."

"If you have all of the financial capability that you have stipulated, why did you tell Mrs. Stone, after you married, that you would no longer pay for anything but Andrew's school fees and the mortgage on your house?"

"I thought she should assume more of the responsibility for herself and Andrew."

"Mr. Rivero, did you commit to provide monthly payments to Christopher Daoud for the accounting practice that you purchased from him when he moved to England?"

"Yes."

"Did you make any payments?"

"I did for a few months, then stopped."

"Why did you stop making payments?"

"The practice I bought was not as viable as I had been led to believe. Not all of his clients stayed with me, so I stopped the payments."

"Mr. Daoud asked you for the payments many times, did he not?"

"Yes."

"Did you know that as a result of your non-payments, Mr. Daoud lost his home here?" Raymond asked.

"Yes," Juan said.

"Mr. Rivero, I would venture to say that given your testimony, perhaps your financial capabilities are not as you have stipulated in your deposition. Would I be correct in saying that you do not have the funds to maintain Andrew as you have previously indicated?"

"Yes."

"Would you say that your home is a peaceful and happy one for Andrew?"

"Yes, most definitely."

"Mr. Rivero, shortly after the birth of your daughter in November, did your step-daughter, Simone, have an altercation with Andrew, and did she cut his thumb with a razor blade?"

"Yes."

"Since this custody case began, Andrew lives with his mother during the week and spends weekends with you. Is that correct?"

"Yes."

"And despite the tension and obvious stress that must be associated with this kind of experience, Andrew has continued to do well in school. His grades have not fallen and they are between A's and B's. Would you say then that Andrew's mother is doing a good job of helping him to maintain his grades?"

"No, I would not. Andrew is a bright boy."

"Mr. Rivero, would you say that Andrew's mother is a good mother?"

"No, I would not."

"Would you say that she loves her son?" Juan hesitated.

"Mr. Rivero, would you say that Mrs. Stone loves her son?"

"Yes, she loves him."

"Mr. Rivero, on October 19th of last year when Mrs. Stone and Andrew were getting ready for bed one evening, their peace was disturbed by nine SWAT team officers, which resulted in a very frightening experience for both of them. The SWAT team had a search warrant and indicated that they were looking for a gun. Did you advise the police of the presence of a gun in their apartment?"

Juan hesitated again. "Yes," Juan mumbled.

"I'm sorry, Mr. Rivero, I did not hear your answer. Did you inform the police of a gun in Mrs. Stone's apartment, an apartment in which your son lived?"

"Yes, I did."

"Mr. Rivero, do you know a woman named Helen Joseph?"

"Yes."

"And is Helen Joseph Mrs. Stone's housekeeper and Andrew's nanny?"

"Not any longer."

"Yes, Mr. Rivero, but until this custody case began, while Mrs. Stone lived at Grandview, was Helen Joseph Mrs. Stone's housekeeper and Andrew's nanny?"

"Yes."

"Mr. Rivero, I would like you to look at this letter, which has been presented as evidence by Mrs. Stone. Do you recognize this letter? It is on your company letterhead."

"No, I do not recognize it."

"In this letter, you state that Helen Joseph is your employee. Further, you make an offer to Ms. Joseph of $10,000 and a visa to the US, if she will testify that Mrs. Stone is not a fit mother. Mr. Rivero, did you write this letter to Ms. Joseph?"

"No, I did not."

"Can you explain how a letter addressed to Ms. Joseph, written on your company letterhead, came to be in her possession?"

"No, I cannot."

"Mr. Rivero, we have no further questions."

Douglas then asked Juan a few perfunctory questions, but was unable to reverse the blood bath that had taken place.

Chapter 23

Judge Warner's Decision

In court on Tuesday, May 1, 1990, Justice Warner made an announcement: "I plan to visit Andrew at school within the hour for a private conversation. All parties are to remain in the courthouse until released." He did not say this, but it was so neither party could influence Andrew's discussion with him. We waited for two hours.

"I will give my decision in a few days," he said when he returned. The court issued a statement the following day to all attorneys that Justice Warner would deliver his judgment on Friday, May 4.

When we arrived at 9:00 a.m. on judgment day, the courtroom was packed.

My dear friend Edward, an attorney, was present, along with many of the attorneys who had stopped me on the street to provide encouragement. Everyone heard that Justice Warner would deliver his judgment, and tension was high.

Justice Warner spoke for two and a half hours. A thunderstorm raged outside, mirroring the thunderous ruling dispensed by Justice Warner. While he couched his language in a carefully worded script, no one was in doubt as to the scathing judgment he delivered.

"If the child is left in the care of Mr. Rivero," Justice Warner said, "Mr. Rivero will continue to disparage Andrew's mother and Mrs. Stone will never see her child again.

"If the child is given to his mother, I am convinced that the mother will abide by the visitation rights and will always speak positively of the father.

"I am convinced that the mother and stepfather will be good parents.

"While financial considerations are important, I am convinced the mother and stepfather will work hard to support the child.

"I will not make moral decisions in this case regarding Mr. Rivero's confusing testimony or dishonesty, especially with regard to his throwing $3,000 at the Inland Revenue for the past few years' tax payments.

"I hereby award complete custody, care and control to the mother and give permission to her to take the child out of the country.

"In addition, all of the mother's attorney costs are to be paid by Juan Rivero.

"Judgment is final and signed as of this day."

There was silence in the room. I looked at my attorneys, who expressed no emotion.

Then the electricity failed and the entire courthouse was plunged into absolute darkness.

It was as if the hand of God slammed the gavel on the momentous occasion. We could not see a foot in front of us and all sat quietly, waiting for directions.

In the dark, Judge Warner stated that no one was to leave the courtroom. After we waited for another fifteen minutes, Judge Warner said that we would not be able to continue.

"I am asking Mr. Roberto Rivero to promise not to take this matter to the appeals court until we can reconvene on Wednesday of next week. Mr. Rivero, do you agree?" Judge Warner said.

"Yes, your honor," Roberto said.

"I am recording this, Mr. Rivero. You are giving an undertaking not to file in the appeals court," the judge said.

"Yes, your honor."

We all felt our way out of the courtroom and into the main central area of the courthouse. The ceiling, two floors above us, was made of glass and there was a small amount of light that filtered down through the panes and into the stairwell. My three attorneys and I sat on the steps under the panes and Raymond dictated as Samantha typed up Justice Warner's judgment.

"What does this all mean?" I asked. "What are you doing? Am I free to leave with Andrew?"

"If the lights had stayed on, we would have been able to conclude the case today," Samantha said. "Because the lights failed, we do have a decision by Justice Warner and we need to make sure it is filed and recognized by the court today. We are typing it up so it will be recorded as of today. We will need to reconvene next week Wednesday, when Justice Warner will formally close the case. You can't leave the country until then."

"Oh, my God, will this never end?" I said.

"Nadean, please be patient. It will be a few more days and then you and Andrew will be free."

"But what if Roberto files in the appeals court? I will be stuck here."

"Nadean, it is unlikely that Roberto would do such a foolish thing. He gave an undertaking today to Justice Warner not to file. To go against the judge would be unwise and a great disrespect to the judge."

"What do I do now? How can we possibly wait until Wednesday?"

"Nadean, you won. Congratulations," Samantha said. "The judge gave you everything. His judgment was scathing to Juan. Justice Warner even awarded that your attorney fees be paid by Juan. This is a huge win. This is the longest custody case in the history of this country at nine months. Try to have a good weekend. We have to go now and file this judgment. We will meet you here on Wednesday."

I called Bill and Aunt Roberta with the news. Both were elated, and Bill could not wait for us to arrive in the US.

I changed our flights to Wednesday afternoon on American Airlines. Andrew and I spent the weekend with Laura, Alex, Karley, Edward, and Edward's wife, Grace, and their children. Laura had all of our friends over for dinner on Sunday night. I had won and we were close, but no one would be truly happy until Andrew and I were on a plane for the United States.

By Monday afternoon, I was at the end emotionally.

Andrew was at school and I was beside myself with worry. I did not trust Juan and Roberto.

I knew I couldn't take much more stress.

"Edward, how long could the case last if appealed?" I asked when I visited him in his office that afternoon.

"Another five years or more, as Juan's attorneys will delay, delay, delay. That will be their tactic."

"Edward, I can't stay in this country any longer."

"I know, Nadean. Let me make a call."

Edward called his friend David, an attorney, who was legal counsel for Rodriguez Auto, one of the country's largest companies.

"Hey, David. How goes it, man? I am sitting here with Nadean. You know the outcome of her custody case last Friday against Juan. Well, they all have to go back to court on Wednesday for Justice Warner to formalize closure of the case. David, Nadean really can't take any more stress. She will need to get out of the country with Andrew immediately after court on Wednesday before Roberto runs and files with the appeals court, which he will do. What can you do to help us?"

Edward chatted with David for a bit longer and then hung up and smiled at me.

"Rodriguez Auto has a private plane that works out of a small private airport near Larico. Keep your flights booked with American on Wednesday afternoon. However, after the court hearing, instead of traveling to Larico for those flights, we will take you to the private airport. Roberto and Juan will probably be looking for you at Larico but they won't think of looking at the private airport. You will leave the country on one of the Rodriguez Auto planes and travel wherever that plane is going. You can figure out how to get to the US from there."

Then the phone rang again, and it was David. Edward listened to David and then hung up.

"David said that his company just found out its phones are tapped. He went to another building and called me to say he is going to go back to his office and will call us from there. He will tell us that the plans originally agreed upon need to be canceled. He has checked, and the plane will not be available. The phone tappers will think the plan is off. However, the original plan will be in force. You are going out on the company's private plane."

We waited a few minutes and David called again, as planned. Edward told me again to keep my flights booked with American out of Larico. He knew Juan and Roberto would be monitoring airline bookings.

"Don't worry, Nadean. I will take care of everything else."

So much rested on all of the elements coming together as discussed, and so much could go wrong.

On Tuesday evening, Andrew and I checked out of our hotel. We made one final visit to Laura, my dearest friend in the world. In front of the children, we acted normally. When I said "Good-bye, Laura," we looked into each other's eyes for several moments, knowing we might not see each other again for a very long time.

Andrew and I spent the night at Edward and Grace's house. I was stressed to the max, but totally committed, whereas Edward was blissfully calm.

Wednesday morning at nine o'clock, everyone was in court again.

Roberto interrupted before Justice Warner could bring the court into session.

"Your Honor, I must inform the court that we filed in the appeals court on Friday afternoon."

There was an instant hush in the room, and no one could believe Roberto had gone against Justice Warner after making a promise to him and the court. I looked to my attorneys, who were ignoring me and watching Justice Warner.

"Mr. Rivero, on Friday you gave an undertaking to this court not to file in the appeals court until we reconvened today. Why have you done this?" Judge Warner said.

"Yes, but we were afraid the mother would leave the country with the child."

Justice Warner then looked at my attorney Raymond.

"Mr. Martinez, this reminds me of another case," the judge said. He cited the case and then said, "Remind me, now, Mr. Martinez, in that matter, the action taken by counsel resulted in the judge being absolved of all responsibility in the case. Is that correct?"

"Yes, your honor, you are correct," Raymond said.

The discussion confused me and I felt a dead weight descend over me. I was now stuck in the country forever!

The proceedings seemed to evolve in slow motion, but as the discussion continued between Justice Warner and Raymond, I sensed something of enormous importance taking place.

"Mr. Rivero," Judge Warner said, "as your action appears to have removed any further involvement by me in this case, my order of Friday morning now stands. Thank you. This court is dismissed."

Everyone rushed out of the courtroom. "What is happening?" I said to Samantha.

"Justice Warner's decision on Friday, which we filed, is good until the appeals court meets at ten-thirty this morning. It is now nine-thirty."

The window of opportunity for escape was still open!

"We need to go together to your office now! I have a car waiting outside," I said.

I had hired Mr. Bissessar, a local driver who used to transport Bill back and forth to the airport, to wait for me outside the courtroom.

Samantha and I jumped into the backseat.

"Samantha, when we get to your office, you need to give Andrew's passport to me immediately."

Samantha was upset and fidgeting in her seat.

"I don't want to know your plans, Nadean. This is not that show *Dallas* or some Hollywood movie. You need to calm down. You can't just do what you want."

"You're right, Samantha. This is my life and right now it is worse than any Hollywood movie. I have an opportunity and I'm taking it!"

"Don't tell me any more," she said.

When we reached her building, both of us rushed inside and up the stairs to her office.

"Please get Andrew's passport out of the vault for Nadean," Samantha said to her secretary.

All of the staff and attorneys gathered around me. This case had consumed their entire office for nine months and they knew it was at an end. There was much crying and hugging.

All of a sudden, we heard shouting on the ground floor.

Roberto Rivero demanded to see me. As I heard him storm up the stairs, I grabbed Andrew's passport, ran to Samantha's office, and locked myself in.

I called Edward and told him what was happening.

"Under no circumstances open Samantha's door," he said. "If those papers are served on you, you are in the appeals court and stuck in this country forever."

Roberto reached Samantha's office and started pounding against the door as he demanded that I open up. With Edward listening on the phone while Roberto screamed at me, I knelt on the floor next to a coffee table and shook.

I heard Harold Colley, senior partner of Samantha's firm, shouting from the other side of the door.

"Roberto, what the fuck are you doing in my office, man? Get the fuck out now!"

I heard Roberto grumble a reply and walk down the stairs. Samantha asked me to unlock the door.

"Samantha, has Roberto left? Are you alone?"

"Yes, open the door."

"Samantha, you must promise that Roberto has left and you are alone before I open this door. Do you promise?"

"Yes, Nadean, I promise."

I opened the door slowly and looked out before I allowed her to enter.

We hugged and I said good-bye and rushed down the stairs to the first floor. I looked outside and saw no sign of Roberto. I ran down the steps toward Mr. Bissessar's car and got in. I locked the doors and gave him directions to Edward's office.

"If all goes well, Mr. Bissessar," I said when we arrived at Edward's office, "you will not see me or Mr. Stone again."

"Good luck, Mrs. Stone, and say hi to Mr. Stone."

Edward's office was across the street from Roberto's partially hidden office. I looked around, left the car quickly and walked up the front steps of Edward's building. Once inside, I bounded up the stairs.

"Okay, Edward," I said when I reached him, "what is the plan now?"

Edward took me out through the back of the building and down the fire escape. Ram, his driver, was waiting.

Edward pointed to his car and opened the trunk. "Climb in, Nadean. You can't be seen leaving my office, as Roberto's office is across the street. Ram will take you to the private airport. I will wait a few minutes so as not to attract attention and then leave my office and follow you there. Andrew will be arriving in Grace's car to meet us."

I climbed into the trunk and Edward closed the lid. As Ram left the parking lot on the ground floor and drove up the ramp and onto the street, the car was clearly visible to anyone in Roberto's office.

The drive took forty-five minutes in sweltering heat. It was completely dark in the trunk except for a tiny shaft of light emanating from one corner.

"Can you hear me, Ram?" I shouted from the trunk.

"Yes, Miss."

If I stretched my damp, tightly cramped body just a bit, I was able to reach a small tear in the corner of the trunk lining just above my head. I stretched upward and gasped for more air. After so much promise, how could it end like this? I arrived an innocent young bride. I was leaving a country and people I had grown to love and was escaping in the trunk of a car! I could only hear loud traffic noises and horns blaring.

"Ram, can you hear me?"

"Yes, Miss."

"How much longer?"

"A while, Miss. Traffic heavy."

When we arrived, Ram opened the trunk and I climbed out. We hurried into the private airport, which was a half-mile from the main airport, Larico. We were the first to arrive. Mr. Mohammed was in charge of the facility and was informed by Edward of what was taking place.

"The flight is going to Curaçao, and you and your son can get off there and make your way to the US," Mr. Mohammed said.

Edward, Grace and Andrew arrived a few minutes later. I was holding my stomach, quaking with fear and kneeling on the floor. I knew that Juan and Roberto were after me.

"It will be okay now, Nadean," Edward said. "You don't need to worry."

Finally it was time to leave. Mr. Mohammed took me and Andrew to a small plane and helped us get seated before he left. The pilots taxied over to Larico for clearance.

While the pilots did a final outside check of the plane, Mr. Mohammed appeared at the side window.

"Mrs. Stone, Juan Rivero is at the airport demanding that you be stopped from leaving. May I have your passports and custody order from the judge? Please stay on the plane. Pretend you are not feeling well. I will talk to the airport officials."

I had to give our only documents to freedom to a man I had met just half an hour before. Mr. Mohammed was away for fifteen long minutes, and I began to believe we would not be allowed to leave.

Mr. Mohammed returned with our documents and a bright smile on his face.

"You can leave, Mrs. Stone. The officials at the airport said the judge's order clearly states that you can leave with your child. You are free to go."

"Mr. Mohammed, do these pilots know who we are and what we are doing?"

"No."

"How long will it be before we are in international airspace?"

"Eight miles."

"Mr. Mohammed, after we are airborne, if the control tower orders your pilots back, what will happen?"

"Don't worry, Mrs. Stone. I will be monitoring all air transmissions. If the tower calls them back, I will override the command and order my pilots to continue on course to Curaçao."

"Thank you, Mr. Mohammed," I said as I cried.

The engines started and liftoff took place. As our plane soared into a brilliant, cloudless sky, I looked out the window at my beloved St. Gustave receding below us.

Will I ever see it again? I wondered.

I anxiously asked the pilots to tell me when our plane crossed into international airspace. I knew that at that moment, my imprisonment would be over and we would finally be free.

A few minutes into the flight, the captain turned to me. "Ma'am, we just passed into international airspace."

Then the plane's radio crackled and I heard Edward's voice.

"Nadean, you are safe, my love. Grace and I are going to Veni Chez Moi to have a drink to you and to celebrate. Take care. We love you."

Chapter 24

Coral Springs, Florida

We could not have been happier to touch down in Florida.
I was so relieved to have finally achieved freedom that I wanted to fall to my knees and kiss the tarmac. I would love to say that all was wonderful after our arrival in Florida, but we faced continuing challenges from Juan.

Within a month he flew to the United States to try to steal Andrew and take him back to St. Gustave. He called on a Thursday when he arrived in Florida.

"I've come for a long weekend," he said. "Andrew is supposed to spend six weeks with me in the summer, so I would like to take him back with me on Tuesday and start our six weeks from then."

Fueled by fear, I took immediate action.

I called the police department in Coral Springs to alert them.

"My former husband is in the city and I fear he is planning to kidnap my son. He has done it before," I said.

The police visited our apartment, listened to my story, and reviewed Judge Warner's judgment. They left us, went to Juan's hotel, spoke to him, and took Andrew's St. Gustave passport from him for safekeeping. They told Juan he could collect it when he was returning to the country. I also called the American Bar Association, explained my need for urgent legal assistance and was referred to Marjorie Sharpton, a family law attorney.

We met on Friday and she started the legal paperwork.

She referred me to a child psychologist, Dr. Kratz, and I spent three hours on Saturday with him. Juan visited us at the apartment, but was only allowed to walk with Andrew in our development while Bill and I trailed behind. Juan also brought the money that Judge Warner ordered him to pay to my attorneys.

All weekend I was in fear, wondering, Will I never be free of this man?

On Monday morning Marjorie and I met in a Ft. Lauderdale court before Judge Watson. We were armed with all of my documentation and a report from Dr. Kratz, recommending that Andrew remain with me in the US.

Judge Watson took me into his chambers an hour later.

"I have reviewed all of your legal documents, which appear to be in order. However, I would like to speak to Judge Warner, as he presided over your case and I would like to hear from him his perceptions of how I might handle your request in the US."

Judge Watson sat at the head of his conference table in his chambers and I sat beside him, trying to remain in control and not cry, as I thought, Now I have to fight this frigging man in another country!

The judge dialed the number for the courthouse, and the call was finally answered after many rings. "Hello, this is Judge Watson in Ft. Lauderdale. I have an emergency custody case that has been set before me and I would like to speak with Justice Warner, who presided over the custody case. The mother and her child are here in the US and the mother fears that the child's father is trying to kidnap the child and take him back. The father arrived in Ft. Lauderdale four days ago."

Judge Watson listened, made a note on his legal pad, and then said, "Thank you, I will call back this afternoon at 1:00 p.m."

"There is a huge rainstorm there and the electricity is out in the courthouse, so Justice Warner left. The clerk is going to go to his house and explain the situation. I am to call him back at his home this afternoon. Can you come back at 1:00 p.m., and we will call him together?"

"Yes, of course. Thank you, Judge Watson."

At 1:00 p.m., Judge Watson called Justice Warner and described our petition. He listened quietly as Justice Warner responded for several minutes. Finally, Judge Watson spoke.

"Thank you, Justice Warner. You have helped immensely. I am so glad that we had this conversation. I now have a more complete understanding of the case and know how I will proceed."

Judge Watson hung up and turned to me.

"I am going to file your legal documents in the United States court formalizing Judge Warner's judgment so that custody, care and control of your son is in effect here. Judge Warner has recommended that you allow Andrew to return to his father in July for six weeks, not now. I asked him what he would do if Andrew's father does not return Andrew to you after six weeks. He said he will have Juan arrested and put in jail for violation of the agreement.

"I am also going to file an order today, that if Juan does not return Andrew to you at that time, he will be arrested at the border and put in jail here if he ever tries to enter the US again. I think that covers us in both countries. If you wait in the room outside of my chambers for a half hour, I will have my clerk prepare a document advising Juan of what has been decided here today. You can give it to him so that he is fully aware of the repercussions should he not return Andrew to you at the end of the summer. It was a pleasure to meet you, Mrs. Stone. I wish you and your family all the best."

That evening when Juan arrived to visit Andrew, I handed the envelope to him.

"Just so you know," I said, "I sought legal advice here and Judge Warner's judgment has been registered in the US court. I will send Andrew to you in July for six weeks. If you don't return him Justice Warner will arrest you. If you ever try to enter the US again you will be arrested at the border and jailed. You will never be permitted to enter the US again. The rest you can read for yourself."

Juan spent some time in Andrew's bedroom talking and then left.

That summer I sent Andrew to Juan for six weeks, somewhat confident that he would be returned to me. The last thing Juan wanted was to be barred from the US.

Andrew started school that fall and played Little League baseball and soccer. I started work with Sealand Shipping and then migrated to management of law firms in Ft. Lauderdale.

Bill signed up as a coach for Andrew's soccer team, which thrilled Andrew.

We settled into our new lives. Andrew visited his father at Christmas, Easter, and for six weeks in the summer.

Although I asked Juan repeatedly to return Andrew to me at least two days before school started in August so he could settle back into life in the US, Juan always scheduled his flight for the day before school started. He still had to have some control over me, whatever way he could.

Juan did as much as he could to disrupt our lives in the US and to destroy Andrew's enjoyment of school and sports.

He called every Monday night to talk to Andrew. When the conversation first started, Andrew would be full of his news for the week about his progress in school and sports. Juan would listen and then once again, speak negatively about me, Bill, school, sports and life in the US. He would tell Andrew that Silvain was living with them and that life would be better for Andrew there. He was buying a sailboat that he and Silvain would sail and if Andrew was with him, he could sail as well. Anna loved him and missed him so much too.

At the end of the conversation, Andrew would always be sad and sometimes tearful. I called Allyson and Samantha to ask for guidance.

Allyson said she was not surprised. Juan would never change. He was out to destroy Bill's and my relationship with Andrew even if it meant sacrificing Andrew.

Both said to record the conversations, which we did.

One would have thought that Juan learned a lesson from letter writing. He memorialized his weekly conversations with Andrew by writing to him each week, regularly regurgitating the hateful things he said on the phone. He referred to Bill as *Stone*, and often told Andrew he did not have to listen to Stone. Juan gave Andrew a three-ring binder so he could insert all of his father's letters and reread them when he missed his father. It was such rubbish and a continuation of the manipulation and belittling we had endured for so many years.

It was very distressing for Bill and me to watch how Juan was willing to destroy Andrew. Bill said he was an evil man. However, I could not in my heart stop Andrew from talking to his father.

Juan was so foolish that he even encouraged Andrew not to study American history, as it was not important. He said only St. Gustavian history would ever matter to Andrew. So, Andrew failed his history course, the only course he ever failed, and had to attend summer school. Both of them lost on that one, as Andrew was only able to spend two weeks that summer with Juan.

In middle school Andrew asked if he could enroll in a magnet school that specialized in science and math, and we happily permitted him to register for the transfer.

Bill and Andrew were both interested in science, so Bill assisted with a project in which Andrew had to build and exhibit Bernoulli's principle of air pressure gliding through a pneumatic tube. Andrew's display was creative and impressive. He was so proud. He was deemed a finalist and was taken by his school to Tallahassee to compete in the state finals, where he came in second in the state.

Andrew was so keen on science that I registered him for a week in early summer at Florida Atlantic University.

He and other magnet students his age spent one week living in the dorm with college-age students, attending classes and working on a science project.

He was so excited about the experience, and told me and Bill that he wanted to go to university at Florida Atlantic.

In the fall of 1995, Andrew tested and was accepted by St. Thomas Aquinas, a highly recognized Catholic high school in Ft. Lauderdale. I was so hopeful that this fabulous school would be a great experience for him and that he would thrive.

However, after living with Bill and me for five years, Andrew started to ask more forcefully if he could return to St. Gustave to live with his father. Juan's five years of denigrating Bill and me during phone calls and in letters and his manipulation of Andrew during Christmas, Easter and six weeks in the summer had affected Andrew greatly. He was now fourteen and no longer as willing to accept our guidance.

During my single days in St. Gustave, I had chatted with Colin, the father of one of Andrew's school friends.

He was English and had a successful business in St. Gustave. Over a drink one Friday evening at Veni Chez Moi, I asked about his life as a child.

"I am from Jamaica originally," he said. "When my parents divorced, my mother took me and my brother back to England to live with her. My brother and I visited my father in Jamaica during the holidays."

"Do you have any regrets about that time in your life?" I asked.

"My only regret is that we never got to live with our father again. We had lots of family in Jamaica, aunts, uncles and cousins. We had no family in England other than our mother. I always wondered what it would have been like if we had stayed in Jamaica. However, we could never have left our mother to live alone in England, so it wasn't an option. But I did regret never having the opportunity to live with our father again, at least for a while."

St. Thomas Aquinas was another adjustment for Andrew. He continued to beg me to let him return to St. Gustave. Finally, after much agonizing thought, many tears and with great reluctance, I agreed.

I recalled my conversation with Colin from Jamaica and his regrets. Andrew had lived with us for five years. His father would have him for the next five years before he set off for university.

"Juan," I said when I called him, "I am sending Andrew back to live with you. I am organizing a flight for the weekend. I hope you will take good care of him, keep him safe. I would like to have him come back to visit us during the holidays, the reverse of what we have been doing."

The last couple of days with Andrew were immensely sad for me. Neither

Bill nor Andrew could believe I was actually going through with it. I cried many tears, once again.

Andrew returned to St. Gustave and Bill and I now had the opportunity to organize fun trips during his holiday time with us. It was especially difficult for me to take Andrew to the airport in Miami at the end of our holidays together.

I would smile as he walked up the gangway to the plane, watch him disappear, and then turn around and sob.

Andrew discovered that life with his father was not as previously promised. As a young man he could now see his father for the man he truly was. They had heated arguments and Andrew rebelled.

I was still so fearful of Juan that I did not return to St. Gustave for seven years. I might never have returned if Bill had not threatened to go alone. When I finally succumbed, I was so happy to reunite with all of my old friends. Laura was thrilled to have us back.

Andrew asked us to come to Grandview.

"Mum, I want you to see my parrot, Brandi. He is just like our parrot, Sam. I asked Dad and he said it is okay for you to visit. He won't be here." When we arrived, Andrew met us at the gate and walked us into the home I'd lived in with him and Juan. It was surreal. Andrew was thrilled with his parrot. Bill and I had bought a larger cage for Sam and shipped Sam's old cage to St. Gustave, so Brandi now had a large home.

As we left Grandview, I presented Andrew with a new camera. "Take some pics and send them to us."

He looked at me and for the first time, I saw the sadness in his eyes as he realized where we were in our relationship and how we had come to this juncture in our lives.

"Andrew, I love you so much," I said as I started to cry. "You have lived with your father now for two years. You know what he is like. Bill and I could never come back to St. Gustave to live. I would love for us to be in the same country, but it can't happen. I was a prisoner in this country. I can't live in the same place as your father. America is freedom to me, and freedom is everything."

"I know, Mum," he said.

During that visit Andrew introduced us to his friends. We took all of them out for pizza. We spent time with him and had dinners together.

We visited again the following year. We followed Andrew in our rental car as we drove to Wakersfield, where he and his friends raced mini cars. Fixing up and racing minis had become their passion.

Andrew drove his Skoda mini much too quickly.

"Bill, if he drives like that he is going to have an accident. I am worried about him," I said as we watched him.

"If it happens, he should be okay. At least the speed limit is lower here."

Chapter 25

Andrew's Skoda

On Friday night, April 16, 1999, Andrew and three friends were stopped at a red light in Southmoorings, near Laura's home. They were in his Skoda. As the light turned green they started through the intersection. A taxi driver to the left of them came speeding through the red light and struck their car broadside. Andrew's Skoda careened down the highway, turning in circles until it came to a stop against the curb a half mile away. Luckily, all of the boys escaped unhurt, but the Skoda was totaled. Neither Juan nor Andrew called to let me know.

Laura finally called me a day later. I was beyond furious that Andrew could have such a serious accident and his father would not call.

"Laura, I am so fearful for his safety. I am afraid for him and more worried that when it does happen, Juan won't even call me. Andrew will die and I won't even know," I said as I sobbed.

"Nadean, that is crazy thinking. Andrew will be fine. You are upset now, but it will be okay. Andrew is coming up to visit you in a few days. Enjoy your time with him. Don't let it be spoiled by this. Andrew and his friends are fine. No one was hurt."

Andrew was scheduled to fly up to the US for the Easter vacation and I was going to pick him up at the airport. The night before, Andrew called to say his dad was flying up with him and would bring him to our home. Juan and Andrew flew to Ft. Lauderdale on Friday, April 23. This was supposed to be Andrew's and my time to spend together, but rather than bring him to me, Juan kept Andrew so they could spend time together in Ft. Lauderdale.

I was hurt, upset and angry. I desperately wanted to see Andrew after his accident and to spend our short week together.

Andrew and I talked on the phone. I expressed my disappointment, hurt and anger.

In a moment of utter anguish, I told Andrew that he could go back to St. Gustave with his dad if that was what he wished, as I was beyond being jerked around by his father.

They were scheduled to fly back on Sunday, April 25. I was extremely upset over our interrupted visit.

On Monday, I called an attorney friend, Paul, and related what had happened. I was embarrassed and ashamed that I had acted in this manner. It was not at all like me.

"Forget all of it, Nadean," he said. "Call Andrew now. Apologize for your behavior and tell him you will pay for a flight today for him to come up and spend the rest of the week with you. Whatever it costs, just do it now."

I emailed Andrew, waited a few minutes, and called.

"Andrew, I am sorry for all of the confusion. I don't care what happened. I love you and I want you to come up and spend the rest of the week with me. Bill is traveling, so it will be just the two of us. Will you come?"

"Sure, Mum," he said and laughed. "Of course! Organize it and let me know. I love you too."

I booked a flight for Wednesday, returning Sunday. In the interim, I started to plan a trip for him that would be memorable. After such a fiasco, I wanted our time together to be special.

I met him at the Miami airport and went straight to News Café on South Beach for a late lunch. We talked about his studies, his plans and his dreams. "I really want to study mechanical engineering, but Dad insists that I complete an accounting course at Lyntech. Even Uncle Roberto thinks I should follow my dreams, not Dad's."

"Andrew, accounting can always help, especially if you ever decide to open your own business. Perhaps you could finish that course and then come up here to study engineering at FAU. Your college is paid for and the funds are just sitting there waiting for you to use them."

We visited the beautiful Venetian pool in Coral Gables and shopped at a record store in Coconut Grove. During the next few days we bought surf jams in Coral Springs, and T-shirts and jeans at the Gap.

He, Juan and Chantal were planning a trip to France during the summer, so we shopped at Borders for CDs and books on France for his trip.

We spent time at the gym working out. I had mailed a book to him in St. Gustave to study for his Florida driver's license. He took the test, passed, and did the driving part in my Volvo.

"This is not a fun car, Mum. Way too slow."

"Yes, but if you lived here that is what you would be driving—an old Volvo, which is the safest car on the road."

We visited the teachers at his old elementary school, then drove to Moroso Park in West Palm Beach to watch Porsche cars racing. On the way back, we stopped at African Lion Safari.

A sports car dealership in Ft. Lauderdale specialized in exotic vehicles, so we walked around and I took photos of him standing beside Maseratis, Porsches, Jaguars and a Viper.

We had meals at some of his favorite places—curry and roti at Shalimar, Chinese food, meatball subs at Subway.

After dinner we went to the movies, a funny, teen version of *Taming of the Shrew* called *10 Things I Hate About You*, and *The Matrix* with Keanu Reeves, which he loved. I had bought the movie *Mambo Kings* because I loved the music and story about two brothers coming to America from Cuba, their struggles and the love story. The ending, in which one brother dies in a car accident, upset Andrew. I explained that it was not based on a true story, but he was still unhappy. I was so sorry to have put that movie on, and apologized.

"I have a girlfriend, Mum," Andrew said one evening over dinner. "Her name is Sandra. We met on New Year's Eve. She is an engineer and is petite and blonde. She exercises a lot, just like you. She has been encouraging me to pursue my engineering studies here in the US. She got her degree here and thinks I should do the same."

We had an absolutely fabulous few days together. Andrew seemed to be more sensitive to me on this trip and to wanting to make it a great time as well.

Bill returned from his trip late Friday night. On Sunday, just prior to our departure for the airport, Isabel and her new husband, Kurt, arrived for a week's stay.

The trip to the Miami airport had always been difficult for both of us. Usually when I took Andrew to the airport, he kissed me good-bye, turned and walked onto the plane.

This time, we joked and laughed. We bought magazines for his trip and had lunch at Burger King.

Just before disappearing around the corner of the gangway he turned, gave me a great big smile, and waved. My heart caught in my throat at his sudden expression of love.

I waved back and waited for him to disappear before bursting into tears.

I called to make sure he arrived safely, and for the next couple of weeks we exchanged emails about the car his father was purchasing to replace his Skoda.

"Mum, it is a secondhand car and is not roadworthy. Anthony's dad, who is a mechanic, checked it out and told Dad it was not a good car. He shouldn't buy it. And it will not travel at ninety miles per hour," Andrew said.

"Andrew, I can't believe your father would buy a car that is not roadworthy. And you shouldn't be driving at ninety miles per hour, anyway. Please promise me that you will be careful. Your Skoda was totaled just a month ago."

"Yes, Mum, but that wasn't my fault. It was the taxi driver."

"Okay, sweetheart. Whatever car your Dad buys, just promise you will be careful, please?"

• • •

The phone rang at 5:00 a.m. on Saturday, May 22.

Bill jumped up and grabbed the receiver. I turned toward him in bed.

I thought of Aunt Roberta immediately, as she had not been well. "What is it, Bill?"

He listened, turned white and looked at me. "It's Silvain. There's been a car accident."

"Is Andrew okay?"

"Andrew was killed in the accident!"

"No!" I screamed.

I jumped out of the bed and grabbed the phone. "Silvain, what happened?"

"Aunty Nadean, I am so sorry. Dad bought a car for Andrew yesterday. Andrew took it out last night. At midnight, he offered to drive a friend home. When they were coming around the Six Shore Highway, they started to race another car. As they turned a corner near Meake's, there were cars stopped ahead of them. They had nowhere to go and could not stop.

"They hit the brakes and the two cars went in two different directions. Both cars were in accidents. The fellows in the other car survived. Andrew and his friend hit the steel pole at Meake's. Andrew's car split in two. Andrew and his friend were thrown from the car. Andrew's friend survived and is in hospital. Andrew lived for a few minutes and died at Meake's."

"Oh my God, no, Silvain. Please tell me it isn't true, please?"

"I'm so sorry, Aunty Nadean."

"Silvain, why didn't Juan call me?"

"He couldn't do it, Aunty Nadean. He asked me to call you."

I dropped the phone and screamed the gut-wrenching scream of so many mothers who have lost their child. I curled up into a ball on the floor beside the bed and rocked back and forth like a wild animal looking for escape.

"No, God, no! Please, God, no!"

Bill tried to grab and hold on to me but I would not let him touch me.

I had gone mad with shock and grief.

When I regained some of my sanity, I permitted Bill to put his arms around me and hold me.

"I have to call the airlines and organize flights for today. I need to get to him as soon as possible. I need to make calls to my family and our friends," I said.

The first person I called was Laura, who was sobbing.

"Fly down this afternoon if you can, Nadean, and stay with me."

"Laura, do you think Juan will let me help organize Andrew's funeral? It will be the last thing I will ever do for him."

"I don't know, Nadean. We can ask."

When I called Aunt Roberta, it took her a while to absorb the news, as it was so early in the morning. She had shared in my joy at giving birth, prayed with me during my fight with ovarian cancer, suffered with me during the separation, divorce, and subsequent custody battle. She tried to comfort me as only a loving, yet grieving family member can.

"Nadean, you might not remember, but Papere died on this same day thirty-two years ago. Andrew is with Papere."

I called one St. Gustavian friend in Miami, who called all of the others. Six of our friends met us at the Miami airport.

Molly, who had pull with the airline, organized a private room for us in the VIP section of BWIA's departure lounge. My friends sat quietly with us while we waited for our flight.

Sometimes we talked about inconsequential things, but not about

Andrew. Other times we were just quiet. In their own silent way, they grieved along with us. When our flight was called we all hugged, and Bill and I walked to the plane alone.

Our flight landed in the dark at 8:40 p.m. We left the baggage area an hour later and as the sliding doors opened, we saw Laura and Isabel standing there waiting for us. They gathered me in their arms and as we cried, I crumbled with grief.

"We called the funeral home, as you requested, Nadean," Laura said as she held me. "There is an attendant waiting to let you in to see Andrew."

While I had always known that St. Gustave was a third-world country, I was not prepared for the funeral home.

Upon our arrival, the attendant approached us carrying a flashlight. "Hello, this is my friend, Nadean Stone," Laura said. "She has come to see her son, Andrew Rivero. Can you take us to him please?"

We followed the man to an area outside the main building. There were long box-like structures, one on top of the other, reaching up to six feet in height. They were refrigerator-type boxes that one would see in a morgue in the US. He reached down and pulled the box that was directly on the ground out toward us. I gasped in horror. Andrew was inside the box. I fell to my knees beside him. I touched his face and his long soft hair. He was cold, but looked so peaceful. Laura, Isabel and Bill crouched down beside me.

"Look, Laura," I said, "he doesn't even have a scratch. He looks so peaceful. He is a beautiful boy, isn't he?"

They all said, "Yes, he is."

I touched his forehead and kissed it. They waited patiently. "Nadean, you've had a long day," Laura finally said. "Perhaps we should go home now so you can rest."

"I can't leave him here like this! It is a horrible place and he is alone. I just want to lie down here beside him for the night."

"We know, but you can't do that, Nadean. Let's go home and we will make plans tomorrow."

Laura made a warm milk drink for me, orange juice for Bill, and put us to bed in her room. I was unable to sleep thinking about Andrew alone in that dark vault and wished I had stayed with him, as crazy as it must have sounded. I was suddenly afraid of the dark. I wanted the light left on, so Bill acquiesced.

I can't remember when I fell asleep.

Chapter 26

Laura

Our friends arrived at Laura's house on Sunday morning to hug, talk and spend time with us. Laura moved around quietly; smiling, greeting friends, making coffee and offering breakfast to everyone.

After Laura answered a knock at the door, she came back into the living room and touched me on the shoulder.

"It is Juan, Nadean. He is here to see you. What do you want me to do?"

"Let him in," I said.

With that, she, Bill and everyone else in the house disappeared. I don't remember seeing them go or where they went. Suddenly I was alone. I stood and walked to the door.

Juan stood inside the entry, waiting for me. I looked at his ashen face, walked up to him, and gathered him into my arms. I held on to him tightly and would not let him go. He relaxed and fell into my embrace. We cried and as our tears mingled together, I touched his face and stroked his hair. I buried my face in his neck.

"It is okay, Juan," I said, as he sobbed. "It is not your fault. It is not your fault."

We stood there and clung to one another for several minutes.

I took his hand and guided him to a chair in the living room. I sat on the sofa close to him and held his hands.

"Andrew loved you very much, Juan, you know that. I loved you too, very much, you must remember that."

He looked at me and nodded. His grief was palpable.

"We had a beautiful, wonderful boy together," I said. "Now, we have to

159

plan his funeral and we must do it together. It will be the last thing we will ever do for him. I hope you will let me be involved in organizing it."

"You can handle the whole thing, Nadean. Organize it however you wish. Just let me know if you want me to do anything."

We talked more about Andrew and his funny little ways. We smiled the sad smile of parents who were grieving and trying to hold it all together. We agreed to meet with the minister to plan the service. We also would meet with the funeral director and visit Andrew together at the funeral home. I walked Juan to the door.

He turned and said, "If you want to see Andrew's bedroom at Grandview, you can come over."

Bill, Laura and our friends reappeared. They had all rushed upstairs into Laura's bedroom to give us privacy.

Bill and I drove to Grandview. We were greeted by Juan, Roberto, Alice and Guillermo.

I had not seen this family for ten years. The irony was not lost on us, but our pain superseded all else. Alice swept me up into her arms. As a mother she could readily imagine my grief. She had just lost her grandson and was visibly shaken.

Juan led Bill and me up the stairs. As we entered Andrew's room I grabbed his pillow and placed it over my face. His smell was still fresh. Juan closed the door. Bill and I sat on his bed. I touched his sheets and laid down on the bed. I walked to his closet, opened the doors and looked at all of the beautiful new clothes I had bought for him four short weeks ago.

I gathered them up and buried my face, breathing in his smell. When I was totally spent, Bill and I walked downstairs to say good-bye.

Many friends visited all day long and into the night.

Isabel would be with us every night and often during the day. That evening Laura and I started planning Andrew's funeral service, the order of the prayers, hymns, who would speak, who would sing and what pieces were chosen. We asked Wanda Perez to read *The Child's Prayer.*

Juan picked us up on Monday morning. I sat in front, and Bill in back. "The car I bought for Andrew was not roadworthy," Juan said as he drove us to the funeral home. "I could have bought a new car that was roadworthy, but I didn't do it." He waited silently.

I couldn't believe he just shared this startling news with us. Was this his full and final confession? Was he looking for absolution from me, or condemnation? I turned to look at him. We had lost everything already. I could not further wound the father of my child.

"Juan, Andrew was going to race any car that you bought for him whether it was roadworthy or not. They were racing, driving fast, and came upon cars that were stopped. They had nowhere to go. Because of how it happened, it was a difficult accident to survive."

The funeral home had prepared Andrew's body for our visit. He was in an enclosed room, on a table. Juan and I stood at the side of the table across from one another. As the sheet was removed, we stared at our beautiful son.

His body had not been damaged in the accident; only his arm had been broken. The cord leading to his spine had been severed, and that caused his death. We marveled at our beautiful child, touched his face and hair, kissed his forehead and left.

Laura picked Bill and me up from the funeral home and we drove to the printing company that would prepare the programs for Andrew's service. "We will need six hundred, Nadean," Laura said. "Juan is a senator in the government. The church will be packed with the entire cabinet, the prime minister, the president, government ministers, his friends, our friends and children from St. Andrew's school."

We did a final review and approved the program for printing.

I asked for a private meeting with Sandra, Andrew's girlfriend, and met her that afternoon at a small cafe. She was as Andrew had described: blonde, petite and pretty.

"We met on Old Year's night," Sandra said as we sat together. "I saw him in the distance. He was absolutely gorgeous! So tall and handsome. He had such a big, beautiful smile and striking brown eyes like yours. I asked my friends who he was. I approached him and introduced myself. He was shy, very polite, and had a great sense of humor.

"After Old Year's, we saw each other often. I called him Drew. He loved being at my place. He talked about you and his father. He said you were very proper, but that you lived in a little protective cocoon that helped you cope. You thought everyone around you was wonderful and everything would turn out all right, but life was not like that. He admired your ability to cope in that way, but didn't think it was realistic. He was very deep in his thinking.

"He had issues with his dad. He didn't want to study accounting. He really wanted to study engineering. I encouraged him, but he could not go against his father. I am so glad that you reminded him of the college funds you saved in the US, and your idea to use them after the accounting course.

"He told me about the confusion on his last trip to the US. He was so glad when you called and offered him a ticket to go up on that Wednesday. He loved all of the special things you organized for him. He loved *The Matrix*, seeing all of those exotic cars and getting his Florida driver's license. I am so happy that you had that time with him. I loved him very much, Nadean.

"Drew also told me about the court case. He said he remembered one afternoon when Juan had him in his arms and was choking you on the landing. I couldn't believe it. Did that really happen?"

I was stunned.

"Sandra, right now I can't remember anything. It must have happened if Andrew remembered it. My mind is a total blank. I can't think right now. Sandra, I need to know, did Andrew know how much I loved him? It is really important to me."

"Oh, yes, Nadean, he knew."

"Thank you, Sandra, and thank you for loving my son. I am so glad that he was able to experience love. Good-bye. I'll see you at the funeral tomorrow."

In lieu of flowers, we asked mourners to send funds that would be used to buy books for a library at a local school. The library room would be named in Andrew's honor.

The church was filled to capacity and overflowed into the street. I stood inside the entry, greeted the mourners and shook hands.

"Hello, I am Andrew's mother. Thank you for coming today," was my refrain.

The St. Andrew's schoolchildren arrived in their school uniforms. I was enormously touched by this outpouring of support and love for our young son. One lone red rose had been placed on top of the casket. I assumed it was from Sandra.

The service was led by the archbishop, who, as bishop, had christened Andrew eighteen years earlier. We had come full circle.

After the service, Juan invited us to join him and his family at Grandview. There would be a large gathering with food and drinks. This was really more than I could bear, but I told Bill and Laura that we must attend. I reconnected with members of Juan's family, his brother Andres, aunts, uncles and cousins.

"I would like to leave now," I said when I found Bill and Laura an hour later.

We had not eaten all day, so we drove to La Coquette for a late lunch. Laura, Karley and her boyfriend, Kirk, Alex, Bill and I sat down and ordered. We had accomplished this last task for Andrew and were emotionally spent.

The grim reality of my life now settled in.

"When I discovered that I had cancer, I made a pact with God," I said to the group. "I asked him to let me live until Andrew was eighteen. If God let me live until then, Andrew would have a good grounding, he would have my morals and be able to get on with his life if I passed.

"Well, God kept our bargain. However, instead of taking me when

Andrew was eighteen, he took Andrew. What do I do now? No children to love or care for, no wedding to plan, no grandchildren, no christenings, nothing. I don't have anything left in my life to look forward to. My life is over."

"Nadean," Laura said as she took my hand, "I love you and I give my children to you to love. They are yours. Their children are your grandchildren. That is my gift to you."

I looked at Karley and Alex and they smiled. They were not surprised by their mother's generosity. In a moment of unbearable grief, my dearest friend, my sister, gave her life to me and I was beyond grateful.

That afternoon, Laura asked me to rest.

"Nadean, we have between forty and fifty people coming over tonight. We are going to celebrate Andrew's life. Our friends and his are coming. Put your nightgown on and go to bed for at least an hour. I know you can't sleep, but just rest. It will be a long night and you have an early flight tomorrow."

Bill had gone to visit our friend Jeremy. Jeremy had had a fall and had broken his leg in multiple places, and so was unable to attend Andrew's funeral. Jeremy was distraught over our loss and his inability to be with us.

Upon his return, Bill said he had never seen Jeremy cry, but Jeremy had cried over Andrew. Jeremy's injury would develop into an embolism, and he passed away ten days later. I have believed ever since that Jeremy and my Andrew are together watching over and protecting us.

Now, when I pray to God and thank him for some kindness, I always thank Andrew and Jeremy as well.

Laura came to the bedroom door when I was in bed and told me that Sandra was there to see me.

"Laura, I feel so weak, I can't stand. Can you ask her to come up here please?"

Sandra stood at the door, grief-stricken. I tapped the bed beside me and she climbed in next to me.

"I had to leave Juan's house. Chantal and Juan are arguing about something and Silvain is being impossible. There is so much confusion and tension over there. On this special day, I thought everyone could get along."

I put my arms around her and held her tightly as she rested her head on my chest and cried.

"I loved Drew so much, and I am going to miss him. I know your suffering is so much greater than mine, but I am hurting so much. I don't know what I will do without him."

"I know, sweetheart," I said. "There is a lot of pain at Juan's house right now. Lots of emotion that they will need to work through. Give them space. We will recover in time. We can't see that now, but it will happen. We all have to go through our grieving."

Laura again came to the bedroom door. "Four of Andrew's friends are here to visit."

"Well, we can't all fit in here. I'll put on a dressing gown and we'll come down."

Anthony, Martin, Justin and Marissa shared so many funny stories about Andrew, we were in hysterics at the joy of the memories. Car mechanics, mini racing, playing his guitar in their band, roller blading, driving around in his Skoda.

Laura's gathering for us that evening was a blessing. A chance for all to reminisce about Andrew and to say good-bye. At 1:30 a.m. Laura and another friend, Jeannette, packed the white roses from the altar at Andrew's funeral for me to take back to the US. She said we could dry them and they would keep forever. I was not sure how we would get these past customs.

"I don't know how I am going to get on that plane tomorrow and resume my life while Andrew stays behind. I am so dreading that flight tomorrow."

Laura drove us to the airport. We clung to one another, said good-bye, and Bill and I started our trip back to the US. I no longer thought of it as home, as my heart was in St. Gustave with Andrew.

The air hostess offered us coffee. I could not speak, so Bill declined for me. He went to the bathroom and returned much later. When the air hostess reappeared, I was crying.

"Mrs. Stone," she said, "I am so very sorry for your loss. I wasn't supposed to take this flight today. My mother is sick and I wanted to stay home with her. One of the attendants called in sick, so I was called out. This is a book I have been reading that I hope will help you. It is called *Chicken Soup for the Soul*. It has really helped me. It is my gift to you. I hope that it will bring you comfort. I wasn't happy about being called out for this flight, but I can see now the hand of God in all of this. God meant for me to take this flight and to accompany you home on this painful journey. I was meant to make sure you arrived home safely. I am going to take care of you and your husband for the rest of this flight. I hope that in time, God grants you peace."

I opened the book and started to read.

Bill completed the customs form. He said he wanted to declare the white roses. I asked him to indicate that we had nothing to declare.

"What will we do when they find the flowers?"

"Go to jail. I don't care. Don't declare and let's see what happens."

As luck would have it, when our luggage slid onto the screen, our customs agent was called to look at another bag. Bill and I watched my bag appear with the flowers clearly visible. Our agent was distracted long enough. When he turned back to the screen, my bag and the flowers were disappearing from view.

As we left the airport with my book and flowers, I smiled at Bill. "God is directing this, you know."

He shook his head in amazement.

Cathie and Molly, the friends who had seen us off when we left, were waiting outside arrivals. We drove to Molly's and they asked me to relate all that had happened. They cried when I cried and laughed at the funny stories Andrew's friends shared.

"I am lost," I said. "I don't know what I will do with my life."

"Nadean," Cathie said, "we pray that you will survive this. You have to. We worry every day now about our children. It is our greatest fear. If you can survive this and go on, we know that we will be able to do so as well if we lose our child."

I found it a heavy burden to place on me.

Two days later, we gathered friends, neighbors and coworkers at our home for a celebration of Andrew's life. On the dining room table I placed photos of Andrew throughout his life, along with the newspapers that reported his accident.

One of the people I had invited was the dean of the engineering department at Florida Atlantic University.

"I read recently, in a book called *Chicken Soup for the Soul*, that what terminally ill children fear the most is that they won't be remembered," I said to the dean. "Andrew enjoyed his week at FAU so much when he was in middle school. My husband and I would like to use his college funds to set up a scholarship in his name.

"It will be called The Andrew Rivero Scholarship Fund and will be for students pursuing a degree in mechanical engineering. We can work on the details later, but that is our wish."

"Mrs. Stone, I am so very grateful that at this time of such immense grief you and your husband are able to find a positive use for Andrew's college funds. You cannot imagine now, but this gift will benefit many young people in the years to come. Thank you so much for thinking of FAU."

Andrew had loved car racing, so Bill arranged to have a commemorative brick placed for him at Homestead Speedway south of Miami. We attended the race and took photos for his friends.

That summer I wrote many letters of gratitude to people who had been so supportive of Andrew, Bill and me. A mutual friend personally delivered my letter to Justice Alfred Warner at his home. When my friend arrived there and told the judge he carried a letter from me, Justice Warner stared at him, took the letter, turned around, and disappeared into his house.

In the letter I told Justice Warner about our life in the US, Andrew's joy in playing baseball and soccer, and his win with the science project that Bill had helped him build. I told him about the flamboyant tree Bill and I planted in our garden for Andrew; the library at the school in St. Gustave; the commemorative brick at Homestead; and the scholarship at FAU.

I told him my reasons for sending Andrew back to live with his father, and that I did not regret my decision, as they had the last five years of Andrew's life to enjoy being together; that I would have regretted it if Andrew had not had the opportunity to live again with his father.

"You cannot know how grateful I am to you for giving my only child to me in 1990. The five years spent with Andrew in the US were the most precious of my life. I don't know what will happen to me now. Andrew would not want me to give up. He would want me to do something useful with my life. So that is what I will try to do. To live whatever life is left to me fully, with purpose, passion and dedication, as Andrew was not able to realize his dreams or goals. I will live my life in such a way as to make him proud, to honor him."

Chapter 27

Annus Horribilis

I called 1999 my horrible year.

No one can prepare you for life without your child. There is no experience upon which to draw.

I watched mothers and their children in the grocery. I stalked them. I wanted to reach out to every mother and tell her to love her child every day, as that child might otherwise pass without knowing he or she was loved. When a child shouted Mum, Mom or Mummy, I turned to look. I was riveted. I longed to hear those words again.

I walked around in a robotic daze. My body was functioning, but my mind and spirit were floating above, watching everything unfold below. I threw myself into work, as it forced me to not think about Andrew during the day, or not to think of him as often. Work became my salvation.

It is impossible to describe adequately, but my heart was literally broken. There was a gnawing emptiness, a great heaviness, a huge weight on my chest that was unbearable. I thought I had gone quite mad and didn't care.

At night, I sat on the sofa and cried. I no longer read, as I couldn't concentrate and it gave me no pleasure. I no longer watched television news or any programs. I cleaned one room in the house each night to give me something on which to concentrate.

After our harrowing escape from St. Gustave, I was haunted for years afterward by the horrendous experience. I would have nightmares in which Juan refused to let me see or talk to Andrew. Juan kept him hidden behind a wrought iron door at his condo, exactly like the day when Isabel and I arrived to take Andrew for the weekend. I would stand outside the front door begging and pleading with Juan to let me see Andrew. I would wake up sobbing after those nightmares. Juan was always trying to keep me from Andrew. This went on for years.

Now, my dreams were of Andrew, and he arrived to tell me he was okay. Sometimes he appeared as a young boy, but more often as a gorgeous, lanky young adult. He stood at the end of my bed, smiling. I walked to him, placed my head on his chest, wrapped my arms around his waist and held him close to me. I found comfort in our visits.

I looked forward to my dreams at night, as it was our peaceful time together.

A reporter called from the *Sun-Sentinel*. He had heard about Andrew's scholarship and wanted to write a story. We met and the story appeared a few days later, but I was unable to find pleasure or enjoyment in anything.

I rarely smiled and never laughed. Friends called. Laura and Isabel wrote. Aunt Roberta called weekly, hoping for progress.

"I don't want to live," I said.

"I know, Nadean," she said, "but you must pray for strength and courage. God will carry you through this as he has done so many times before. You must believe."

"I am not talking to God anymore. I am very angry with him. We made a pact that he would let me live until Andrew turned eighteen. Then he took Andrew when he should have taken me. Then I would have happily given my life for Andrew. I want God to take me too. I want to be with Andrew."

"Nadean, it isn't your time."

I was a lost soul; desolate. Bill was patient, kind, comforting, but he could not help me. He moved around me gingerly, waiting for me to return to him.

• • •

We planned a visit to Sault Ste. Marie that summer so I could spend time with Aunt Roberta. In advance of our visit, I wrote to the hospital where I was born, explained that after the birth of my son I'd begun my quest to find my birth mother, and asked for an appointment.

Aunt Roberta, Bill and I met with Judith Dupois, the administrator of the hospital in Blind River.

"Thank you for meeting with us, Ms. Dupois," I said. "As I explained in my letter, I lost my only child, Andrew, two months ago. I do not have a single blood relative anywhere in the world that I know of. I would like to find my birth mother, if that is possible. She probably married and had more children. I could have brothers and sisters. I have written to all of the adoption agencies in Ontario and none of them can find an adoption record for me.

"If I find my birth family, I have no expectations for any relationship. I would just like to meet them and then I will go away. Can you help me?"

Judith sat to my right, very close to me. Our knees almost touched.

She held a file on her lap.

"Nadean, I have your birth record here," she said, and lifted the file. "I can't understand why it still exists. You were born forty-six years ago.

"Most records have been destroyed by the hospital, but when I received your letter and started my search, I found yours.

"In the record, your mother clearly indicates that she wanted you to be adopted. Whether an adoption actually took place or not does not factor into this. The law in Canada has not changed. We are not permitted to share adoption info with adoptees at this time."

"Surely you must understand that my situation is unique," I said. "I have no one in the world. Is my birth mother's name in that record?"

"Yes, it is."

"And you won't give it to me?

"Nadean, I am so sorry for your loss. I do understand your desire to be reunited with your birth mother. However, the privacy laws in Canada are very strict and I cannot break that confidentiality."

We all sat quietly. I looked at Judith. The urge to reach out, grab that file and run out of the hospital was overwhelming. I didn't care about the consequences. To be so close and then denied this wish was unfathomable. I had to fight for control and to hold myself back.

I looked at Bill and Aunt Roberta and then at Judith.

"Well, there is nothing left for us to do here. Thank you for your time."

Isabel flew to Coral Springs that December to spend Andrew's birthday with me. Bill and I flew to St. Gustave for Christmas and Old Year's. It was the millennium. Aunt Roberta made me laugh for the first time in many months. She was convinced that trains, phones and computers would fail at the midnight hour and the world, as we knew it, would end. She had stored up cans of food and bought a gas mask. She was totally taken in by the hysteria surrounding the millennium. Nothing Bill or I said could convince her otherwise. We called her on January 1 to ask if she was wearing her gas mask.

"Well, Aunt Roberta, you will have cans of food to eat for many months ahead."

Laura, as always, took great care of Bill and me.

Although the holiday week was tinged with sadness for me, I soldiered on.

One year after Andrew's passing I felt that I was no further ahead than I was on the day he died. The night before the anniversary of his death, I sat down at our breakfast table and wrote letters to Bill, Aunt Roberta, Laura and Isabel.

I am not getting any better, I wrote. *I am as grief-stricken as I was a year ago. I will never be whole again. I cannot go on. I hope you understand and will in time forgive me for the pain I am about to cause. I love you, but I need to be with Andrew.*

I sealed the letters, grabbed a bottle of aspirin and a bottle of wine, and sat at the table waiting for the strength to swallow the pills and follow them with the wine. I worried that I might not be successful. I might throw up and then be left in a vegetative state. I didn't want Bill to have to care for me in that state because he wouldn't pull the plug. That would be worse than death.

As I sat and cried, asking God for guidance—which after some time I had begun to do again—Andrew's cat Bonkers jumped up onto my lap. He rubbed his whiskers against my face and neck. I put him on the floor. He jumped back up. He would not go away. I pleaded with him to leave me alone but he kept jumping back up.

I contemplated my choices for two hours. I took a sip of wine, then more. I remembered Cathie and Molly's words: "If you can make it, then we know we can if it happens to us."

I knew that I would disappoint many if I took the pills. How had I been brought so low that I lacked the courage to go on? If I couldn't make it through this unbearable challenge, they would lose all hope.

The clock struck midnight. It was the anniversary of Andrew's death. I realized that death was the easy way out. It took more courage to live. Finding faith, hope and strength to reengage in life took more effort and determination. I held Bonkers close to me, stroked his fur and kissed his head.

I hid the letters in Andrew's bedroom. "Not tonight, God, not tonight," I said.

The first three years after Andrew's passing were the worst.

I took stock on each anniversary as to where I was and whether I could go on. Many mornings as I lay in bed, paralyzed with sorrow, I prayed to God to give me strength to get through the day.

My work kept me sane. During the day I was needed, had to think of others and perform in my role as a legal administrator. It kept me grounded. During the day, I was not overwhelmed with thoughts of Andrew and my all-consuming grief. I forced myself to get up each and every day, go to work and perform my job. Many evenings I thanked God for helping me get through the day.

"Now, God, please help me get through tomorrow."

Years earlier, when applying to universities, I had considered pursuing a degree in journalism. It was my first choice before switching to French and English literature. In 2002, I decided to fulfill my dreams. If Andrew could not realize his, I would pursue mine in his name.

I enrolled at The Connecticut School of Broadcasting in Davie, Florida, and completed a certificate in journalism. I shared with Bill and my friends that my goal was to work at NBC in Miramar. I saw the skepticism on their faces, but they did not discourage me. I was forty-nine years old.

Bill was more vocal. As we sat with Dave and Laurie at dinner, he said, "Nadean, you need to accept that it will probably never happen."

One Saturday, I paid for and attended a broadcasting writing workshop at a local hotel. A famous CBS news producer and author was the featured speaker.

During the breakout lunch session, we were asked to gather in groups to discuss writing techniques for making news stories more powerful. I deliberately joined a group that included the news director for NBC, Jeff Thein, whose name tag I had noticed earlier. The group sat together over lunch and talked about writing techniques. Jeff asked where I worked and what I was doing at the workshop as we walked back to the ballroom together for the afternoon session.

A couple of months later when I, along with five other applicants, interviewed at the NBC station for an intern position, Jeff remembered me.

"I was really impressed that you would pay for the course and give up your Saturday to attend," Jeff said. "I thought that you were taking your career change very seriously. We would like to have you join us here at NBC as an intern.

"We think you would be a great addition to the team. We have many different departments and opportunities for an intern in news production, weather, editing, sports coverage and photography. In which department would you like to work?"

"I would love to work on the news desk."

"Then, it is settled."

On my first day we were short a reporter so Andi, the assignment desk editor, asked me to drive out to Janet Reno's campaign headquarters with a photographer and interview her about a breaking story. Janet was running for governor of Florida and I had worked on her campaign as a volunteer. Although I had resigned my campaign work upon taking the position with NBC, Andi nevertheless reminded me that I needed to remain impartial during the interview.

"In reality, I should not be sending you out as your political leanings are obvious, but no one else is available."

She had to ask Jeff to sign off on this assignment before we left. Andi forewarned me that we might have to go live and I should be ready. We didn't go live but it was great experience on my first day at work. I was able to obtain some great sound bites during the interview that were released in a news package that afternoon.

Andi, Jeff, the other assignment desk editors and the reporters trusted my judgment and professionalism from the start. I was mature and serious about my career. For the next six months I worked closely with the assignment editors and in that short amount of time, with their guidance, developed a keen sense of stories that were newsworthy.

I performed beat calls on a daily basis, reviewed incoming faxes and emails to determine if coverage was required, accessed the wire services throughout the day and monitored police and fire scanners for breaking stories. I summarized developing stories, input relevant data to INews, booked satellite trucks and, with Andi's approval, ordered helicopter coverage when needed.

In addition, I attended the morning producer meetings and pitched story ideas, which were sometimes developed, or managed the assignment desk alone while the editors attended the meeting. Throughout my internship I contributed heavily to NBC6's increasing contact and Rolodex list, a lifeline for any station. When we were short-staffed, I ran the teleprompter for the afternoon broadcasts.

On numerous occasions I was sent with a photographer to cover high-profile federal and civil trials in Ft. Lauderdale and Miami, as well as many breaking stories. I conducted interviews, selected appropriate sound bites and prepared tracks for the afternoon reporters' packages. Although not required, I often worked on Saturdays on the assignment desk and traveled with the reporters and photographers to cover news stories.

Around the station, I was affectionately referred to as the Super Intern. Andi would often say, "I can't get by without you. You have a nose for news."

"Your work ethic is exemplary and your attitude to your internship has been fantastic. You have raised the bar and set a new standard for all future interns and for a quality of work that we will now routinely expect," Jeff said.

I loved being at the station and working at NBC. I was passionate about our work and getting the scoop before another station. The tight timelines involved in capturing the stories was exhilarating. I had reengaged in life and I was finding happiness once again.

When my internship ended, there were no full-time positions open at NBC Miramar. Jeff advised that while my work as a field producer was exemplary, the station no longer had a budget for that position. The reporters had to make do with reporting in the field as best they could without assistance from a field reporter. If I wished to work on-air as a reporter, I would need to relocate to a smaller market and over the next two to five years, work my way back to the Miami market.

I was not keen on uprooting us to a small city, so I returned to law firm management, my second career choice.

Within six months I received a call from Fran Mires at NBC. The station was launching *The Rick Sanchez Show*, a live one-hour daytime talk show.

"If you want the show to succeed, you need to hire Nadean Stone," Jeff said to Fran.

At my interview, Fran offered me a position as booker.

"It is one of the most important positions on any show," Fran said. "A good booker makes the show."

As I had never heard the term, I didn't even know what a booker did! She offered me a salary of $25,000, which was half of what I was making managing law firms. I countered that if she could make it $30,000, I would accept.

Fran was the executive producer and I was the booker/celebrity producer, one of five producers and Fran's right-hand person. Fran tried to alleviate my stress and to encourage me in my new role.

"Right now, you are the most important person in television in South Florida," Fran said. "No station has ever tried a one-hour live talk show, five days per week. Your decisions as to which guests to book and how to convince them to appear is crucial to the show's success."

This only served to frighten me even more. The pressure to succeed was enormous. Failure was not an option.

I booked guests at little or no cost to the show, such as celebrities, chefs, authors, musicians, singers and people with interesting stories. I obtained clip clearance, bios, books and press kits from authors, booked flights, limos and hotels and trained our interns.

We started with computers and an empty database. With the help of the four producers and the interns whom I trained, we created a database of book publishers, public relations contacts, reps for actors and actresses, and experts in diet, exercise and science throughout the United States that was extremely valuable. Every topic was welcome on Rick's show.

In addition to nurturing relationships with them via email and phone, I created an email e-blast every two weeks updating our contacts on our progress and successes with recent guests as well as format changes and new hires. Some nights I stayed at the station until 1:00 a.m. creating my e-blasts. Some of the publicists wrote back with glowing feedback.

When Rick and his cohost were unavailable, I traveled with our photographer and conducted celebrity interviews in the Ft. Lauderdale and Miami area.

Our movie critic, Maria Salas, took me to Los Angeles one weekend to meet some of her celebrity contacts.

Maria traveled to LA every weekend to interview movie stars whose pictures were being released. We shared a room at the Four Seasons. As we waited to catch the bus to that weekend's movie screening, Maria introduced me to Morgan Freeman and his wife, Myrna. Myrna had just written a book and they were on their way to the home of a producer who was hosting a party to celebrate its release.

That evening we sat through the screening of the movie *The Clearing*. The following day, Maria introduced me to its first-time director, Pieter Jan Brugge, and the president of Fox Searchlight Pictures, Peter Rice, who were distributing the film. I helped her prepare questions for her interviews with the stars of the movie, Robert Redford, Helen Mirren and Willem Dafoe.

It was all very new, interesting and exciting for me. I had never experienced such fun at work. I asked Robert Redford if he would appear on Rick's show when he attended the Miami Film Festival in a few months. He readily agreed, as he was keen to promote his latest projects at Sundance.

My persistence as booker resulted in an exclusive one-on-one interview for Rick with John Kerry, who was running for president in 2004, and Paul Burrell, Princess Diana's butler. Everyone was clamoring to book them and I secured it for Rick. Although our show aired locally in South Florida, it had national content and flavor and therefore tremendous appeal.

On numerous occasions our senior line producer, Leigh, who had worked on *Oprah*, *The View* and *Oxygen*, told me, "I have never seen a booker like you—you are a monster booker! If you were in New York, you would be the number one booker in the city. None of my producer friends in New York believe what you do for our show. I appreciate what you do each and every day."

As booker I received invitations to movies, plays, restaurant openings, and the Rockettes Florida tour. I took advantage of all invitations. If Bill did not wish to accompany me, I took my girlfriends. I was given great seats at no cost and we would often go backstage after a show to chat with the stars who had appeared on Rick's show earlier that day.

Gianni Versace's South Beach mansion was sold after his death and made into a private catering and event venue. My girlfriends and I attended the evening launch, sipped champagne, ate great sushi, among many other offerings, toured the house and fully enjoyed this amazing affair. The girls loved our outings.

However, with little fanfare, NBC suddenly canceled our show one afternoon in July of 2004 because Rick had accepted a position as news anchor with CNN in Atlanta. I surmised that he edited the tape from his interview with John Kerry and sent it to CNN.

NBC department heads appeared at 1:00 p.m. with Rick, shared the news of his departure, but not of his new employer, and gave us four hours to cancel all booked guests, pack up, and clear out. We were informed that we had to leave the station by 5:00 p.m. Fran had given birth in late May and was on maternity leave with her family in the Bahamas. I called her and broke the news.

I was left with the nightmare of terminating our staff, packing up our offices and calling the guests who were at a hotel next door preparing to walk to the station for the 2:00 p.m. taping.

I had booked the following guests in June prior to the termination of Rick's show and had to call their reps to cancel: Spike Lee, promoting the Black Film Festival; Bill Clinton, promoting his book release; Robert Redford;

Stephen Baldwin; and Teresa Heinz Kerry, wife of John Kerry.

When Fran returned from maternity leave, we met for lunch and talked about opening our own company to produce local shows. We both needed a regular income, though, so we dispensed with that plan. I tried to obtain a position with television stations in South Florida as a producer.

However, after working in such an exciting environment with Fran, I found it difficult to work as a producer in a news department. Once again, I returned to law firm management, which offered me stability and a significantly higher income.

Chapter 28

DNA Testing and Olivia

Aunt Roberta passed away on January 19, 2017, four days after her ninety-third birthday.

I lost the loving, caring woman who replaced Grandma as my mother, and I was crushed. Who would I chat with every Sunday? Who would make me laugh? A yawning emptiness lay before me. At the family lunch following Aunt Roberta's funeral, my cousin Bev, a nurse, offered to help find my birth mother. When I returned home, I thought about her offer. Was it worth one last shot?

In 1973, I applied at the Registrar General's office in Toronto for my long form birth certificate, as I had been told that it would contain the name of my birth mother. In completing the form, I was required to indicate the names of my parents. I explained to the officials that I did not know the names of my birth parents, only my adoptive parents.

They instructed me to place those names on the forms. I was confused.

Ten days later, the administrative staff at the Ministry in Toronto provided me with a Delayed Statement of Birth and a small birth certificate indicating that my name was Nadean Rita Russell and that I had been born to Sydney Russell and Lorida (Rita), *nee* Tessier. The letterhead stated it was from the Office of the Registrar General, Province of Ontario, the Vital Statistics Act.

The bottom section of the form said, "I register this birth by signing this statement," and it was signed by an administrative official. I told them the information was incorrect, that I had been adopted. They looked at me, perplexed, and said that was impossible as I had never been adopted and the Russells were my parents. I was visibly upset as I left the office.

In 1980, after Andrew's birth, I wrote to numerous agencies in Ontario inquiring about my adoption. Once I had a child, I wanted to know about our background. The agencies responded that they could not find an adoption record. I thought it must be a mistake. Surely official documents had been signed and filed. You can't just give a baby away!

My cousin Heather contacted me in 2011 via email.

The law had changed in Ontario, Canada, providing adoptees the right to access their birth records.

Heather and I were over the moon with excitement.

She was overjoyed that she could finally fulfill a childhood promise to help find my birth mother. My birthday wish every year since I was a child was that I would meet my mother one day and learn of my history. Heather and I worked solidly for the next three years, from 2011 to 2014, trying to find her.

Heather visited the hospital and spoke to the records custodian. She was initially willing to answer Heather's questions about my birth and to assist. However, after an investigation of the hospital records and a consultation with the CEO of the hospital, she contacted the hospital's attorney and subsequently refused to communicate further with Heather. She would communicate with me only.

I completed the required government forms for Service Ontario applying for Post Adoption Birth Information under Section 48.1 of the Vital Statistics Act and forms for the Adoption Disclosure Register.

I wrote to agencies such as Children's Aid Society in Algoma District and Toronto; Catholic Children's Aid; Ministry of Community and Social Services; and to Parent Finders and Origins Canada seeking information on my adoption and assistance in my search.

Service Ontario in North Bay provided a response to my request in August 2011:

After reviewing your application, we have determined the following:
Your application for disclosure of adoption information cannot be completed

because there is no adoption order registered with Ontario's Office of the Registrar General that matches the information you have provided.

Your file has been closed and no further action will be taken relating to this request.

Heather visited the town hall in Blind River. Every birth at the hospital must be registered there. She searched for girls born in December 1952. There were no girls registered for the month of December. There were two boys born and registered in December. So, the hospital was registering births as they were required to do, by law.

She looked in January, February and March 1953 to see if there was a late registration, but could not find one for any girls.

"Odd," she said. "Why wasn't your birth registered?"

I placed my story on numerous Canadian adoption websites.

I called a representative at the Office of the Registrar General in Toronto, where I had once again submitted forms asking for my long form birth certificate. I asked the rep to confirm if an adoption had ever taken place.

She said she would check their records, consult with her supervisor, and call me back.

She advised, "Nothing in connection with your birth was done correctly. You were never registered with the Canadian government as having been born. The hospital should have registered your birth as required by law."

She looked at my file and said, "Until you applied for a birth certificate in 1973 we had no evidence that you existed. By virtue of supplying the only parental names and birth info that you knew of, you unknowingly registered your own birth.

"The hospital should have called in the Children's Aid Society to supervise an adoption and schedule visits to the Russells' home. Nothing was done according to law."

She said that I had "an actionable case against the hospital."

In December 2011, I hired an attorney, Paul, in Sault Ste. Marie to file a complaint with the information and privacy commissioner against Blind River District Hospital (previously St. Joseph's Hospital) asking for my personal health records and for Release of Adoption Information under the revised law for adoptees.

After many months and numerous letters back and forth I was sent a letter and a document from the records custodian on hospital letterhead. She wrote the following:

As it pertains to you only, I am able to share this information. The document was signed by Sister Dympna and Sid and Rita Russell as follows:
January 11th, 1953.
"We, the undersigned Mr. & Mrs. S. E. Russell have adoped [spelled incorrectly] to-day a Female Babe of three weeks from The St. Joseph's General Hospital, Blind River, Ontario."
Rita Russell S E Russell Sister Dympna

A second letter arrived a few weeks later from the hospital regarding our Request for Release of Adoption Information:

The threshold in this case is that we are not reasonably satisfied that the records we have on file relate to yourself. There is no conclusive evidence of this in that the female child, adoptive parents, and natural mother are not in any way linked. Only the date of birth and discharge date correlate with the information provided. The information recorded is too vague and unreliable for us to conclusively determine the relationship between all parties.

The records we do have on hand relate primarily to a birth mother and we cannot release any identifying information about her, including her name. If we were satisfied that the birth records did relate to you we would have to sever the record obliterating the birth mother's personal information. Absent a court order or the birth mother's consent the Blind River District Health Center has no authority to disclose this information.

Despite that assertion, a few weeks later a second document was sent to me, in error, by the hospital.

It was my birth mother's hospital doctor chart with her name, age, religion and nationality redacted.

It indicated that a healthy female child had been born on December 18, 1952. Birth mother was admitted at 3:50 a.m. on December 18 and discharged at 1:00 p.m. on December 24th.

S. W. W. D. – S for Single.

Working Diagnosis: Normal Pregnancy. Result: Cured, Improved, Unimproved, Died

Observation – Cured!

Physician – J. Pigeon Pregnancy cas (which meant Children's Aid Society).

Doctor's notes in his handwriting – *Normal delivery and postpartum baby discharged good condition. F/C Dec 18/52. F/C stood for Female Child.*

The Ontario Privacy Commission then stepped in and asked Paul, my attorney, to prevail upon me to withdraw my complaint against the hospital, or the commission would render an opinion on my complaint that might seal my records forever. The commissioner did not actually state this on record, but indicated such to Paul via telephone.

Further, I had till 5:00 p.m. that day to confirm the withdrawal. Paul said I would not have future access to the records or any future legal recourse. The privacy commissioner's office was prepared to deny my complaint on the basis that I had "no legal right to access the third- party records of my birth mother."

The commissioner was furious that my birth mother's hospital doctor chart had been mistakenly sent to me. On one hand the hospital denied the connection between me and my mother. Yet the hospital's records custodian was confident enough in our mother-baby link to send this document to me.

Paul advised me to withdraw my complaint.

"We can always refile in a year or two but we don't want the commissioner to render an opinion that will seal your file forever. This woman is really annoyed and she will do it."

I viewed it as an unjustifiable threat from my own government and after an angry, heated argument with Paul, I agreed most reluctantly. He withdrew my complaint prior to the 5:00 p.m. deadline.

However, I continued to communicate with the hospital on my own. I argued that I had been left alone in their facility for three weeks, from December 24, 1952, to January 11, 1953, and so a separate medical record should exist in my name or the name of a Jane Doe. I asked the hospital for access to that record. Request denied.

I hired a detective agency in North Bay to find my birth mother. Clarissa, a detective at the agency, was assigned to my case. I provided the info that was given to my grandmother by Mother Superior Dympna in 1955. Clarissa was not able to find her.

I had been informed by a reliable source that the nuns kept separate records for unwed mothers and their babies at the Motherhouse in North Bay. I wrote to the Mother Superior asking if any records of my mother and my birth existed. I asked them to research all documents in storage and offered to pay for same. They wrote back indicating they had conducted thorough research and no such records existed.

After completing government forms in 1973, 1980, 1999 and 2011 through 2014, fighting the hospital and the Privacy Commission, registering my story on all Canadian adoption sites, contacting Parent Finders and Origins Canada, and hiring an attorney and a detective agency, we discovered that in fact, I had never been formally adopted.

I had simply been given away. It was like going to the pound and picking up a puppy!

I can only be grateful that Sister Dympna did not send me to an orphanage but waited three weeks for the Russells to appear!

Now I was caught in a catch-22. Had I been formally adopted I would have all the rights accorded other Ontario adoptees, such as access to my birth records. I was being discriminated against through no fault of my own by my own government.

I argued with my attorney that the law was discriminatory in its application and in the spirit of the intent of the law. As a Canadian citizen, I should have been entitled to the same justice that is accorded other Ontario adoptees; access to the birth records should extend to illegally adopted children like me. He understood, but was powerless to help any further.

In addition, if my birth parents were still alive and trying to find me, they would be experiencing similar difficulties. At the end of 2014 I finally accepted, with great reluctance, that I might never find my birth mother. It would never happen. Everyone involved in and after my birth had failed me.

Within days of Bev's offer of assistance, the desire to find my birth mother resumed with increased intensity. This would be my final effort. I returned to the Canadian Adoptees Registry and G's Adoption Registry websites and updated my contact information with my personal email address.

My previous email, set up in 2011, directed respondents to contact me at my former law firm, but I was currently semi-retired. I updated my info at Origins Canada and Parent Finders and ordered a DNA kit from Ancestry.

I wrote to the hospital in Blind River and put them on notice:

Annette, hello again,

I have decided to revive my efforts to find my birth parents. Please keep all of my records in a safe place. If you retire please email me so that I know my records are being maintained by your replacement. Please confirm receipt of this email.

Thank you,

Nadean Stone, MBA, CLM,
DOB December 18, 1952 at St. Joseph's Hospital in Blind River

Vicki, a volunteer with G's Adoption Registry, corresponded with me about the efforts I had made thus far in my search.

When I shared that I had received my mother's doctor chart from the hospital in error and that the hospital's records custodian had redacted her name, age, nationality and religion, Vicki responded immediately:

Nadean,
In the past when I received similar documents, I have held them up to the window with sunlight streaming in behind them. That works sometimes. Try it. Let me know.

I rummaged through my box of documents from 2011 to 2014. I had made so many copies of the chart sent to me in the mail I wasn't sure I would find the master.

Finally, amongst all of the papers, I found the doctor chart with the word *Original* I had written at the top. I ran to the window and held the paper up, with the sun streaming in behind it.

Unbelievably, I could clearly read that she was European, R. C., for Roman Catholic, age 26, and that one of her names at the end of the name line looked like Ann, Anne or Janes, a Croatian name.

I was beyond ecstatic. It was a gift from God. Vicki was overjoyed. Now my focus settled on deciphering her full name. It became my obsession.

Many days thereafter I stood by the window trying to see more letters in the name.

Bill said, "I don't see anything that you are seeing. If you don't stop that, you will go blind."

I was not deterred.

On February 7, one week after updating my website posts, I received an email from a woman named Olivia.

She had been born in Canada and after reading my updated posting felt a strong urge to reach out to me. Olivia called and we spoke for an hour.

"Nadean," Olivia said. "I am a DNA genetic genealogist. It is my second degree. I am also a volunteer 'Search Angel.' We are a group of people who help reunite adoptees with their parents. I have helped five people before you and, in each case, we found their birth parents. All of my previous clients were men. You would be the first female I am working with. I am retired. I am not looking for anything from this, except to help you. It has become my passion, reuniting adoptees with their parents."

"Olivia, this won't be as easy as your previous clients. I was never formally adopted."

When I related my story, she was shocked.

"There is no way that could have happened. The hospital could not simply have given a baby away without recording the transfer, calling in Children's Aid and filing adoption papers."

"Well, it happened with me. Do you still want to help?"

"Absolutely. It will just be more challenging!"

Another gift from God! And off we went.

I had taken a DNA test with 23 and Me in 2012, but did not know how to interpret the results or what to do with them. Olivia gave me a quick primer on centimorgans, DNA, SNPs, haplogroups and how to review and understand the connections with my new third and fourth "cousins."

Olivia provided this analysis of my 23 and Me results:

You are 49.2% Balkan, or a total of 56.4% Southern European. So next step was to check those closest to you with .50% or more DNA that matches yours — 3rd cousins. You have one very close match at .95% who could be a 2nd cousin, however, they are anonymous and a female. Six people listed where their mothers and fathers were from and it was Croatia and/or Slovenia. Serbo-Croatian suffixes for last names are ic, cic, kic, vic, vac, sic, or end in ar, ak, ja, za.

Most have the acute accent over the c, any s, or letter z. So, we know your birth mother is Croatian with a like surname.

"Nadean," she said, "with adoptees, because we don't know the parents, we have to start in the 1850s with great-great-grandparent connections and work our way down to your parents, making connections through your third and fourth cousins down to second and hopefully first cousins. That is why we need to communicate with them and ask them to cooperate with us."

Olivia and I divided our responsibilities. I would send messages through the 23 and Me portal to all of my cousins asking them to share their DNA and any family surnames as well as residences in Europe, the US or Canada and any other info or family tree, explaining that it was to help find my birth mother.

A contact in Blind River who had worked at the hospital shared that she had seen my birth record and thought my mother's first name might be Teresa with a last name ending in ski or skie.

I sent a message to more than a hundred cousins:

Hello, my mother was Slovenian. She emigrated to North Bay in late 1940s. She became pregnant with me in 1952 and traveled to St. Joseph Hospital in Blind River to give birth to me on December 18, 1952. She left me behind to be adopted. Birth Father was an intern at St. Joseph Hospital in North Bay. She was 26 in 1952, her first name was Teresa or Tereza or Theresa. She was from Croatia or Slovenia, was a nurse and or worked in housekeeping at St. Joseph Hospital in North Bay. She would be 90 now. I am hoping to reconnect with her or with any full or half siblings. I have no blood relatives that I know of. I am 64 and started my search in 1973. Would you be kind enough to share haplogroup for your

mother, and or father, and if you have a family tree with descendants? It would be
immensely helpful to me. Thank you so very much.

From the responses, Olivia created spreadsheets of the "cousin" DNA connections, their family surnames and the towns, or parishes, in Europe in which they were born.

The majority replied quickly, sharing as much information as they had. We didn't hear back from some for months, as they didn't visit the 23 and Me site on a regular basis.

I sent repeat requests to the ones who hadn't replied. We also asked those who had initially responded to download their DNA results to GEDmatch, a website created for adoptees. DNA results for 23 and Me, Ancestry, Family Search and other DNA testing sites could be downloaded to GEDmatch.

Olivia would then compare all the data and run further tests to determine the connections to me and my birth parents.

As the months progressed, many of the "cousins" became invested in my search and sought out other relatives to provide additional information. They started communicating with us on their personal email and provided their cell numbers so we could talk to them.

One cousin's aunt was a close connection to me. The aunt was in the hospital, dying.

My cousin told her my story and asked her aunt if she could share her aunt's DNA with Olivia. The aunt, on her deathbed, kindly agreed.

Her DNA results, when downloaded to GEDmatch, greatly furthered our journey toward 1952.

"Nadean, so many of your cousins are moved by your story," Olivia said. "When I talk to them they refer to the baby, you, and of wanting to help. You might not have parents at the moment, but you have this amazing growing family of cousins who care so much and are doing their utmost to help us. It is really quite incredible. In all my years helping adoptees I have never seen such an outpouring of care and compassion. They want you to succeed."

The cousins' kindness encouraged Olivia and me immensely.

Olivia and I researched all we could on North Bay, Slovenia and Croatia.

Olivia found a link to the 50th Anniversary booklet published by St. Joseph's Hospital School of Nursing in North Bay. It had ninety pages with illustrations. Based on Grandma's discussions with Mother Superior Dympna that my mother worked at the hospital in North Bay, we assumed that my mother was a nurse or a nurse aide.

Class of 1956 – nurse Anne Frachinski. In the Honor Roll section Ann's name is spelled without the "e" at the end, however, under her picture it is Anne.

Didn't you say on the redacted copy of the Dr. Chart you could see "Anne"? Could her name have been Teresa Anne and she used her middle name? However, Frachinski is a Ukrainian name. She would not have married him after.

Could there be a possibility your mom was perhaps Ukrainian and it's your Dad maybe who was Croatian or Slovenian?

Olivia and I were all over the place with speculations.

All we knew for sure was that the DNA indicated that one of my parents was Croatian.

After days of research I emailed Olivia.

Olivia,

I found the connection between Mother Superior at the Hospital in Blind River and my Mum. If you look at page thirty, former nursing graduates sent congratulations to newly graduating nurses. Sister Dympna, class of 1923, sent congrats on page thirty.

She was the Mother Superior who signed the adoption letter on St. Joseph Hospital letterhead on January 11, 1953. Look at the first document that I sent in the package to you. She knew my Mum. Grandma had the correct info. Sister Dympna is also on the Board of St. Joseph Nursing School. She was in constant contact with the hospital in North Bay.

Also, one of the Graduates, Sister Josepha, class of '51, went to work at the hospital in Blind River after her graduation. Both nuns knew my mother. We have to find Sister Josepha and talk to her.

Alas, Sister Josepha had passed in 2012.

My cousin Heather, who lives in Algoma Mills, seven miles from Blind River, called former nurses who had worked at the hospital in Blind River, but they either did not remember my mother or they started working there after my birth.

The booklet shows every graduating class from 1907 to 1970, with photos. The book begins, after introduction, introducing pictures of staff. Note housekeeping: it's a nun. Don't think your mom was in there. Olivia

I created an Excel spreadsheet of each nursing class by year from 1947 to 1956, noting first, middle and last names and their former residences in Canada, looking for a Teresa or someone with a last name ending in -ski, -skie or anything Croatian. I also created a spreadsheet of the doctors looking for an intern who might have been my father.

After a review, Olivia sent her comments to me:

Class of 1948 has a picture of Theresa Duchaud and I would say no.

Class of 1951 Sister M. Josepha is shown—maybe when your mom began working?

Class of 1955 has a picture of Theresa Mayor who I keep being drawn to. Maybe Mom started nursing school in '51, stopped working when baby started to show, lost weight, got into shape, returned later in '53 and graduated '55?

Chapter 29

Ontario Privacy Laws

I contacted my detective, Clarissa, in North Bay. She was thrilled that I had not given up—Clarissa had also been adopted.

Hi, Nadean,

I talked with a source who used to work for government registrations, including births. She made a few good points, but maintains the government role of being fair to all sides of the triangle. She called your registration of birth "Delayed Registration" since you did it yourself.

She definitely said to request information from Adoption Disclosure Register, as well as the Children's Aid Society which I said you had done. She also said to keep applying to the Adoption Disclosure Register because things can change or someone could be looking for you.

I guess there is no use pursuing the court records, since there probably was no court case for your adoption. The "doctor's card," she called it, might have been enough for your grandmother to get the Baby Bonus. Of course, now things are different. She did mention that you should not tell the government that you have your birth info from the hospital in Blind River.

As for your baby bonus, she said that in those days you may not have needed a birth certificate, a "doctor's card" may have been enough. She said that this document should never have been released. This is the protection that birth mothers are promised when they give up their babies.

My source also cautioned that should you get your non-identifying information to be aware that information is often vague or incorrect.

She warned about repercussions when you have your information, but again she is coming from the government side of things. I can certainly help you here as can others who have experienced the highs and lows of the adoption journey.

I would love to walk through the hospital with you when you come here. I could also show you around the city where your mother lived. Clarissa

On Clarissa's recommendation, I reached out once again to all the Ontario government departments and Children's Aid agencies.

Hi Nadean,

As requested via telephone, I am following up with you via email to clarify what information/services are available to you as an adult adoptee:

Non-identifying Information: The agency that placed you for adoption can provide you with this information. This is social history and medical information regarding the birth mother/birth father that was compiled at the time of your birth. This includes information such as their age, ethnicity, education, family etc. It also includes information about you such as your birth records, developmental milestones, time in the agency's care (if any). I will send you a form for Non-identifying Information which you can fill out and send back to the Custodian of Adoption Information. The Custodian of Adoption Information has a record of all of the adoptions that took place in Ontario. They will advise you which agency placed you for adoption. You can then write to that agency for Non-Identifying Information.

It is my understanding that if the adoptee is placed for adoption through a private adoption agency the Custodian of Adoption Information prepares the Non-Identifying Information.

Identifying Information: You are eligible to apply for your Original Statement of Live Birth and Adoption Order through the Office of the Registrar General. This will provide you with your name at birth as well as your birth mother's name. (The birth father's name can sometimes also be found on there but this happens rarely).

I will send you the form for this as well. The form is called Post Adoption

Information and should be filled out and sent back to the Office of the Registrar General.

If you are interested in a possible reunion with a birth family member, you can also register your name with the Adoption Disclosure Register (or A. D. R.). If a birth relative is also registered you will be advised and provided with that person's contact information and vice versa.

I will send you this form which should be returned to the Custodian of Adoption Information. I hope this is helpful. If you need clarification, or have other questions, please feel free to call me. Disclosure Services

Hi Nadean:

I just received a call from the Custodian of Information following-up with respect to your request for records. They have advised that they are in receipt of your request for adoption records and are still working on it.

They directed me to advise you that they will be in contact with you directly, in writing, with respect to the outcome of their search. As a search of our CAS records failed to reveal any record of your adoption; please be advised that I will be closing your disclosure request at this time.

Respectfully, Children's Aid Society of Algoma

I emailed Olivia:

They know everything about every birth from inception. Or they are supposed to know. I wrote to them in 2011 and they had nothing back then, but I provided more information this time, such as Sister Dympna's document giving me to the Russells, a copy of the doctor chart, my baptismal certificate and baby book info. They will have a harder time denying my existence this time.

All responded once again with the same information: no adoption had ever taken place, so they were unable to help me.

Again I emailed Olivia:

Olivia, I have written to every Canadian governmental agency for any info they could find. Heather at Children's Aid confirmed that I had completed all possible forms in search of my records. In summary, the only info that is available are the records at the hospital in Blind River and whatever we can find through DNA testing and investigative work.

As responses came in from the 23 and Me cousins, I created a spreadsheet of their family surnames going back to great-great-grandparents from A to Z. Then I accessed the North Bay telephone directory online for 2017 and entered the data for current relatives with those last names.

The names, Cop, Chop, Janes, Knauss, Kovac, Malnar, Stimac, Wolf, appeared with increasing frequency from the cousins. I emailed the Library in North Bay and The North Bay Museum. I called the Croatian Church, Croatian Hall and the Croatian Recreational Center.

I left messages that I was conducting research and would like their assistance in finding history on my ancestors.

Only the library responded.

Hi,

Thank you for your question. Attached are directories with the J and K sections. Please note that the library only had the 1951/52 telephone directory. Both the 1951 and 1952 Henderson's Directory (reverse directory) J and K sections are attached. Also attached are various newspaper articles pertaining to local nurses in 1951, 1952. The only other place we could think of to contact would be the North Bay Museum. Unfortunately, you have already done so with no results. We hope this information can assist you.

Unfortunately, we cannot provide info related to all of the other letters of the alphabet. It would be too time consuming for our small staff as it would involve copying hundreds of pages of the 1951/1952 directory. It would be best if you visit our library and conduct your research here.

Thank you, Resource Library

My latest obsession of finding my birth mother's name from the redacted doctor chart took me to camera photo shops, the home office of a former FBI official in Coral Springs, and to audio-video specialists. All took the original document, placed it under their sophisticated magnifying equipment and together we tried to discern more of the letters. All to no avail.

I researched and found the name of a forensic software redaction specialist in North Carolina.

I took a morning flight to Raleigh, North Carolina, and a taxi to his home. He walked me upstairs to his home office, placed the document on his sophisticated equipment, and started up the lighting process. He moved the document this way and that, changed the ultraviolet lighting, and enlarged the doctor chart. I was hopeful that this time we would discover more of the letters.

"Nadean, they did a good job with the redaction. I can see some letters but I can't state for sure that they are accurate."

After my return late that evening, I told Bill that it was still worth the trip.

Olivia and I were emailing and texting one another all day long and well into the night. Bill would walk into the kitchen at 3:00 a.m. to find me at my laptop.

"What are you doing at this hour?"

"Emailing Olivia."

Bill jokingly began to question my obsession and sanity.

In addition to filing all of the information in folders on my laptop, I had the research scattered and piled up on the kitchen table and chairs so I could access it quickly—nursing school graduating classes in North Bay from 1947 to 1956,

North Bay *Henderson's* phone lists from 1951 and 1952 of names ending with J and K, lists of doctors in North Bay in 1951 and 1952, all legal correspondence between me and my attorney Paul from 2011 through 2014, letters to and from Blind River District Health Center, Clarissa's detective report, all correspondence between me and Ontario government agencies in connection with my Post Adoption Request, letters to and from Origins Canada, Children's Aid, Parent Finders, Catholic Children's Aid, and North Bay Library, North Bay Obituary and North Bay Social News Indexes from 1952 and 1953—which consisted of 1,250 pages of birth, marriage, and engagement announcements, some of which could have information about my mother—other nursing schools in Ontario and their graduates, updates to adoption websites, and Olivia's spreadsheets of 23 and Me and Ancestry cousins, including their parents' names, grandparents, and cities where they lived.

"Olivia, I am going to find a job with a law firm to keep me busy during the day. I need to concentrate on something else besides this search. It has taken over my life. I need perspective. I will work during the day and then with you at night and on weekends."

I sent emails to my legal recruiters and started a three-month assignment with a Fort Lauderdale law firm the following week. Working brought some sanity to my life as it provided a daily reprieve from this all-consuming obsession.

When Bill started booking flights to Sault Ste. Marie and Vermont for our vacation from the end of July to mid-August, I asked him to schedule two days in North Bay following the interment of Aunt Roberta's ashes in Blind River. He conducted research on flights. He was not happy.

"Why are we going to North Bay?" he asked. "What do you hope to accomplish there? This will take time and money from our vacation in Vermont. Not only that, but we will have to travel on some podunk airline called Bearskin Airlines. It is the only one that fits our already packed schedule."

"I'm hoping that by that time, Olivia and I will have found my mother and I will be able to meet her."

"Nadean, do you realize how unlikely that is?"

"It might be, but I would like to do it anyway. Who knows what can happen between now and then? There are three more months before the trip."

One of the 23 and Me cousins recommended I place my story asking for assistance on Croatian and Slovenian Facebook websites. These are closed groups, but she convinced the administrators to accept me due to my Croatian DNA. I submitted my info to the nine groups.

As the months passed and we had not found any first or second cousins, frustration began to set in.

Olivia regularly asked me to seek legal counsel again.

"What happened to you should not have occurred. Everything that was done was illegal and now you are being denied access to your records due to the Privacy Commission. You should sue that hospital and the provincial government."

"I know, Olivia. I am being discriminated against because there was no formal adoption. Everyone failed me . . . the nuns at the hospital, Children's Aid. I should have the same rights as every adoptee. Every person born has the right to knowledge of their history, their roots, their heritage, their ancestry. I have been down this road before. I promise you that I will leave no stone unturned in this quest for my identity. If DNA doesn't produce results, suing the hospital and government will be my last option, and I will do it."

She was so angry at the system and so unrelenting that she registered me for a free consultation with an attorney on an Ontario legal website. "I have never heard of a case like that," the attorney said after hearing my story, "though I am in no doubt that it happened to you and others. Your charge of negligence on the part of the hospital and discrimination by the provincial government is an intriguing premise. I would be interested in taking on such a case but you should know what you will be up against.

"You are challenging the Privacy Laws in Ontario, which are very strict. You are asking the court to set aside the law and make a special concession for you. You would need a judge who is sympathetic to your case and courageous enough to go up against the Privacy Commission.

"Also, the Ontario government would hire the best lawyers to fight you. They would be afraid that once that Pandora's Box is opened, other non-adoptees will come forward asking for the same access to their birth records. In addition, once we file our petition, the other provinces will hear of it and they will petition to join the Province of Ontario to stop you.

"They won't want you to succeed. So, all of the resources of all of the provinces will be against you. This case won't be settled at Mediation. It will go to trial.

"If that happens, you will need at least $50,000 to see it through to the end. It could take months or years. If you win, you can apply for and could be reimbursed for between sixty to ninety percent of your legal fees and costs. If you lived in Canada we could get publicity for you and you could start a Go Fund Me account. Many Canadians who are sympathetic to your cause would help finance your legal costs. It is your decision. I just thought you should know what you are up against."

I thanked her and said I would wait to see where DNA took us. Olivia was somewhat mollified.

Chapter 30

Ancestry DNA

Olivia emailed me on Saturday, May 20. She had logged on to my Ancestry account, and a first cousin connection at 98% certainty had suddenly appeared.

Her name is Vivian Sayer, I just did some quick research.

She lives in Brampton near Toronto. Her father was Viktor Tomaskovic and her mother is Irene. Viktor died in 2000. Irene had no sisters, only one brother named either Franjo or Frank Marjetic.

If Vivian is your first cousin, Frank could be your father.

However, the first thing I will ask her to do is upload her Ancestry data to GEDmatch as that will verify and prove first cousin. Ancestry shows no chromosome breakdown or DNA proof, just their confidence and estimates. Plus of course, she may or may not have a story. Vivian could have done this test to find her mother's family or perhaps her father's as there doesn't seem to be much on him. She may know members of the Marjetic family.

Everything is an unknown at this time.

We were shocked and ecstatic. It was the break we needed. Olivia and I talked about our approach.

Nadean,

I know how to handle the phone call. Been there, done that plenty of times for others who hit a situation like this and are not sure. I won't say much and will let her do the talking. I will just say there is a match, however, Ancestry has been known to be in error and GEDmatch is a genetic site that verifies or disproves by showing exact matches and to what degree, which is true. I will ask her to upload to GEDmatch.

I also found a public tree in Ancestry with a link to the Marjetic family. Might be some relative of Vivian and Irene. I wrote to the administrator of the Marjetic tree. I'll see how she responds.

Olivia waited until Monday evening to call Vivian, as it was a long holiday weekend in Canada. She emailed me after they spoke.

Nadean,

It was a really weird phone call. Vivian seemed surprised and kept asking if you were connected to her mother. I said no, you were connected to her only. She was concerned that her Mother was not showing up on Ancestry as her mother. I said sometimes it takes Ancestry a few days to publish their results. She said she didn't know about DNA and told me to call Ancestry and find out why they weren't showing as related.

Then I decided to call the mother, Irene Marjetic Tomaskovic. She is eighty-five and a very nice, alert woman. She felt a lot of compassion for your story and said no child should be without their mother. She swore on her heart that she was very sure you could not be from her brother Frank. He lived most of his life with her and her family. She said he was not a lady's man. He was boring, a loner, and did not date much at all, and when he did, it didn't last long - because he was so boring. She said Vivian had told her about the test results and your match to her. Irene said she did test at the same time with Vivian.

She said she did not understand this at all and it was just awful if it was wrong, and she so sweetly asked me if I could ask Ancestry why she and Vivian weren't showing up as daughter/ mother relationship.

She asked me as well if you showed up as being related to her. I said no.

I explained how I had asked Vivian to upload to GEDmatch and told her what it was and that I could prove the relationship with that data. I promised I would follow up with Ancestry and get this cleared up.

Then I called Ancestry. They said they are so backlogged it could take a month before Irene and Vivian show as a mother/daughter match. They are 98% sure Vivian is your 1st cousin.

Nadean, I find this a bit strange. When I spoke to them, both were most concerned with whether you matched up with Irene and why they were not showing up as matching. That was their primary focus.

I received a message from Shirley, the administrator of the Marjetic public tree along with her cell number. Shirley had a lot of information.

She is married to Irene's first cousin Walter and it is Shirley who maintains the family tree. We went through that entire family line. Shirley stopped and asked me if I thought of looking at Irene's husband or his family, Viktor Tomaskovic. I said no because they have him as coming from the Federation of Bosnia. She said that they weren't Bosnian, but Croatian. She explained he was from Mostar, which was Yugoslavia then, and when it moved to Bosnia, they moved over to Croatia. She said that he was born in 1925, so he would be a year older than your mother.

Then she added that he was married once before and had a son, but couldn't remember either of their names.

Then Shirley told me he didn't marry Irene until 1958, Vivian was born in 1960, and her sister Elizabeth in 1962. I told her Viktor could not be your father because then Vivian would show as a half-sibling and she asked if Ancestry even does that. Good question! She also told me that he has a brother and sister as well – Stipe and Mila, but doesn't know if they ever left Croatia. She also gave me his parents' names –Marian Tomaskovic and his mother was Ljubica Tomaskovic, maiden name before marrying was Krulic. This family comes from a very small area in Bosnia and are Bosnian Croatians. I already had their info because Viktor died in Florida. He and Irene were snow birds. Shirley said if the brother and sister are still alive and never left Croatia, they would be over by Livno. I thanked her for her help, got her regular email and promised to keep her updated.

So, this is where we stand. Irene insists her brother Frank is not your father. If you are 1st cousin to Vivian then Viktor's brother Stipe or his sister Mila is your parent. Or if Ancestry is slightly wrong, one of Viktor's cousins could be your parent. I keep checking and Vivian has not uploaded her Ancestry data to GEDmatch. I don't understand why she hasn't done it. Irene said no child should be without its mother so I would think she would encourage Vivian. I would know exactly if the parental connection we have found is through the father or mother line, however, I am leaning on the father side. Olivia

I responded to Olivia:

Firstly, sperm doesn't care if you are boring, so Frank could still be my father. Let's wait a few days more to see if Vivian uploads.

Olivia and I exchanged texts and emails for days researching Viktor's family. We were speculating like crazy as to why Irene and Vivian tested. Did Irene have a daughter out of wedlock before she married Viktor?

Was it Viktor's child or another man's? Was Irene looking for her daughter? Was that why they were asking if I matched Irene? Did Viktor have Vivian with another woman and brought Vivian home to be raised by Irene? Was that why Irene and Vivian did not match? Crazy stuff!

Olivia found a flight manifest that showed Viktor flying to Halifax, Canada, in May of 1951—nineteen months before my birth. Did his brother or sister follow him? We wrote to cousins on Ancestry and 23 and Me asking about the Tomaskovic family in Croatia.

Olivia wrote to me again when she received more news.

Your fourth cousin Jean on Ancestry wrote back to me. All three of you are a match on Ancestry – you, Jean and Vivian. Jean has no idea how you are all related but it has to be through Tomaskovic.

They are all from the same area in Bosnia and are the only ones matching with you that are. So, it's pointing to the father. Jean knows the name Tomaskovic. Her parents were Croatians from Bosnia and Jean and her parents live just outside of Toronto.

I want more information before I call Irene again. I think Irene may have been holding back, and Vivian too in not responding. Irene knew her husband was married before and didn't say a word or even bring him up. Maybe the daughters don't know about his past. I don't want to stir things up and get her angry with me.

I want to have direct questions to ask her. Now I can use Jean as the reason for pointing to her husband. But I need to find another way to bring up his marriage. There is a good possibility that Vivian can be your half sibling. I did some reading and it has happened.

Of course, they all recommend in these cases to upload to GEDmatch or FTDNA. There is no way to know unless she uploads to GEDmatch and she hasn't, and there must be a reason why. I think they know and they think I don't because I focused on the uncle, Frank, Irene's brother even when talking to both of them.

I played very stupid and upset with Ancestry as if they made an error because in no way did I want Irene to hang up or become angry, and she didn't. I kept focusing on how awful this has been for you, and how you just want to find your mother and she followed with that and agreed.

Remember I said, This is where it gets delicate. You don't want to burn bridges, upset people, or cause family problems. I need the doors of communication to stay open. I need more facts and ways to get around where I obtained the information.

We really don't know anything about this family. There may be a good reason for their acting this way. Maybe it is me. What I mean by that, is perhaps they are wondering why they aren't hearing from you. Some people don't like intermediaries. At first yes, maybe, but afterwards no.

If you want to attempt to call and no one answers, leave a message, let them hear your voice. Be kind and sweet like you are with friends and me.

Say something like, Hello, my name is Nadean Stone and I am the one who matched as a cousin and I am related to your father, or your husband Viktor Tomaskovic. I need your help to find his brother or sister, who would be my parent. Don't add anything else, because they both know already you have absolutely no family. I have been through everything with them, especially Irene.

On Saturday, June 3, I sat on my bed with a pen and note pad, gathered my courage, and dialed Irene's number. She answered after the second ring and I introduced myself. She seemed warm, pleasant and happy to help. I explained that it would appear from the DNA results that Viktor's siblings might be my parent. I asked her if she would tell me about Viktor, his family and how she met him.

"Viktor was born in 1925 in the city of Mostar in southern Bosnia and Herzegovina. He was the middle child. There were only two siblings. His father was Mate and his mother Ljubica.

"He had an older brother named Stipe, born in 1922 or 1923. He married and had a son and daughter.

"He never lived in Canada, but visited Viktor and me in Toronto. He remained in Bosnia and died in the 1990s.

"His younger sister Mila was born around 1930 or 1931. She married a Muslim, whom she divorced. She then married an Italian and lives in Belgrade. Mila visited me and Viktor in Toronto but never lived in Canada. Mila has a daughter."

I thought that if neither of them came to Canada until after Irene and Viktor married in 1958, they are not my parent.

Irene continued:

"Croatians like Viktor fought in WW2 on the part of the Axis, who were aligned at the start of the war with the Germans. The Serbs fought with the Allies, the British and French. Viktor became a fighter pilot. Before the war ended he defected to the other side.

"He crashed his plane in Slavonski Brod, a city in Eastern Croatia. Partisans found him injured and carried him to a jail. His head was split open. Nuns nursed him in jail.

"His brother Stipe knew one of the Croatian guards working at the jail and asked him to help Viktor escape. Viktor and one other war prisoner escaped and walked over the mountains into Austria where they were placed in a DP, Displaced Persons Camp."

I did the math as she related the story. Viktor would have been 20 in 1945 when the war ended. So, he was only 18, 19 and 20 when he was a fighter pilot.

"Did Viktor ever marry while he was in Europe?" I asked.

"After the war, Viktor married a woman named Mila, yes, just like his sister Mila. They had a son. Viktor applied for immigration to Canada after the war. He had to wait a long time to be accepted. When he left for Canada sometime in the early '50s, Mila remained behind. She was supposed to join him but didn't. Eventually they divorced, but that took a few years."

I couldn't resist and interrupted at this juncture.

"Irene, where did Viktor settle when he landed in Canada?"

"Oh, after he landed in Halifax he went straight to North Bay."

Bingo! I started to shake with the realization. I knew it. I felt an instant connection. Viktor was my father. Of all the towns he could have gone to in Canada, he chose North Bay. I don't believe in coincidences! Now, I had to keep her talking and obtain more info without alerting her to what she had just given up.

"Why did he choose North Bay?" I asked.

"When he immigrated he had to commit to working for the Canadian government for one year to satisfy his immigration requirement, so he worked in the bush camps outside North Bay cutting trees. After one year he was free to live and work wherever he chose in Canada."

"Where did he work?"

"He worked for Peterson Electric as an electrician."

"How long did he live in North Bay?"

"I don't know, a year or two. I didn't meet him until 1953 at my cousin Johnny's wedding in Toronto. Viktor was a groomsman and I was a bridesmaid. He was still living in North Bay at that time. We got married in 1958 and Vivian was born in 1960."

I noted that she didn't mention her other daughter, Elizabeth.

"In Toronto Viktor worked for Perry Electrical as an electrician. His friend, a Croatian in Toronto, encouraged him to work for himself, so he bought a large truck and went into the trucking business.

"Then his friend in California, Vlad Stimac, and his wife, Olga, encouraged us to move to California, so we moved to Long Beach, Los Alamedos, where we started a concrete pumping business. It did very well. Vlad had known Viktor when we all lived in Toronto before Vlad and Olga moved to California. Viktor liked California as Mostar was hot, so he was comfortable in California.

"After we retired, we bought a place in North Port, Florida, and lived there for 20 years. Viktor developed Parkinson's, then liver cancer, and he died on Nov 9, 2000. He is buried in Englewood, near North Port.

"Viktor was consumed with Croatian politics and I could have cared less. He talked about it all the time and said how everything in Croatia was better than anywhere else. I visited Mostar when we were younger but I didn't like it very much. The people there were very different! Most of Viktor's friends have passed now. Lots of Croatians live in Toronto.

"Who could your parent be if Mila and Stipe never lived in Canada?"

The question surprised me and I had to scramble.

"Does Viktor have any other relatives—cousins?"

She supplied the names of three of his first cousins, but added: "I don't think any of them ever lived in North Bay."

Why did she say that? Neither Olivia nor I ever mentioned that my mother was from North Bay.

I was not about to inform her that the Ancestry results of first cousin status with Vivian could be incorrect and Vivian and I could be, in reality, half siblings.

"Irene, my husband Bill and I visit Toronto on occasion. We would love to take you and Vivian out to dinner the next time we visit."

"That would be nice."

I couldn't wait to call Olivia.

"Olivia, I just got off the phone with Irene. You won't believe. Viktor is my father! I just know it. Guess where he went to live after he landed in Canada?"

"North Bay?"

"Yes!"

"Oh my God!"

"Olivia, I have an entire story to type up now from my notes. Let me put it down in writing to send to you and then we can talk again. You will understand from what Irene says that Viktor's siblings or cousins could not be my parent. It's Viktor. Ancestry is wrong. We just have to prove it, Olivia. Vivian and I are not first cousins, we are half siblings!"

Chapter 31

Viktor Tomaskovic

One week later, I laid in bed thinking about Vivian and Viktor. The coincidences were overwhelming. He had to be my father. As I could not sleep, I got up at 5:30 a.m. and opened my laptop. Olivia usually worked late, as she was one hour behind me in Minnesota, so I started to respond to her emails from the previous night. As I was typing, an email appeared from Olivia asking if I was awake.

I'm up, but not awake.

She replied:

Make coffee, sit down and call me.

Olivia is not dramatic, so I knew she had something. I made coffee, sat on the sofa and dialed her cell.

"Good morning, sunshine. What happened?"

"Nadean, you won't believe it. I could not sleep last night and kept thinking about Vivian and why she hasn't uploaded her DNA results to GEDmatch. It doesn't make sense to me if they really wanted to help you.

"Anyway, I climbed into bed around 2:30 and couldn't sleep. Those Ancestry results had me puzzled. So, I started reading a forum where people have posted complaints about Ancestry's latest website upgrade, which took place a couple of weeks ago. Many posts mentioned that it was difficult to clearly see results between cousins, as Ancestry just lists the connection, like you and Vivian are first cousins, and nothing else.

"They complained further that most people don't know they now need to click on an icon with the letter *i* to obtain information. Get it, *i* for information? The icon is not that noticeable. Well, after reading that I jumped out of bed, started my laptop, logged on to your account, found the *i* icon next to Vivian, and clicked it. First, let me remind you of centimorgan connections.

"When we started this search, we were happy to find a cousin on 23 and Me with 33 or 34 centimorgans across three segments. Those are big chunks.

"If you and Vivian share 75 centimorgans, your relationship would be fourth cousins. If you and Vivian share 200 centimorgans, your relationship would be third cousins. If you and Vivian share 400 centimorgans, your relationship would be second cousins. If you and Vivian share between 600 and 1,150 centimorgans, your relationship would be first cousins. If you and Vivian share between 1,150 and 1,450 centimorgans, your relationship would be half siblings. Well, you share 1,298 centimorgans over 44 segments. Vivian is your half-sister. Viktor is your father."

"I knew it, Olivia. That is unbelievable!"

"It was there all along, Nadean. I just didn't realize that since the upgrade, I needed to click on that new icon for the information. Duh!"

"Olivia, I never thought we would find my father. If my Mum is ninety or ninety-one now, I figured we would be lucky to find her alive. Or she might be in an assisted living facility without the mental capacity to remember me or my father. Finding him was a real long shot. And now we have found him first. This is a miracle, Olivia! Another gift from God. Just like you!

"Where do we go from here? There is no way I can call an eighty-five-year-old lady and break the news that before Viktor married her, he had an illegitimate child with another woman. That the Ancestry results were incorrect and now we have proof of the relationship. I can't do it. Will you call her?"

"Nadean, they might know about you already. Perhaps that is why Vivian never uploaded her DNA results to GEDmatch. They might have known all along that a child existed but didn't expect to find you so soon. I don't really know their reasons for testing. I will call Irene this afternoon after church."

Olivia spoke to Irene that afternoon and called me after their conversation.

"Nadean, she was very kind and gracious. After I explained the significance of recent DNA findings of half sibling she said: "Welcome to the family. I did not meet Viktor until 1953, and he was in North Bay before that, so he would have had a life there. In the forty-two years of our marriage, he never mentioned a baby, so maybe he did not know.

"If he knew and his friends knew, the friends would have told me, but they didn't and they have all died now. Vivian and I would be happy to meet Nadean. She mentioned coming to Toronto when we spoke last week. She said she would like to take us out to dinner. That would be nice. We will bring pictures of Viktor and tell her all about him."

"Wow, Olivia, that is an amazing response. I am so glad. I would love to have a photo of Viktor as a young man."

"Well, Irene promised. That is the story so far. However, before we go any further I am going to ask Vivian to upload her DNA results to GEDmatch. That will prove beyond a doubt that you are half siblings.

"Irene said further that Vivian is a secretary in a school and has been busy with the end of year. Also, each weekend Vivian and her husband go to their cottage. So, she has probably not logged on to Ancestry since June 2 because she is so busy.

Irene said they only tested to see how much of Viktor's Bosnian Herzegovina genes Vivian had versus her mother's Croatian genes.

"We need to confirm Vivian as half sibling on GEDmatch and continue the search."

I asked my friend Ralph, who is an eye surgeon, if the magnifying equipment at his office might be able to help me see more of my mother's name on the doctor's chart. We sat in his office with his assistant and moved the chart around under the microscope, without result.

"You need to stop looking at that paper in the sun or you will go blind," Ralph said. "You know, Nadean, the outcome of this search might upset a lot of people. Your mother will have gone on with her life. She will be in her nineties. She might not wish to reconnect with you, and her family might not wish to either. Perhaps you should let it go."

"No way am I stopping now, Ralph! We have come too far. I don't care about the outcome. You don't know what it feels like not to know your nationality, history, birth names or parents. It is beyond your sphere of reference.

"I am going wherever this search takes me. I am going to see this to the end. Whatever happens was meant to be. We just found my father, and I never expected to find him. That is a miracle! Why would I stop? We have momentum now. We can't stop. The outcome might be joyful." I knew that Ralph truly cared and didn't want me to be hurt, but he had no understanding of what was driving me onward. I was willing to accept any pain that might result, just to know the truth.

Olivia continued to message Vivian on Ancestry, asking her to upload on GEDmatch. It would be the definitive way of confirming our half sibling relationship, though I was in no doubt that Viktor was my father. Vivian never uploaded to GEDmatch and stopped logging on to Ancestry.

Olivia and I both called Ancestry to discuss the results.

The reps confirmed that given the centimorgan and segment levels, there was a strong likelihood that our relationship was half sibling. They would not commit absolutely, but said that based on their experience with similar results in the past, a half sibling relationship was likely.

Olivia continued to monitor Ancestry and GEDmatch to see if Vivian uploaded her DNA. She observed Vivian logging on to Ancestry, but nothing else.

Olivia and I began to speculate that the offer of meeting Bill and me for dinner in Toronto might never materialize. Perhaps Ralph was right after all.

Olivia continued with her research and found that Viktor's uncle, Lucca Krulic, who was Viktor's mother's brother, had immigrated to North Bay. Lucca was born in 1899 and came over to North Bay in 1928 from Mostar as a single man. Perhaps that was why Viktor had chosen North Bay. He had family there already. Viktor might have stayed with Lucca and his wife and not had his own address or telephone number.

I looked at the J and K telephone directory names from the North Bay library and found an address for Lucca and his wife, Pauline, in 1951 and 1952. They lived at 325 St. Vincent Street.

Olivia also found their son Lloyd and sent a message to him asking him to call or email her. He might remember Uncle Viktor and his women friends.

I contacted Clarissa, my detective. She was thrilled to hear of my Viktor news and asked how she could help.

"Out-of-the-box thinking here, Clarissa. Would it be possible to visit the Croatian church, Croatian recreation center, Croatian homes for the elderly and explain that you are doing research for the daughter of a person who resided in North Bay in 1951 and 1952?

"What we are looking for here, Clarissa, are ninety-year-old Croatian males and females who might have known him when he lived in North Bay. They might know with whom he associated.

"One of them might also be my mother if she is ninety. Are there any people living on 325 St. Vincent Street who are in their nineties and have lived there since 1951 and 1952, when Lucca and Pauline Krulic lived there and Viktor stayed with them? They might remember him and his friends. What do you think?"

I sent an email out to my Ancestry and 23 and Me cousins on Father's Day.

Hello, dear cousins,

There are so many of you to thank. Firstly, Olivia and I are immensely grateful for all of your assistance over the past four months in trying to find my birth parents.

What is so moving is that on this day that is so special to so many of you, we have FOUND MY BIRTH FATHER!

His name is Viktor Tomaskovic. DNA testing linked me as a half sibling to his daughter. I am keeping the names of his daughter and wife private out of respect. Viktor did not know, or at least never shared with his wife, that he ever knew of my birth.

The search continues for my birth mother where it all started, in North Bay. So, we are once again asking if any of you have ever heard of Viktor Tomaskovic and if you know of any connection to a woman he would have met in 1951 or 1952 in North Bay, Ontario, Canada. It is amazing that all of the stories told to me were true regarding North Bay!

Below is info on Viktor in a book called "Croatian Aces of WW2." I bought the book, of course! With all of our sincere gratitude for your caring and assistance, Nadean

The news astounded and stimulated the cousins, who responded with renewed vigor. With this startling discovery, everyone was reinvested in helping find my mother. Email continued to pour in with additional family information.

For the next month Olivia and I focused on establishing where Viktor lived and worked while in North Bay. The bush camps had closed many years ago. If we could contact elderly residents who knew him in 1951 or 1952 we might find my mother.

Olivia and her little team of genealogists, which had grown to three—Olivia, Kate and Evelyn—kept researching the parishes in Croatia and my third and fourth cousin DNA connections. Kate didn't know DNA that well, but knew the history and families of the Upper Kolpa River and of Croatia. She is fluent in Croatian. Using the family trees sent to us by the cousins, Kate translated parish records and created a list of 3,000 names with connections to me from that region.

Olivia sent me an email with her assessment of Kate's work.

It is amazing. She connected all of the lines way back to the 1850s starting with Janes, to Ozbolt, to Jeselnik, to Miclik, with Zagar and Kovac. We couldn't see your mother in any of these links, but OMG the work. So professional.

Then, she did another that we think may lead us to her if we just had a couple of closer matches and I am laughing so hard because it is the Knavs [Knauss] line. So, I think now I will call you Melania as in Trump—hahaha.

Chapter 32

Roberta's Interment

Prior to leaving on our trip to Vermont, I called Irene one last time. She didn't answer and I left a message:

Hello, Irene, it is Nadean. Just calling to let you know that Bill and I are traveling to North Bay in a few days, continuing the search for my birth mother. I also wanted to reiterate that I am not looking for anything from you and your family, except a photo of Viktor as a young man, which would be much appreciated. I hope all is well with you. Thank you, Nadean.

Within a few minutes a call came in on my cell from an Unknown Number and I answered.

"Hello, this is Elizabeth, the mean sister. I am calling to tell you to stop calling our family! Do you hear me?"

As she screamed into the phone, Bill walked into the bedroom and heard her shouting from the bedroom doorway.

"You need to stop calling and harassing our family. Do you hear me?"

"Yes, I hear you, Elizabeth."

"You need to stop now and forget about coming to Toronto for dinner and getting a picture of Viktor! That will never happen! Do you hear me? Do you hear me? Am I shouting loud enough?"

I thought that perhaps this is why neither Vivian nor Irene ever mentioned this daughter. She is crazy.

She continued to scream at me, so loudly that Bill could hear the whole conversation from the doorway. Finally, I interrupted her rant.

"Elizabeth, neither Olivia nor I harassed your family. I'm sorry you feel that way. Good-bye" I said, and hung up.

This would be the last interaction with Viktor's family. So much for Irene's "Welcome to the family."

Bill was more upset than I at the way she treated me. Although I was initially hurt for a few hours, and actually shed a few tears, I was undeterred and continued on with our journey.

When Uncle Joseph died, he left the family farm to his son, Charles, who sold it in 2008. Aunt Roberta's wishes were that some of her ashes be spread at the farm under the hazelnut tree on the hill. She was worried that because the farm had been sold, we would not be allowed access.

I had reassured her repeatedly, saying "Don't worry, Aunt Roberta, I will organize it. You will get your final wish no matter what."

I emailed the funeral director, Terra, and my high school friend Ben, who was a real estate agent and had sold the farm:

We would like to bury my Aunt's ashes on Monday July 31st in Blind River. Would you please organize the grave digger for me and ask the town priest, Father Ignatius, if he would be available to say a few words at the grave site?

We will be driving to Blind River from Sault Ste. Marie on Monday morning so would probably arrive at the grave site just before 10:00 a.m.

I will pick up the urn and the small package of her ashes early Monday morning. Would you kindly organize, as well for me, please, three arrangements of flowers for the family graves? Is there anything else I need to think of and organize in this regard? Thank you.

I then sent an email to Ben:

Ben, I know it might be an imposition, but would you ask the owners of the farm if we can do a final walk in the fields?

This will be hugely emotional for us as we will never be back. But going into the fields will help us revisit many joyful past experiences. There will probably be six of us.

Bill and I started our three-day drive to Vermont on July 26. More time would be needed for the trip, as we had to stop every 2½ hours to charge his Tesla. He loves that car, which is the source of many affectionate jokes that I tell to my girlfriends.

"So," Bill said, "do you have a plan for our two days in North Bay?"

"No, when we booked the flights in April, I thought I might have found my mother by now, so right now I don't have a plan. It will evolve."

I am always optimistic. Glass half full.

"We are going to waste two days in North Bay without a plan? Well, I suggest that you and Olivia come up with something."

But I didn't have a plan.

Olivia and I sent texts to each other during the trip north. Bill was very tolerant of this six-month project, which became an obsession. He worried that I would have difficulty coming to terms with my life if we didn't find her. He observed me at my laptop all day and into the night researching, breaking only for a gym class or to take a walk. Waking up at 2:30 a.m., unable to sleep, as my mind raced. Getting up and emailing Olivia at 3:30 a.m. Up again at 5:30 a.m. to get onto the iPhone and laptop to email Olivia or my 23 and Me cousins.

After settling in at our friend Melinda's house we visited Dave and Laurie, who were having a family gathering.

They asked Bill if I was sick.

"She has lost so much weight, and looks so much older. Is she sick?"

"No," he said, "just obsessed and stressed. She had a diverticulosis episode in June and was really sick. Since then she has only eaten enough to survive! She's down to 100 pounds. But she won't listen to me. Maybe you can talk some sense into her."

He reiterated the conversation to me, hoping the *looking old* part would have an effect. I was not moved.

On Sunday afternoon we flew into Sault Ste. Marie. The interment of Aunt Roberta's ashes was set for the next day at 10:00 a.m. at the family plot in the cemetery in Blind River. Father Ignatius would say a few words, and we would visit the farm afterward. I wanted everything to be perfect, as it would be the last thing I would do for her.

At 8:00 a.m. on Monday we picked up her urn, ashes, and three arrangements of flowers at the funeral home and drove to Blind River, eighty-four miles away.

I placed the flowers beside Aunt Roberta's, Grandma and Papere's, and my mother Rita's tombstone. Father Ignatius met us at the cemetery, along with my cousins Charles, Heather, and Bev and her husband, Brian. It was a beautiful sunny day. Father Ignatius conducted the lovely service.

I took photos of Grandma, Papere, and Mon Oncle's tombstones, my mother Rita's, and her son Beverley's. The cousins posed for photos, as we didn't know when all of us would be together again. Then we drove to the family farm for a final visit. The new owners gave us permission to visit and they were away for a long weekend. We were in shock upon arrival.

The farm we remembered had completely changed.

The well-manicured fields, apple orchard and three gardens were totally overgrown. There was no longer a single field to be seen. Trees and underbrush were everywhere. There existed just a small plot of land where the new owners had placed a large barn-like shed and a small vegetable garden.

"Nadean," my cousin Heather said, "there is no way we will be able to find the hazelnut tree or even the hill. It is a half mile away through all of this brush. And there is a tick infestation in Blind River right now. I would not recommend that we walk into that brush."

I was so disappointed.

"Well, what did you expect after forty-three years?" Bill said. "There was no one to do all of the work that was needed to maintain 160 acres of land."

"Okay," I said. "I think Aunt Roberta will be happy that we were able to get onto the farm."

We walked where the old barn, chicken coop, pig shed, blacksmith shop, wood sheds, dairy house, rhubarb patch and house used to be and each of us dropped some of her ashes onto the ground.

We marveled at the 200 evergreen trees Mon Oncle had planted, which were still standing strong in the field along the road leading to the farmhouse. We talked and laughed as we remembered Aunt Roberta. We knew that she would be so pleased.

At lunch in town afterward, Bev, Heather and I tried to make out more letters of my birth mother's name on the doctor's chart. From his looks I saw that Bill thought it was such a waste of time but he said nothing. I had been studying that piece of paper for six months. The cousins were just happy to be together and assisting in the search. Heather, Bev and I did a final walk of the town all the way to the high school. I thought, sadly, that I would never be back and wanted to capture everything in my mind one last time.

The drive back to Sault Ste. Marie was a nightmare because of an accident on the highway. We needed to be at the airport by 5:00 p.m. to catch a flight to Toronto and then on to North Bay. We were forced to take a detour on back roads through rural farm areas, but we made it to the airport by 5:00. Bill has an obsession with being on time, so the stress and frustration were palpable in our rental car.

At check-in we discovered that there were problems with our flights and Bill spent more than half an hour at the Air Canada desk. Bearskin Airlines had canceled our flight a few months prior, as they did not have enough customers booked to make the flight. Bill had worked with them then to transfer our flights to Air Canada, and it had not been done properly. We finally got tickets and went through security.

As we sat in the departure lounge, I took hold of his hand.

"Wow, can you believe we got through after that horrendous drive and ticket mix-up? Now on to Toronto and North Bay. Woohoo!"

The loudspeakers came on and airport officials announced that all flights to Toronto were canceled due to thunderstorms.

We left the departure lounge and went back to the check-in and car rental counters. Bill scrambled to rebook our rental car so we could drive the hundreds of miles to North Bay, which was eight hours away.

Although Bill never wanted to make this trip to North Bay, he was now doing everything possible to get us there.

I tried to persuade him otherwise.

"Bill, I don't want to drive hundreds of miles in bush country at night to North Bay. The only semi-significant town between Sault Ste. Marie and North Bay is Kenora. We won't get there till 3:30 a.m. This is crazy. We don't know the area and the roads. We have had an emotionally packed day and I am worried that we will have an accident, as we are both exhausted."

Bill dismissed my concerns.

No rental cars were available, and our return had been given to another driver, who had already left the airport. No other cars were available, and all other rental agencies were closed. Thank you, God!

It was 6:30 p.m. and there were no taxis to take us back into Sault Ste. Marie. We were stuck at the airport. Bill canceled our flights on Air Canada and we tried to figure out a plan B.

"Bill, it just wasn't meant to be. Let's just bypass North Bay, go on to Toronto when we can, and forget about North Bay. I can come back on my own in September. You didn't want to go there anyway, so it will work out."

All of this time, I was texting Olivia about our developments and she was as stressed as we were. We had been looking forward to this trip since April, when Bill booked the flights. To abort now would be a huge disappointment and further delay our search.

At 7:00 p.m., officials announced that the weather in Toronto had cleared sufficiently for pilots to fly. Everyone had to go through security immediately as there was a very short window of opportunity. The flight crew needed to leave within fifteen minutes or they would exceed their allotted hours and the flight couldn't leave until the following day. Bill jumped up and rushed back to the Air Canada desk. Attendants rapidly reissued tickets and we hurried through security a second time.

"We don't know if the weather will be clear enough for you to make your ongoing connection to North Bay tonight, but hurry up and good luck!" the airline attendant said.

We were not seated together on the flight, but we were lucky enough to get two seats. I ordered a much-needed glass of Pinot Grigio. There were further delays in Toronto, which was provident as our plane to North Bay had not left.

Although we had tickets for the flight, Bill had to fight with the attendants to allow us onto the plane. Earlier flights were canceled and now those customers wanted to get onto our plane, the last one into North Bay. We finally boarded and arrived at our hotel at 1:30 a.m. We were exhausted. Nevertheless, I was up at 6:00 a.m. I couldn't wait to get to the library.

Chapter 33

North Bay

Bill and I arrived at the library as soon as it opened. We told the librarians that we were doing research on my father, Viktor, his life in North Bay, and his work in the bush camps and asked for their guidance in establishing that he did in fact live there from 1951 through 1953.

They opened a locked door and carried out the *Henderson's Directories* from 1951 through 1953. These volumes are so precious that we were required to leave our driver's license with them until the books were returned.

Olivia believed that Viktor might have been sponsored by his mother's cousin Lucca Krulic and his wife, Pauline. He might have lived with them as well when he arrived in North Bay.

If he did, some of the Krulic neighbors might remember Viktor, and one might remember his friends and his girlfriends. One neighbor might be my birth mother.

Olivia was obsessed with the Krulics and finding them.

In looking at the *Henderson's Directory* for 1952, we discovered that it also listed the names of all residents who lived on the same street as the Krulics, as well as their addresses and telephone numbers. I took a photo of the page with my cell and emailed it to Olivia, who sat by her laptop and waited for information from us.

We were thrilled with this find.

Bill asked the librarians if they had a current North Bay telephone directory that we could buy and they said no. We spent the entire day at the library taking photos of lists of names in the *Henderson's*. Bill concentrated on 1951 and 1953; I worked on 1952. Olivia provided names that we had discovered through DNA testing on 23 and Me and Ancestry, as well as from family trees supplied to us by the village of 23 and Me cousins over the past six months. We tried to find the same or similar names in the *Henderson's*. One of them could be connected to my birth mother or related to her.

Bill thought this was a waste of time but went along with it. Hours later, one of the librarians returned to us with a current North Bay telephone directory.

"We found an extra copy. You can have this one," she said.

Bill finished with his names for 1951 and 1953 and started online research on North Bay while I continued to work on 1952. By that time, it was late afternoon and Bill kept interrupting me with his latest "find": "Hey, Nadean, look at this book called *The Fridge Sales and Repair Man*. It is about a Croatian man who fought in WWII, was imprisoned in Europe for years after and then immigrated to North Bay. His son Joe wrote it with him. His name is Antonio Trobic. He would be about Viktor's age."

I opened our North Bay telephone directory, found a phone number, called, and left a message.

At 7:30 p.m. we left the library to have dinner, talk about our achievements and develop a plan for the next day. I was emotionally drained.

"Bill, we haven't achieved anything really. The info is out there but how to grab on to it? Viktor lived here. We just need to prove it. If we can prove that, then maybe we can find the name of my birth mother. If she was the same age as Viktor, she might have passed already, but if we can just find her name, we are further than anyone could have envisioned six months ago."

"I don't want to do the library again this morning," I said to Bill when we awoke the next day. "Let's think outside the box about Viktor. We only have one day left. We have to find links to his life here today. We need to find some elderly Croatians who might have known Viktor. We need to forget the DNA for now and think like detectives."

Bill had researched the names, telephone numbers and addresses of all things Croatian online and in the North Bay telephone directory the night before, so we set off on our mission.

First, we visited the Krulic home at 325 St. Vincent Street and took photos of the house and all surrounding buildings. I noticed that it is near St. Joseph General Hospital.

We visited the Croatian Hall on Chester Street. It was an old building, locked, and no one was present to answer any questions. We found the Croatian Catholic Parish on Harris Road. It was locked with a sign noting that there would be no morning masses Monday through Friday during the month of August.

"It's August. When did that happen?" Bill said as he read the sign.

We had been so obsessed with our work that the month had changed the day before, unbeknownst to us. We visited the site where St. Joseph General Hospital was located in 1952. It is no longer the hospital, but a rehabilitation clinic. We entered and asked to speak to an administrator.

I was trying to establish how names were placed on doctor's charts to determine if my mother's name is last, first and middle or some other configuration. We were passed from the receptionist to a representative in medical records.

"Well, I don't know how it was recorded in 1952, but today we record names as last, first and middle. But my friend works at the new hospital in medical records. She has worked at hospitals for years. She might be able to tell you. This is her number," she said.

As we walked back to our car, Bill noticed a sign on a building that read "North Bay Multicultural Association."

"Hey, I think they might be able to help us. They might have Croatian info; after all, it says *multicultural*," Bill said.

"I don't know; we can try," I said as we walked toward the building.

On the first floor there was a classroom filled with Syrian men and women taking English classes. We described our research to the teacher, who sent us up to the second floor.

"The Director might be able to help," the receptionist said. "She is on her way to a meeting but might have five minutes. If you wait, I can see if she has time for you."

Cathy, the director, arrived and took us into her office as she let us know she didn't have a lot of time.

We told her about Viktor and the search for my birth mother, whom DNA had noted as Croatian.

"Oh, that happened a lot back then. People were so secretive. I know of quite a few families with illegitimate children," Cathy said. "I have this ancient Rolodex of Croatians, Slovenes, Poles and other nationalities. Back in the day when Europeans immigrated to North Bay, we would call on these people to help us with assimilation, in translating documents and in teaching English. We don't have much use now for those nationalities. But we have some elderly Croatians in this Rolodex who might be able to tell us if they ever heard of Viktor Tomaskovic. Delores and Gerald Radetic have always been especially helpful. If anyone knows of Viktor, it would be them."

Delores answered her telephone, and Cathy put the call on speaker phone.

"Mrs. Radetic, it's Cathy Woodward from the Multicultural Association. How are you? I have a woman in my office who is looking for info on her father, who was Croatian. He lived in North Bay back in the early 1950s. His name was Viktor Tomaskovic. I told her how you and your husband used to help us. Do you remember a Viktor Tomaskovic?"

"No, I don't remember a Viktor. Gerald, do you remember a Viktor Tomaskovic?"

Gerald answered in the background that he didn't remember Viktor. "Well, we are sorry," Delores said, "but we can't help you, Cathy." Cathy tried Vino Sisko, but he too did not remember my father. Vinko Humar, who is Slovenian, also had never heard of him.

We thanked Cathy and met my former detective, Clarissa, for lunch. I had renewed our relationship in February when Olivia and I started the search. Clarissa had worked on my case for the past six months at no cost. We told her about our work in North Bay.

"Clarissa, what is needed is to contact elderly Croatians who might have known Viktor and my mother," I said. "There is still a Croatian church in operation. If we were staying the weekend, I would go to all of the masses and find some way of introducing myself to the elderly group. I might come back at the end of September for the weekend and do it anyway."

Clarissa provided a written report of her recent findings and talked about two points in the report.

"It's funny that Cathy called Delores and Gerald Radetic, as I called them as well," she said. "They said they did not know Viktor. I also spoke to my friend who is Slovenian and is our generation. She is married to a Slovenian. She said the organizations begun by their parents are no longer in existence. She asked her aunt, who would be your mother's generation, about the names Chop, Cop, and Wolf. Her aunt said Cop was the maiden name of a family friend. The Cop woman is Slovenian and came to Canada in 1952. She came alone and has no relatives in Canada."

Bill and I thanked Clarissa and set off back to the library. As we drove along now-familiar streets, Bill noticed a sign for Peterson Electric. Viktor worked there in the 1950s.

"Bill, please stop here," I said. "I want to go in."

I explained my search to the manager and asked him to look for HR records from when Viktor worked there.

"Well, you are in luck," the manager said. "We are in the process of closing down the business. I am shredding all HR records but I have not gotten to these yet. You are welcome to go through them to see if you can find your father."

I ran outside to the car while the manager pulled the records and told Bill I would be a few more minutes.

Alas, there was no record for Viktor.

"Well, the company was sold in the '60s, so maybe the new owners destroyed all those old records," the manager said.

Another disappointment. I felt that we were so close; that it was within our grasp, but we just couldn't get to it.

"What about *The Fridge Sales and Repair Man?*" Bill said as he started the car.

I called again, and a woman answered the phone.

"You have the wrong Antonio. You are calling his son Antonio." She gave me the father's number and I called him.

"Hello, Mr. Trobic. Your daughter-in-law gave your number to me. My name is Nadean Stone. My husband and I are in North Bay searching for info on my father, who was Croatian. He immigrated to North Bay in the 1950s and worked in the bush camps. He died in 2000. As you come from similar backgrounds, I was wondering if you ever met Viktor Tomaskovic?"

"I don't remember his name. My memory isn't that good anymore with names, but I am good with photos. Do you have a picture of him? If I see a picture I might remember. How long are you in North Bay?"

"Today is our last day. I do have a photo of Viktor, but it was when he was older."

"Well, if you want to come to my house, I can look at it."

"Mr. Trobic, thank you for that offer. Let me discuss it with my husband. We don't have a lot of time left so if we decide to visit you, I will call back."

"What do you think you are going to accomplish with an elderly man who can't remember Viktor's name?" Bill said.

"At this point, we have nothing, so nothing to lose" I said, and laughed. "Come on, let's go. It might be fun."

I called Mr. Trobic and asked if we could come over. He lived a few miles out of town on acres of land. When we arrived, we were greeted by Antonio, his son, Joe, another son and daughter and his granddaughter.

Antonio was tall, still fit and handsome at ninety-one, warm, kind and anxious to help. I sat beside him on the outdoor patio and shared that my real focus, after establishing Viktor's residence, was to find my birth mother. The family listened to my story in silence and said they would help in any way they could.

"I also worked in the bush camps for my first year and then I worked at St. Joseph General Hospital for five years as an aide," Antonio said. "I had medical experience from years of giving needles during the war."

"Antonio, you might have met my mother, as she was working at the hospital in 1951 and 1952."

I opened my cell and showed Antonio two photos of Viktor that I had found. "He looks familiar, but I can't say for sure. It was so long ago, and looks change over the years. I would really need to see a photo of him from the '50s."

We chatted a few minutes more and thanked them for their time.

I hugged Antonio and started to cry as I wished his family was mine. They are lovely people.

As we walked to our car, Antonio followed. He hugged me again, wished me luck in my search, and stood in the driveway as he watched us drive away.

"You know, I found telephone numbers for the Croatian Recreational Center online yesterday. It is so funny. It is actually in the listing to call one number and if no one answers, lists another number to call. Who puts that in a directory?"

"What is the number, Bill?" I said.

"It's there on my notepad with my 1951 and 1953 names."

I called the first number and as no one answered, I called the second number. A man named Paul answered.

"I am not old enough to remember Croatians from the '50s, but if you want that era, Leonard Petrovic is the man to call. Leonard knows everything Croatian."

I called and left a message for Mr. Petrovic.

232 NO STONE UNTURNED

"Okay, Bill," I said as I looked at my watch and saw it was already 4:00 p.m., "back to the library."

We made ourselves comfortable at our familiar table with laptops open and notepads beside them. Then I looked at Bill and said, "It was worth coming here, Bill. I know we didn't accomplish what we set out to do, but I am glad that we came. Look at the great people here at the library who have helped us, and that lovely Trobic family we just met. I am going to come back in September and attend the Croatian church services. Someone there will help me."

My cell phone rang at 6:30 p.m. "Hello. Did you call me? It's Leonard." He spoke with a heavy accent.

"Yes, I did, Leonard."

"You're looking for info on your father, Viktor?"

"Yes, I am. I am trying to learn about his life in North Bay in the '50s."

"I know Viktor very, very well. Viktor was a very handsome man. All the ladies in North Bay loved Viktor," he said.

"Is that true, Leonard? What do you remember about Viktor?"

"Viktor worked in the bush camps like me. I saw him on weekends at the bars. Viktor and other Croatians got into arguments about the war. They were still fighting the war.

"Viktor was very good to me. I was younger than Viktor, but he was good to me."

"Leonard, do you know where Viktor lived? His mother's cousin was Lucca Krulic. Lucca's wife was Pauline. Did he live with them?"

"I only know Krulics that lived on Argyle Street. Nice people; nice family. I don't know if Viktor ever lived with them. Back then most Croatian boarders lived in Croatian homes. What did you find so far?"

I told him about the closed Croatian Hall, the Croatian Church that has no morning masses in August and our visit to Mr. Trobic.

"I know Antonio very well," Leonard said. "He is my good friend. I was in the fridge sales and repair business just like Antonio. He got out of the fridge business before it went bad. That's how I know the Krulics. I fixed their fridge on Argyle Street. Antonio knows Viktor. Same age. Antonio just doesn't remember. Croatian mass is still on Sunday during August, just not Monday to Friday. How long are you here?"

"Today is our last day. If we were staying for the weekend I would attend all of the masses at the Croatian Church on Saturday and Sunday, as I thought some of the elderly Croatians might remember Viktor."

"Too bad you're not staying. Yes, some would remember Viktor. Delores Radetic remembers Viktor. She told me many years ago that she liked Viktor very, very much. But the relationship ended. I don't know why. Tell me, did Viktor have a wife in Croatia?"

"Yes, he was married to a woman called Mila and they had a son. When he came to Canada she was supposed to follow him but she didn't. They divorced."

"So, it's true. That explains why Delores didn't marry Viktor. Viktor was already married."

I was shocked. Delores was the lady Cathy called from the Multicultural Association and the same woman Clarissa called. She and her husband Gerald said they didn't know Viktor.

"I went to Toronto like Viktor. I didn't like Toronto so I came back to North Bay."

"Leonard, did you visit Viktor in Toronto?'

"No, I know he married, but I didn't visit. So, you were born in Toronto?"

I was caught now. I couldn't lie.

"No, Leonard. I was born in Blind River."

There was a long silence and I sensed I was going to lose him. "Well, I don't want to know about that. I know nothing about Blind River, nothing. I must go now. I'm busy."

"Leonard, wait. Thank you for talking to me. May I call you again?"

"Yeah, sure," he said and hung up.

I recounted the conversation to Bill.

"I had him, then couldn't lie and lost him."

"But you established that Viktor lived here and many Croatians knew him."

"Bill, I think Delores Radetic might be my mother. What do I do now?"

I sat on the stairs of the library and called Olivia.

"Olivia, can you research Delores Radetic, find her maiden name and see if it fits into any of our 23 and Me names? Bill and I are exhausted. We are going to dinner and then back to the hotel. We leave tomorrow. It might be her, but we have to be certain."

During dinner I received a text from Olivia informing us that Delores's maiden name is Fajdic or Phajdic. The name did not connect to any of the cousins, but Olivia had always said my mother could be an outlier. We needed to establish Delores's birthday to see if it fit with the age of twenty-six on the doctor chart in 1952.

I sent Clarissa a text and asked if she could find the birth date of Delores Radetic. I also gave her the details of my conversation with Leonard Petrovic.

Meanwhile, Olivia replied to my text.

Find Delores's address and go over there and knock on the door. Use the pretense that you are looking for information on Viktor Tomaskovic, as he is your father. Don't say a word that you may think she is your mother.

If she asks if you called, say yes, but you are only in town one day and need all the help you can get and tell your story. Maybe you just seeing her face to face and what she looks like, or really her seeing you face to face and what you look like, might cause something to happen.

When we finally arrived at our hotel at 9:00 p.m., I called Olivia. "Olivia, are you crazy? I can't ambush an elderly lady like that. She might have a heart attack. We are losing perspective from the stress. I just have to go on to Vermont tomorrow and we need to work on establishing whether she is my mother or not. I am going to come back in September, the week after Labor Day, and meet and talk to some of these elderly Croatians. I know now that Viktor lived here and was involved with Croatian groups. Some of them must have known friends he associated with."

Chapter 34

Our Cottage in Vermont

I woke up alone in bed crying.

I was dreaming of Andrew and feeling very sorry for myself. Bill came into the bedroom.

"Happy anniversary," he said as he sat down beside me. He leaned in, wrapped his arms around my shoulders, raised me up, and gave me a hug. As he lowered me back down on the pillow, he stared at me. "Why are you crying?"

"I realize that in the end it is just us, you and me, Bill, and I need to be happy with that. I am so lucky and blessed to have found you and to have you in my life loving me as much as you do. You are my family. God brought you to me. I am a better person because of you."

"Wow, I am bowled over. Wasn't expecting that."

"We didn't accomplish all that we wanted in North Bay, but I am glad we went. We established that Viktor lived there, and that was the focus of our visit. It is a start. We have come so far. And you, who didn't want to go to North Bay, were the one who found all those people and connections."

"You know, Nadean when you started this up again in February with Olivia, I never thought you would find either of your parents. I thought it was a lost cause, especially after the three years you spent writing to all those organizations, Children's Aid, fighting the hospital, hiring an attorney, fighting the Privacy Commission and then hiring a detective. Then you found your father. I am amazed at what you and Olivia have accomplished in six months."

I was physically and emotionally drained and sobbing at that point.

Aunt Roberta's interment and North Bay had all taken their toll.

"Bill, when I think about it, I feel that Nadean is someone else, not me. She is over there and I am watching her in shock, awe and utter amazement. There is no way that I could have gone through what that woman has endured and survived it all with any level of sanity. It is beyond unbelievable."

"Well, the sanity part is questionable!"

"Not funny," I said, and laughed.

"I think I should write a book. Maybe it will give people hope and courage to continue to persevere no matter what. Some good has to come out of all of this. It can't just end here."

"That is a great idea. Go ahead write your book."

At our anniversary dinner that evening I raised my glass of champagne to Bill and we toasted us.

"Bill, I have been thinking."

"Please don't do that, it always worries me," he said, and we laughed. "Bill, you and I both love Vermont. You have said for years that if it wasn't for me you would live here full-time. I'm the one who can't take the long winters. I have decided that I would like to spend a few months each year in Vermont rather than just two to three weeks in summer. It is time for us to enjoy our lives. Why don't we try to find a place we can rent for longer periods of time?"

"Are you serious? How much time?"

"Five months."

"Really, five months?"

"Yes, let's do it."

That morning I decided that I wanted this lovely man who had stood beside and supported me all these years through all of our challenges to be truly happy. It was time to fulfill his dream in life—more time in his beloved Vermont.

The next morning Bill logged on to his laptop and looked for long-term rentals. After returning from North Bay on Thursday, we were once again staying with our friend Melinda until our rental cottage became available on

Saturday at noon. The three of us sat in her living room, while Bill browsed numerous websites. Properties in the islands were difficult to find on a long-term basis.

"Why don't you look at properties to buy if you are going to spend that much time here? If you look further up the islands you might find properties that are less expensive," Melinda said.

"Melinda, we have been down that road so many times without success. We have discussed buying before, as you know, looked at properties every year and then it has never worked out," Bill said.

"It will this time," I said.

Bill started scrolling through properties for sale in the islands north of Burlington. He saw a cottage available on Grand Isle.

"Look at this property, Nadean. It is reasonably priced."

It was a one-story, red cottage on Lake Champlain near the drawbridge. It had a western view for sunsets.

"I am not really attracted to it, Bill. Keep looking."

"Hey, there is a second one for sale on the same road, right next door to the red one. Look, Nadean."

This one was a two-story, blue cottage with a large deck on the second floor.

"That one has potential, Bill. We are moving into our cottage at 12:00 noon so let's call the agent now and make an appointment to see it this afternoon."

Just fifteen hours after sharing with Bill my desire to spend more time in Vermont, we might have found our dream cottage.

We loved the cottage. It was built in the seventies and needed work, but was livable with a good cleanup. The deck on the second floor had all-around seating and a superb sunset view. The cottage was 100 yards from the lake with 100 feet of shoreline. It was perfect for us! Bill told the agent we were interested, and the negotiations began.

Two days later, Bill and I sat at our rented cottage on South Hero and watched television. I couldn't concentrate. I kept thinking about my only conversation with Leonard Petrovic. Leonard knew more than he shared with me. I had to talk with him again.

"Bill, I'm going to call Leonard again. I don't care anymore. I have nothing to lose."

I walked into the bedroom with my notepad, closed the door, sat on the bed, and dialed Leonard's number.

"Hello, Mr. Petrovic, it's Nadean Stone. We spoke last week. Do you remember me?"

"Yes, you're Viktor's daughter."

I knew this had to be persuasive or he might hang up on me.

"Mr. Petrovic, I am going to tell you my story. The reason I was born in Blind River and not in Toronto is that I am a child that Viktor had before he married his wife, Irene. Viktor had me in 1952 with a woman who lived in North Bay. I don't know who she is. We found Viktor in June through DNA testing. I matched up with his daughter in Toronto. His family in Toronto doesn't want to have a relationship with me.

"The reason I went to North Bay was to research where Viktor lived in hopes that it would help me find my mother. I am sixty-four years old. The mother who took me after my birth, Rita, died when I was two years old. My grandmother who raised me, Rita's mother, was told by the Mother Superior at the hospital in Blind River that my birth mother was from North Bay. After she gave birth to me she returned to North Bay.

"On every birthday since I can remember my only wish has been to find my birth mother, to know her name and to find out my history. I want to find her before I die. It is my last wish in life. Once I know that, I will go away and they will never hear from me again if that is their wish. My mother might have passed already if she was Viktor's age, or she might still be alive. We don't know. Will you help me find her?"

There was silence as he digested the information and I waited for his response.

"Yes, you have a right to know your mother. I will help you." Leonard said he didn't know the bush camp where Viktor worked, as they did not talk about it. He did not know how Viktor got to Canada, by boat or plane.

Leonard sailed from Germany. He said Germany was close to Croatia so after the war he and another friend went to Germany and applied for immigration to Canada. Leonard arrived in Canada in April of 1954. He worked at bush camps outside of North Bay and moved to North Bay in 1955. Viktor was still there in 1955, working at Peterson Electric.

He thought Viktor moved to Toronto in 1957, but was not sure. As Leonard did not arrive in North Bay until 1955, Leonard did not know about any girlfriends back in 1952.

Viktor and other Croatian men would get into arguments about the war. Some, when they arrived in North Bay, were classified as aliens, as they had fought on the wrong side of the war because of their country's alignment with the Axis or the Allies and changing allegiances. Arguments became heated, and fights broke out.

Leonard said once again that Viktor was very, very handsome. Many girls liked him. He repeated that Delores Radetic said she really liked Viktor but heard he had a wife in Croatia, so she ended the relationship. She later married Gerald.

"Leonard, do you know where Viktor lived?" I asked.

"No. Maybe he lived in a boarding house."

Like many other Croatians, Leonard moved to Toronto but returned to North Bay and opened his fridge business.

Leonard reaffirmed that he did not get in touch with Viktor while in Toronto.

"Who else in North Bay might have known Viktor?"

"All have died except Delores Fajdic, who married Gerald Radetic, and

Antonio Trobic, but Antonio does not remember. Gerald had a women's dress store in the '50s. Gerald's mother had a boarding house where many Croatians lived."

"Leonard, if Gerald had a women's clothing store in the '50s he would have known all the Croatian ladies and he would remember one who left North Bay in 1952 for four to five months and returned."

I did not mention to Leonard my suspicions that Delores, Gerald's wife, might be my mother.

We made a plan and exchanged email addresses.

Leonard said he would stop at Delores and Gerald's house and talk to them about me. He was going to ask what they remembered and if they knew any of Viktor's girlfriends who could have become pregnant with a child in 1952 and gone to Blind River. He would also stop at Antonio's house and try to jog Antonio's memory of 1952.

He said Antonio was the same age as Viktor, probably worked at the same bush camp, and as Antonio worked at the hospital for five years after bush camp, he might remember a woman who worked there, left the hospital and returned five months later.

I sent an email to Clarissa.

Clarissa, would you be able to find out Delores Radetic's birth date? I have spoken to Leonard Petrovic twice now and both times he mentioned how very handsome Viktor was and how Delores had told Leonard that she liked Viktor very, very much, but ended their relationship when she found out about his wife in Croatia. I don't know if Delores really does not remember Viktor or deliberately lied to you and Cathy. I am wondering if Delores could be my mother.

On Thursday, August 10, at 5:49 p.m., I received a text message from Leonard:

I have a story: one Croatian man was going with a Slovenijen girl. Her name in Slovenia, Sabina in Croatian: Martha Last name Pavlec. She left North Bay in early 1952. PAVLEC is the way to say it properly. Has a little mark on top of the letter "C."

I had no idea what he meant and forwarded the text to Olivia. I sent my response to Leonard:

Leonard, where did you get this info? I am wondering, as well, could Viktor have lived in Gerald's mother's boarding house?

He replied the following day:

No way Viktor lived at the Radetic place. Gerald and Viktor were going after the same girl, Delores. I asked Delores about Viktor and she doesn't remember, she said she had lots of boyfriends. Gerald remembers Viktor and said Viktor had lots of girls. Gerald Radetic thinks Viktor stayed in the Krulic home. Delores or Gerald told me about the Pavlec person, but that's not a name to tell anyone.

I sent this additional information to Olivia. She couldn't make a connection to the Pavlec woman based on DNA results so far.

"I always said your Mum could be an outlier," Olivia said. On Sunday night I received a text from Leonard:

What proof do you have that your mother died?

I replied,

Leonard, I do not know if she is alive or if she has passed. She had me on December 18, 1952, and the doctor chart from the hospital shows her age as 26 which means she was born in 1926 so would be 90 or 91 now. The chart says she is European and Catholic. The chart has her name blacked out.

Leonard was on to something. He was rattling the cages. I sent another text to him Monday morning.

Hello, Leonard. My only wish in this search is to connect with my mother and to hear her story of how she came to Canada, how she met Viktor and her life after Viktor. Also, to tell her about my life if she would like to know. That is all I am looking to do. Also, to have a photo of her as a young woman if she is willing to share.

Chapter 35

Christie

On August 14, I received the following email at 8:48 p.m.:

Good evening,

I have a friend whose mother is looking for a child she gave birth to in 1952 in Blind River, Ontario, Canada. I saw your post on Croatia roots wondering if you have more information regarding your birth and adoption. Hope to hear from you soon. Kristie McKnight

My response was quick:

Kristie hello,

I was born on Dec 18, 1952 at St. Joseph Hospital in Blind River. Does that birth date correlate with your friend who is looking? After my birth there, no formal adoption was completed. I was simply given to a young couple on Jan 11, 1953. Please let me know if I could be the daughter of your friend's mother. I have been searching for my birth mother for many years.

Thank you, Nadean Stone.

I ran out of the bedroom to share my news with Bill. Then I sent another email to Kristie with my cell phone number and told her that my only wish in life was to meet my mother and that I was not, in any way, looking for anything else from her.

Kristie responded quickly.

Nadean,

I just got off the phone with my friend and she is calling you now. Her name is Christie also, spelled different. Kristie

My cell rang.

As soon as I said hello, Christie replied: "I don't know where to start." I could hear the excitement and apprehension in her voice.

"It is okay, Christie, start by asking me questions."

Christie related how she believed that her mother and I were connected. Her mother's age did not correlate with the doctor chart, so I was skeptical.

"Christie, DNA has established that Viktor Tomaskovic is my father. Will you ask her please if Viktor is the father of her baby?"

"Will do. She is asleep now. This is a huge emotional event for her, as it is for you. I can only imagine what both of you are going through."

We agreed to share photos that night. We stayed up late emailing one another. And thus, it began.

Christie, please see photo attached. I think this is where your Mum lived or worked in Blind River. Back then, unwed women lived with the nuns at the convent and worked at a home for the elderly that was near the hospital and church which were all close to one another. Please ask your Mum if that was the arrangement for her. There was a ward on the third floor of the hospital for unwed mothers. They had their babies there and then signed papers giving them up for adoption. She had me on December 18, 1952 and was discharged from the hospital on Christmas Eve 1952 at 1:30 p.m. per the doctor's chart. Did she take a train back to her home that afternoon? As you can see, we have done a lot of research to find my Mum.

After lunch, Bill and I talked to a banker about a small mortgage for our cottage. I heard my cell's text notification chime. I checked quickly and saw that it was from Christie. I excused myself from the meeting and read her text.

I will try calling you later today. Just spoke to my mom, yes, it was Viktor. She is a little foggy about how she returned home. I think she is still in a little shock today. I told her you are beautiful, successful and educated. She loved hearing that.

Unbelievable! I responded. *Christie, will you and your Mom take DNA tests? We need to confirm what we all believe to be true. I have come too far to have any uncertainties.*

Christie wrote back and said that she was interested in the testing. I looked up at the banker and Bill.

"Christie just confirmed that the father of her mother's baby was Viktor," I said to Bill. "They are having a family meeting tonight for her mother to tell the other siblings."

Bill's eyes widened.

"We think we have found my wife's birth mother! It has been a long search," Bill said to the banker.

Christie and her mother agreed to take a DNA test to confirm the connection. Christie ordered the kits from 23 and Me.

The kits arrived on Friday, August 18. They did the tests and Christie mailed them that afternoon.

"The earliest that 23 and Me has ever completed tests is four weeks," Olivia said. "It usually takes between four to eight weeks."

I looked at my calendar.

"Olivia, 23 and Me will receive the kits on Monday, August 21. If it takes them four weeks to process, my mother's results could come out as early as her birthday on September 18. Wouldn't that be something?"

"Yes, Nadean, it would, but it will never happen. That is the earliest day they could possibly be processed and released."

"From your lips to God's ears, Olivia dearest!"

"Nadean, you always say there are no coincidences. I know the age on that doctor's chart bothers you, but Viktor could not have had two women pregnant at the same time. She is your mother."

Christie and I continued to communicate as we waited for the DNA results. She was totally invested in the story. She emailed me every day and continued to send photos. My mother and I wouldn't talk or meet, per her wishes, until DNA confirmation. I agreed. Too traumatic for both of us to invest emotionally and then find out we were not connected. I do not trust hospital records.

Chapter 36

Englewood, Florida

Bill, his sister Debi and I visited Viktor's grave in Englewood, Florida, on Sunday, September 3. Although I never had an opportunity to meet Viktor, it gave me comfort to spend time at his final resting place. We took photos and as we dropped Debi at her assisted living facility and got back into the car, I saw a missed call at 5:06 p.m. on my cell.

It was from the woman who might be my birth mother.

I grabbed note paper and called her back. With car noises and a storm raging outside, it was difficult to hear clearly. While I was initially apprehensive about returning the call, I was not overly emotional. I realized that if I was certain she was my mother, my reaction would be totally different.

She told me about her family and how she had traveled to Canada. She said that when adoptive parents came to take babies, the nuns would ask one of them to stand in the glass window of the hospital.

As she related this to me, I remembered the story Grandma had shared when I was a child:

When your mother Rita left the hospital with you, she and your father Sid saw a young woman standing by the windows on the upper floor watching them leave. They couldn't make out her features. They thought it must be your birth mother.

I explained that my birth mother had already left the hospital when I was given to the Russells on January 11, 1953.

"I know," she said, "but I think they just asked any of us to stand in the window to make the adoptive parents feel they had seen the birth mother."

She said there were three or four pregnant women living at the convent with her. They did not share their stories or their real names. They were told not to do so by the nuns.

"Did Viktor know about me?"

"No," she said.

The conversation took an hour and a half and we were both drained. She said she wanted me to fly to her town and meet with her alone, in a private setting: no siblings and no Bill. She did not want to wait for DNA. I told her I would discuss it with Bill and would call her again.

The irony of the possibility that I had visited Viktor's grave on the same day that my birth mother called me for the first time was not lost on me.

The potential for the doctor's chart not being correct was still troubling me. If DNA did not come back positive, I knew I would be a mess.

I emailed our conversation to Olivia and Kate and asked for their advice. Kate replied first:

Now that I have wiped the tears from my eyes, yes – her maiden name is a viable name in the DNA matches. Rare, but viable. I only have a few, but what I do have is right in your DNA region.

My 4 names are in the highlighted towns. I don't want to get over-excited, so your plan to wait for the DNA is a good one. I hope this all works out and you two can build a relationship!

Olivia replied next:

That doctor's birth chart has bothered me since you found her, to be honest. It just doesn't seem to add up, though it is redacted. I have sat here and looked at it close up a few times and just can't seem to see her name fitting. It had me worried that perhaps from the start, the hospital was aware they made a mess of it all. It doesn't mean that your mother is not your mother and of course the DNA will prove or disprove that, however, the facts just seem to be against you at this point.

I can understand her memory being vague. It was pure trauma for her. She handled that entirely on her own and at a young age. Her faith got her through it, and I am so happy to hear the nuns were so kind and helpful to her.

You are doing the right thing in waiting. If she or your siblings ask why, be honest with them. Tell them about the redacted birth form, and how this has been a disaster since the very beginning with your birth never being registered, your adoption never being completed or legalized - that you have to be so very cautious.

Seriously, if the DNA turns out to be positive, I still think you have one hell of a major law suit on your hands against that hospital.

On September 12, I sent a birthday card to my possible birth mother.

Olivia called me on September 17: "Christie's 23 and Me results just posted. She is your half-sister."

"That is wonderful, Olivia. You watch. My mother's results will post tomorrow on her birthday! Won't that be the best birthday gift ever?"

Olivia sent me a text message at 6:00 a.m. on September 18:

Her DNA results have been released. She is your birth mother.

I was overwhelmed with joy and excitement. My greatest wish in life had just been fulfilled. It was unfathomable that with so many unbelievable challenges we had actually found her. It was truly a miracle! I looked upward to the heavens and with tears in my eyes said "Thank you, God. Thank you, Jeremy. Thank you, Andrew."

With trembling fingers, I emailed my "new" siblings:

Good morning. This is a truly momentous day in our lives, but especially mine and our mother's.

Our mother's DNA results posted today and it clearly shows 49.9% Mother connection. Viktor is the other 50%. My laptop is on the fritz again so Olivia texted me. Olivia was crying. I said to Olivia weeks ago that if 23 and Me posted as early as 4 weeks what an amazing gift if it was to appear on her birthday!

One really has to see the hand of God in all of this. Our search has been a miracle in coming! Today for the first time in my life, I will be able to utter the words I have been longing to say for 62 years: "Hello, Mum! Happy birthday!"

I will be calling her shortly. Flowers that I ordered yesterday morning, before all of this happened, are on the delivery truck now. I cannot wait to meet her and all of you. With much love for a truly spectacular day with our mother!

Then I called my mother.

Her response about the DNA match was simply, "I knew that it would."

She had told her doctor and attorney about me in February, the same time Olivia and I started our search, and asked for their help in finding me.

Olivia sent an email to our genealogist team:

Good Morning Everyone,

Yesterday Nadean's sister appeared on 23 and Me as a match.

Today is Nadean's mother's 86th birthday, and she showed up as a match as her mother at 50% which is the most beautiful birthday gift that could be given. So, it is now verified that she is indeed Nadean's mother.

The next step is a meeting between only Nadean and her mother, which as all of you can imagine will be extremely personal, intimate and emotional. I haven't stopped crying since I saw the results this morning, for I am truly happy beyond words, as her mother has been searching as well. It was her hope and dream to find Nadean also and both their nonstop hopes and prayers came true on her mother's birthday.

As I have told Nadean, this was the last case I was ever taking—I am hanging up my hat. It has taken a toll on my family and my time. I promised my daughters, as I have let too many things go that I need to finish. It was a beautiful ending to my years of helping others.

Chapter 37

The Family

Bill worked on booking tickets. As my mother wanted to meet with me only in a private setting in our hotel room, Bill said he didn't want to accompany me. "What would I do while you spend time with your mother?" he asked.

"Bill, I have no idea, but I can't do this alone. It will be way too stressful for me. You have to come with me. No question about it."

He booked our flights for September 29, ten days later. We would spend the weekend and return on Monday. As our connecting flight left Toronto, I became anxious.

I received a final text from Christie just before takeoff:

Our mother has changed her mind. She is coming to the airport to meet you.

This is the day I dreamed about for sixty-two years, since Rita's passing. During the flight I worried that the plane would crash before we got there. Then I told myself that I was crazy and that everything would work out.

As Bill and I walked through the arrivals area on the second floor, we approached an opaque sliding glass door. As the doors opened, we immediately saw an attractive, petite European lady sitting upright on a bench directly in front of us. She was in a tailored two-piece suit and was holding a small handbag on her lap. A very tall, handsome young man sat beside her. As we approached, Bill stopped walking. The young man rose and stepped away from the bench. She stood up and clutched her handbag to her stomach.

My mother and I stared at one another.

There was a small anxious smile on her lips. She watched as I approached. I held out my arms, engulfed her in a soft embrace and said the words I had longed to say for so very many years: "Hello, Mum."

As we released one another and turned toward Bill, the young man snapped a photo of us. He was my mother's son-in-law, Christie's husband.

As introductions were made, he turned to Bill.

"Bill, this weekend is all about Mum and the siblings. We are just window dressing."

We discussed plans for the remainder of the evening. Bill and I shared that we hadn't eaten since lunch. My mother suggested that we pick Christie up and that we go out for a late dinner.

Christie was delightfully warm, intelligent and funny. We shared stories of our past at the restaurant and finally ended the evening close to midnight.

When we arrived at our hotel we were greeted by a beautiful bouquet of flowers from my siblings.

The next morning, Bill and I drove to my mother's house. Mum has a lovely home in a quiet neighborhood, decorated with beautiful art.

On Saturday morning, Mum served the first breakfast she'd ever made for me. She put on a huge spread of homemade breads, eggs, bacon, tomatoes and an assortment of mixed fruit for us. I could see that she made a special effort at laying out an attractive table.

My other siblings arrived and were introduced to us. The morning was quite surreal as we looked at photos, talked about our past and became acquainted. We were not being thrust upon one another. Everything evolved slowly and quite naturally.

They asked what we would like to do after breakfast.

"I would like to see where you lived when you first arrived here, Mum, where you worked and where you and your family lived after you married," I said.

The family climbed into one car and Bill and my brother-in-law into the second. Cell phones were linked so we could hear one another as we traveled around the town.

Mum pointed to various rooming houses where she lived after her arrival there.

The siblings excitedly took us to the schools they attended and talked about their music and sports activities, the festivals in which they marched in their traditional costumes, the house, now a museum, where the lady who hosted dinners for new immigrants lived—and where Mum met both her husband and Viktor—and St. Joseph Hospital, where Mum worked.

As we approached one rooming house, Mum asked us to stop the cars.

"Do you see that window on the second floor facing the street? After I returned from Blind River, your father came to visit me. I was in my room on the second floor. The landlady knocked on my door and said a gentleman was asking to see me.

"I looked out that window and saw it was Viktor. He was standing on the stoop outside. It was January. I walked downstairs and opened the door. We looked at one another, but there was nothing to say. He was still married, with a wife and son in Croatia. I had not told him about the pregnancy; the nuns had told me never to tell anyone about the baby. There was no future for us.

"So, I turned around, closed the door and walked back upstairs. When I looked out the window again, he was gone. It was the last time I would ever see him. I never told him about you."

There was palpable silence in both cars. We were all struck by the profound sadness in her retelling of their final encounter.

That evening the siblings hosted an early Thanksgiving dinner for the family at Christie's home. The entire family was warm, welcoming and gracious. If they felt at all uncomfortable, it was indiscernible to Bill and me.

Our final evening was a family dinner in the private room of a restaurant. Bill and I drove Mum home afterward.

As we sat at her kitchen table, she started to cry as she talked about Viktor.

"He showed a picture to me of his son in Croatia. So, there was nothing we could do," she said.

"You do not need to worry or feel bad about the past," I said as I took her hand. "You did the best you could do at that time. You were eighteen years old when you left home for a new country, a young immigrant to Canada who barely spoke English.

"You made the right decision. Back then you would have had a very difficult time with a baby. You went on to build a wonderful life with your husband and children. All of them are well educated with challenging careers.

"They have lovely spouses, beautiful homes and children who are all making their way in life. You made a wonderful life for all of them. You should be proud of what you have accomplished. I was fortunate to have Grandma raise me. She too valued education and I was the first and only grandchild to graduate from university with a master's degree. My life has been good. You don't need to worry about me. I have a wonderful husband who loves me and now that I have found you, I am at peace. I am just sorry I was not able to meet Viktor."

She looked at me with tears in her eyes and said, "Well, when we die, you and I will meet Viktor in heaven."

Christie and Mum came to the airport the following morning to see us off.

As we sat on the plane, Bill turned to me.

"If I had not come with you, I could not possibly have ever appreciated how warm, welcoming, kind and generous this family was to you. No matter what you would have told me, I could not have grasped it fully. The whole weekend was unbelievable! I am blown away by their hospitality and kindness. I think your mother is worried that now you have found her, you won't wish to have a continuing relationship."

"Right now, I am so emotionally drained, Bill. I can't even think."

A few days after returning home, I mailed a letter to Viktor's wife, Irene.

Hello Irene,

I thought that you might like to know that I have found my birth mother and she and her family have very kindly welcomed me into their lives.

We visited them this past weekend. My mother shared with me that after giving birth she saw Viktor only once. They did not speak and so she never told him about me.

I hope that this info gives you peace and comfort. I only wish good things in life for you.

Sincerely, Nadean Stone

Olivia and I continued to email one another, and she was beyond happy for us.

I need and want to tell you about a conversation Kate and I had. I have looked at the work she has done, and all the names that we found so many times, however, there is still no connection to anyone. It is because the correct people have not been found yet. So, I said to Kate, we would have never ever found Nadean's mother through records, and only possibly through DNA if someone closer tested. Kate fully agreed.

I told Kate that what really sent things into motion was finding your father, which was by chance with his daughter testing. I told Kate that the entire situation seemed to really motivate you and you persevered like never before, like a private P. I.

That trip you and Bill took and your website posts turned the entire situation around, as well as your mother and siblings searching for you as well. To me, the entire thing was brought on by miracles, which I believe is a result of the positive spirit, love, compassion, and never giving up that people have inside of them.

This should make you feel good, no, wonderful. Your love for your mother and never giving up, and your mother's love for you and never stopping and finally opening up brought you together.

This entire journey with you has been so absolutely unbelievable. I feel someone selected me to choose to help you, and from then it went off on its own preordained journey.

The gift for me, a truly happy, inspiring end to my helping so many. It was meant to be, so many of us met throughout this process.

I am still so very close to Kate and the rest of our genealogist team. I am doing all I can to help them with DNA and we are all friends, which is so nice for me. I am thankful every single day for you entering my life. It has only become better for it."

Love, Olivia

I sent a text message to Clarissa:

Clarissa, you were so very close in August but we did not realize it. When you contacted your friend, who is our age to ask if she could help in our search, your friend asked her aunt if she knew of a woman in her social circle who could have given birth to a female child in 1952. Do you remember? Well, her aunt, after whom she was named, is my birth mother.

Mum and five of her family members visited us in Florida over the first week of December. Bill and I wanted it to be a memorable vacation for them.

Bill and I pulled out all the stops decorating the house for Christmas. I had placed the photo that Christie's husband took of Mum and me at the airport in a frame on the kitchen counter so they would see it upon arrival.

A second photo of Mum, me, and my siblings, taken by Bill at her house, was placed beside it. In the living room, I placed a photo of Mum as a young woman between one of Rita and one of Bill's mum, Arlene.

On Friday, the day after their arrival, Bill served an amazing brunch.

We swam in the pool afterward. Then we visited the local flea market and Butterfly World and had an early Christmas dinner at home.

Our friends gathered at our house on Saturday for dinner.

Mum, the siblings and I had grown more accustomed to the relationship as the weeks progressed and we exchanged emails, texts and calls.

Our friends, however, were overwhelmed. As they arrived and were introduced, both the women and men cried upon meeting and hugging our new family.

My siblings moved to a hotel on the beach before dinner, leaving Mum to stay with Bill and me. They thought bonding time would be good for us.

Bill and I spent the next two days showing her Andrew's schools, walking around the local farmer's market, walking among the gorgeous yachts at Bahia Mar, and shopping at Sawgrass Mills Mall.

We met the family for dinner on Sunday evening. I made a reservation at Sea Watch, a local seafood restaurant. The evening couldn't have been more perfect. We were seated at a table next to long windows that looked out onto the beach. It was a full moon, so the moonlight flickered onto the swaying palm trees and the sea below. It was a magical setting.

On Monday, our final evening together, we sat at the kitchen table and shared Bill's many leftovers.

"Mum, do you think you could show Bill and me the town you come from? Bill should be able to find it on Google."

Bill started up his laptop and went onto Google Maps, which worked much better than Google World. Maps takes you along the actual roadways of any town or city.

As Bill zoomed in to the geographical area and then to the town, my Mum said, "Look, Bill, that is our family home. Right there."

The next morning, I dressed for work as Mum finished her packing. Bill was taking her to the airport to meet the rest of the family for the flight back.

Someone told me years ago that life is never perfect; however, one can experience many perfectly memorable moments.

As Mum and I hugged and said good-bye, she held me by the shoulders and looked at my face.

"I am looking at your eyes," she said. "Do you know why?"

"Yes," I said, and laughed, "You are looking for Viktor."

"Yes," she replied, as she smiled with a twinkle in her eye.

I remembered Aunt Roberta's words to my mother Rita upon meeting me for the first time:

Rita, that is the homeliest baby I have ever seen. She has huge eyes and is so skinny. She looks like a hungry bird.

"Mum, sixty-four years ago you had one little chick in your nest. She was always hungry, adventurous, kept jumping up and down anxiously waiting for you to return. One day she fell out of the nest. You went on to build a wonderful life and to have more baby chicks. You have spent the last sixty-four years searching for that little lost bird. You have found her now and you have all of your babies safely back in the nest. It is time for you to rest and to be at peace."

Epilogue

Who am I?

I am the sum total of my rich life experiences, and the unyielding love and support over the years from my many mothers and the many girlfriends who became my sisters in life. You know who you are. Bill is my rock! I am forever thankful for his constant love and support. 2017 was my year of miracles. In the year that I lost my beloved Aunt Roberta, I found my birth mother. On Sundays I would call Aunt Roberta to chat and catch up. Now I call my birth mother. She wishes to remain anonymous, and I am content with her decision. I am only too happy to be able to forge a loving relationship with her and her family.

I wrote *No Stone Unturned* to provide faith, hope, strength and courage to readers seeking inspiration to persevere in the face of daunting life challenges.

A portion of the proceeds from the sale of my book will be donated to St. Jude Children's Research Hospital, The Salvation Army and to a scholarship fund in Andrew's name that Bill and I established at FAU.

In July 2018 I filed a petition with the UN Commission on the Rights of the Child illuminating numerous Articles of the UN Convention that the Province of Ontario has violated in its treatment of illegally adopted children. The Committee met in September and October 2018 in Geneva to review and deliberate all submissions. The Committee will assemble questions to present to the Canadian government delegation, asking for its response to the allegations.

I will be filing a petition with the Province of Ontario to amend its current law, thereby enabling access to birth records for thousands of illegally adopted persons like me. I will also be petitioning the Catholic Church in Ontario, Canada, to unlock its secret archives regarding illegal adoptions.

The work continues.

(top left) Rita Russell. *(top right and below)* Rita and Sid Russell.

(top) Mon Oncle and Grandma in 1952.

(left) Rita and Sid Russell's Confectionery store in Sault Ste. Marie.

(below) Rita's Packard in front of their home, "The Old Stone House," now a museum in Sault Ste. Marie.

(left top) Mon Oncle and Nadean.

(left bottom) Mon Oncle with captured fox.

(above) Nadean modeling, front page of a St. Gustave newspaper.

(right Nadean and Andrew after his christening.

(below) Andrew.

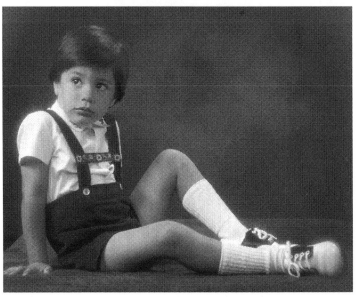

Acknowledgments

I am grateful to Julie Woik, whom I met at an art fair.

Julie is the author of *The Life and Times of Lilly the Lash*, a series of fascinating children's books, in which an eyelash teaches life lessons and the importance of self-esteem.

Our serendipitous meeting resulted in an introduction to Christine Rockwell, my copy editor par none.

To quote Julie, "Christine is a literary guru who is wicked brilliant!" Christine's belief in this project, unending encouragement and insightful editing of my manuscript resulted in a gripping and emotionally uplifting and inspiring narrative.

Lastly, I am eternally grateful to my beautiful mother Rita who, with the toss of a coin, took a chance on me.

About the Author

Nadean Stone is a legal management consultant and an author. She works as an advocate for children and adoptees, with an interest in public policy and legislation.

She is currently exploring the transformation of *No Stone Unturned* into a film or television series and is also working on several children's stories about her adventures on her grandmother's farm.

She and her husband, Bill, divide their time between their home in South Florida and their cottage on Lake Champlain.

Nadean can be reached at her website, nadeanstone.com.

Made in the USA
Middletown, DE
21 April 2021

37560032R00161